Land, Nation and Culture, 1740–1840

*Palgrave Studies in the Enlightenment, Romanticism and Cultures of Print*

General Editors: **Professor Anne K. Mellor** and **Professor Clifford Siskin**
Editorial Board: **Isobel Armstrong**, Birkbeck; **John Bender**, Stanford; **Alan Bewell**, Toronto; **Peter de Bolla**, Cambridge; **Robert Miles**, Stirling; **Claudia L. Johnson**, Princeton; **Saree Makdisi**, UCLA; **Felicity Nussbaum**, UCLA; **Mary Poovey**, NYU; **Janet Todd**, Glasgow

*Palgrave Studies in the Enlightenment, Romanticism and the Cultures of Print* will feature work that does not fit comfortably within established boundaries – whether between periods or between disciplines. Uniquely, it will combine efforts to engage the power and materiality of print with explorations of gender, race and class. By attending as well to intersections of literature with the visual arts, medicine, law and science, the series will enable a large-scale rethinking of the origins of modernity.

*Titles include*:

E.J. Clery
THE FEMINIZATION DEBATE IN 18TH-CENTURY ENGLAND
Literature, Commerce and Luxury

Peter de Bolla, Nigel Leask and David Simpson (*editors*)
LAND, NATION AND CULTURE, 1740–1840
Thinking the Republic of Taste

Mary Waters
BRITISH WOMEN WRITERS AND THE PROFESSION OF LITERARY CRITICISM, 1789–1832

*Forthcoming title in the series*:

Adriana Craciun
BRITISH WOMEN WRITERS AND THE FRENCH REVOLUTION

**Palgrave Studies in the Enlightenment, Romanticism and Cultures of Print Series Standing Order ISBN 1–4039–3408–8 (hardback) 1–4039–3409–6 (paperback)**
*(outside North America only)*

You can receive future titles in this series as they are published by placing a standing order. Please contact your bookseller or, in case of difficulty, write to us at the address below with your name and address, the title of the series and an ISBN quoted above.

Customer Services Department, Macmillan Distribution Ltd, Houndmills, Basingstoke, Hampshire RG21 6XS, England

# Land, Nation and Culture, 1740–1840

## Thinking the Republic of Taste

Edited by

Peter de Bolla, Nigel Leask and David Simpson

First published 2005 by
PALGRAVE MACMILLAN
Houndmills, Basingstoke, Hampshire RG21 6XS and
175 Fifth Avenue, New York, N.Y. 10010
Companies and representatives throughout the world

PALGRAVE MACMILLAN is the global academic imprint of the Palgrave
Macmillan division of St. Martin's Press, LLC and of Palgrave Macmillan Ltd.
Macmillan® is a registered trademark in the United States, United Kingdom
and other countries. Palgrave is a registered trademark in the European
Union and other countries.

ISBN 1–4039–2047–8

This book is printed on paper suitable for recycling and made from fully
managed and sustained forest sources.

A catalogue record for this book is available from the British Library.

Library of Congress Cataloging-in-Publication Data
Land, nation and culture, 1740–1840 : thinking the republic of taste / edited
    by Peter de Bolla, Nigel Leask, and David Simpson.
        p.   cm. — (Palgrave studies in the Enlightenment, romanticism, and
        cultures of print)
    Includes bibliographical references and index.
    ISBN 1–4039–2047–8 (cloth)
    1. Great Britain—Civilization—18th century.   2. English literature—
    18th century—History and criticism.   3. English literature—
    19th century—History and criticism.   4. Nationalism—Great Britain—
    History—18th century.   5. Nationalism—Great Britain—History—
    19th century.   6. Great Britain—Civilization—19th century.   7. Aesthetics,
    British—18th century.   8. Aesthetics, British—19th century.   9. Art,
    British—18th century.   10. Art, British—19th century.   I. De Bolla,
    Peter, 1957–   II. Leask, Nigel, 1958–   III. Simpson, David, 1951–   IV. Series.

    DA485.L35 2004
    306'.0941'09033—dc22

                                                                    2004052826

10   9   8   7   6   5   4   3   2   1
14   13   12   11   10   09   08   07   06   05

Printed and bound in Great Britain by
Antony Rowe Ltd, Chippenham and Eastbourne

*For John Barrell*

# Contents

# List of Illustrations

# Acknowledgements

We would like to express our gratitude to all those who helped in the preparation of this text. Emily Rosser was extremely encouraging and efficient in seeing the project move towards publication, and Paula Kennedy has been equally helpful in seeing it through the passage into print. Evelyn Arizpe was indispensable in handling the technology of the final preparation of the copy.

PETER DE BOLLA
NIGEL LEASK
DAVID SIMPSON

# Notes on the Contributors

**Ann Bermingham** is Professor in the Department of the History of Art and Architecture, University of California, Santa Barbara.

**John Brewer** is John and Marion Sullivan Professor in English and History, Department of English, University of Chicago.

**T.J. Clark** is George C. and Helen N. Pardee Professor of Art History, University of California, Berkeley.

**Thomas Crow** is Professor of Art History in the University of Southern California and Director of the Getty Research Institute, Getty Centre, LA.

**Stephen Daniels** is Professor of Cultural Geography, School of Geography, University of Nottingham.

**Peter de Bolla** is Lecturer in the English Faculty and Fellow of King's College, Cambridge.

**Frances Ferguson** is Mary Elizabeth Garrett Chair in Arts and Sciences, Department of English, Johns Hopkins.

**Harriet Guest** is Professor in the Department of English and Related Literature, University of York.

**Nigel Leask** is Regius Professor of English Language and Literature of the University of Glasgow.

**David Simpson** is Professor and G.B. Needham Fellow, Department of English, University of California, Davis.

**David H. Solkin** is Professor of the Social History of Art, Courtauld Institute, London.

# Introduction

*Peter de Bolla, Nigel Leask and David Simpson*

The study of the 'long eighteenth century' – usually understood to span the years 1688–1832 – has for some twenty years been shifting its focus and reassessing its touchstones. The change in orientation is perhaps most noticeable for historians of culture. Scholars working in this field have challenged previous tendencies to study literature or art as autonomous disciplines with their own internal laws of development, in a more or less inert relationship to a historical 'background' – the latter taken to represent a foreclosed body of historical 'events', be they political, social or religious. Furthermore, where, say fifty years ago, historians and scholars interested in the long eighteenth century kept pretty much within their disciplinary formation – art history, literature (or even more narrowly, drama, poetry or the novel) – more recently the terrain of culture has been understood in its widest sense. And this sense of culture in an expanded field requires an approach that not only works from within a particular discipline, or across adjoining disciplines, but also brings forward an array of techniques, interests, knowledges and training from the assembly of different disciplines. It requires a multidisciplinary approach.

Of course it might be said that there is nothing new under the sun – scholars of the period working in the early twentieth century were far from being immured in mono-disciplinary interests even if they derived their professional identities from the traditional disciplines. Exceptions which might prove the rule would be the theatre historian Allardyce Nicoll, the historian of landscape aesthetics Christopher Hussey or the literary historian Marjorie Hope Nicholson, all of whom were certainly promiscuous in their materials, ranging over printed texts from many fields – poetry, philosophy, history and so forth – images of varying sorts, diverse historical records, and even material objects such as scientific instruments. Some fifty years later this promiscuity is displayed in an influential 1965 volume of essays entitled *From Sensibility to Romanticism* (edited by Frederick W. Hilles and Harold Bloom) which contained essays on Pope's garden aesthetic, portraiture, vernacular linguistics and the picturesque, as well as poetry and poetics.

However, it is significant that the collection (presented as a *festschrift* for Frederick Pottle) did not contain any prefatory explanation of its inclusiveness, precisely because the disciplinary boundaries between 'literature' and 'background' remained unchallenged, despite the range of subject matter. Such confidence in the settled nature of the methods and protocols of scholarly investigation pertaining to different disciplines begun to be shaken somewhere around the late 1960s.

This sense of things being settled was nowhere more glaringly evident than in the field of eighteenth-century historiography, which had long been dominated by a 'Whig' and Naimierite consensus emphasizing 'Augustan' political stability, social hierarchy and economic prosperity. As E.P. Thompson quipped in 1974, 'historical conferences on eighteenth-century questions tend to be places where the bland lead the bland'.[1] But from the 1960s on a transformation began to be wrought by Thompson and Raymond Williams which, more than just challenging this 'Augustan' political consensus, also questioned the methodologies and protocols governing the historical investigation of 'culture' itself (Christopher Hill did important work on the seventeenth century along similar lines). Although Thompson and Williams (along with Hill) inhabited and contributed to a broadly defined socialist or Marxist tradition they did not necessarily share a common sense of the lineaments of the concept of 'culture'. Williams, for example, provided a rigorous historical etymology of the word itself, tracing its meaning from 'the general state of intellectual development, in a society as a whole', through 'the general body of the arts', to 'a whole way of life, material, intellectual and spiritual'.[2] In a series of books starting with *Culture and Society* and including most notably *The Long Revolution, Keywords* and *The Country and the City*, Williams focused the attentions of a generation of scholars on the complexities of both culture itself and of the uses made of that term in political and aesthetic traditions. Despite his strictures on the political evasions of the 'Culture and Society' tradition, Williams found critical and even revolutionary potential in 'culture's' usefulness in *relating* rather than *separating* material and symbolic production. In contrast Thompson, while standing up for the integrity of a working-class life system and belief, brought the full weight of his sceptical empiricism to bear upon a concept which made him suspicious that 'the very term 'culture', with its cosy invocation of consensus, might serve to distract attention from social and cultural contradictions, from the fractures and oppositions within the whole'.[3] Differences of emphasis notwithstanding, Williams and Thompson were both instrumental in deepening and widening our senses of the meaning(s) of 'culture'. Their endeavour was at once challenged, informed and complicated in the 1970s by a popular Althusserian Marxism that proposed a rigorously repressive function for all aspects of the state and ideological apparatus, including culture. Williams and Thompson both resisted this thesis, in their different ways, but some sort of navigation between and among these extremes has been incumbent upon us ever since. For the generation of scholars who followed, an urgent sensitivity to the complexities of culture in both theoretical and empirical-historical senses, and as potentially both restrictive and democratically expressive, was to become foundational.

Of that generation John Barrell stands out as an early, perhaps the first, scholar to fully embrace the need for, and implications of, a multidisciplinary approach to the history of cultural forms: his influence pervades the essays assembled in this volume which celebrates his distinguished career. Barrell's early work placed the politics of culture at the centre of enquiry and drew inspiration from both Williams and Thompson, combining their approaches to the history of culture with the training of a literary critic. It was this combination of close textual analysis, especially in regard to poetry, and a keen political and historical sensitivity, which began to open up eighteenth-century cultural forms to hitherto unseen and unremarked filiations. In Barrell's early work the public and political frequencies of the cultural domain – the location of culture for both Williams and Thompson in their different ways – began to be reformulated in terms of the self-consciousness of eighteenth-century writers themselves: 'what was it that most struck them about what was happening in their society, and in what ways did they try to comprehend what was happening as an historical process?'[4] What emerged from this was a new and urgent sense of the traffic between the public and the private in an increasingly commercial society. How does the 'private' individual both draw sustenance from the 'public' social world and, at the same time, resist or refuse its embrace? What kind of culture promotes or encourages such traffic, and which cultural forms result from these interchanges? All of the essays in the present volume ask these questions, albeit in different ways, and all of them follow the path that Barrell has carved out so consistently.

Barrell, of course, has not been alone in forging a new sense of the cultural-historical terrain. Others, also working in the shadow of Williams, Thompson and Hill, took off in similar directions, drawing upon Williams' commitment to understanding how all the media – highbrow and popular – carry culture's messages, and Thompson's and Hill's decision to write history 'from below'. And so, surprisingly quickly, the settled paving stones of the canonical long eighteenth century began to be uplifted. In place of Pope or Johnson or Reynolds or Wordsworth, a new *dramatis personae* moved to centrestage: Stephen Duck, George Morland or John Clare, say, or (when the challenge of feminism, by no means central to the work of Thompson or Williams or Hill, began to make its impact), Mary Collier, Mary Wollstonecraft or Mary Shelley. In place of the political and constitutional history of Britain – geographically centred on London, Oxbridge and the great houses of England – a new cultural history, based in the lived experience of ordinary British men and women in the country or the city, as well as the overseas subjects of Britain's colonial power who were located even further from the metropolitan seats of government, began to challenge our accepted versions of the eighteenth-century world.

While these developments were underway in the sequestered glades of eighteenth-century scholarship, new and different challenges of a more philosophical and methodological kind also began to impact upon scholars in the diverse fields of art history, literary studies and social history. It has become a commonplace to describe this intervention as 'the linguistic turn' and to derive its major components from the debates pursued, mainly in Europe and more specifically in France, which developed out of mainstream European philosophy in the years following the Second World War. While not all of these initiatives were exclusively 'philosophical' – still less simply 'structuralist' or 'post-structuralist' – the impact they had on the *methodologies* of the distinct disciplines was to prove substantial and long-lasting. The methodological scepticism often associated with the work of Barthes, Derrida and Foucault, and sharpened by the challenges posed by Althusserian Marxism, further contributed to breaking down the disciplinary boundaries which governed scholarship in the long eighteenth century. However unevenly distributed across the disciplines, it has nevertheless proved to be of significant importance.

Something of the force of these changes can be observed by taking a snapshot of one particular discipline, literary studies. In the late 1960s the eighteenth century was subdivided into smaller periods – the 'age of Walpole', 'of Swift' or 'of Pope', the 'Augustan Age', the 'age of sensibility'. And these smaller segments when combined were understood to provide a counterbalance to the romantic period, which was itself bifurcated into early and late, keeping Wordsworth, Blake and Coleridge apart from Shelley, Keats and Byron. Each literary genre was presided over by uncontested 'giants' – Richardson and Fielding over the novel, Pope and Swift over poetry and Johnson over criticism – and their borders seemed to be impermeable: there were no 'hybrid' texts, nor were the animadversions of natural philosophers or rhetoricians deemed to be of much interest to the study of such literature. Perhaps to our eyes now the absence of virtually any women writers (with the exception of Jane Austen) seems the most bizarre and the most embarrassing of various oversights and omissions.

Throughout the 1980s, literary scholarship on the eighteenth century was becoming more varied and open to new approaches – deconstruction, feminism, reader-response criticism and so on. By 1987, when Laura Brown and Felicity Nussbaum co-edited *The New 18th Century*, a decade's worth of new work revealed a distinctly different set of keywords, interests and methodologies. The editors challenged the then-current state of eighteenth-century studies and its 'resistance to theory' by championing 'new feminisms, Marxisms and historicisms' against the neo-formalism and 'old' historicism which they claimed still seemed to dog the field. The new priorities are signalled everywhere in the titles of the essays they collected: terms such as *empire, performance, consumption, spectralization, contradiction, authority* are read as historically-embedded practices of culture. Pope, Johnson and Swift are still there, but they sit beside Mary Collier, Laetitia Pilkington and Stephen Duck. Locke and Hume no longer provide the sole tutelary spirits of philosophical prestige: now we have also Marx, Bakhtin and Barthes.

It would be wrong to characterize the more recent change we are highlighting as merely an extension of or revision to the canon. Brown and Nussbaum's list of contributors was almost exclusively comprised of literature professors then teaching in the United States (the exception being the co-authored contribution from John Barrell and Harriet Guest), and at that time American literary studies was indeed hypersensitive to questions of canonicity. But the subsequent recasting of the terrain of the long eighteenth century has *not* been primarily concerned with the question of the literary canon, since its revisionary force has impacted upon almost every aspect of the history of culture and society, and has therefore involved a more thoroughly multidisciplinary turn.

The important changes that have occurred really fall between rather than within discrete disciplines. To some the impact of theory on the humanities is something to be deplored, to others it provides a welcome intervention and enabling strategy; some claim its day to be over, others argue for its continuing power to shape work within the humanities and beyond. Yet there can be no doubt that the gradual spread of theory through the humanities, unevenly but unignorably (the chronology is inevitably murky) into literary studies and anthropology, into art history, social history, media studies and human geography, has resulted in a more permeable division of the faculties. As evidenced in this volume the 'new' long eighteenth century eschews identification with any single privileged discipline.

The work which we have in mind is thus, to begin with, already interdisciplinary: for example, techniques of close reading originally developed within literary studies by I.A. Richards or William Empson have already been usefully carried over to the study of what is now known as 'visual culture', the content of which most obviously falls within the discipline of art history. But the new terrain of the long eighteenth century is not only now excavated by previously distinct disciplinary interests, it is also subjected to what we wish to call a 'multidisciplinary' turn. A whole variety of materials – legal documents, statistical surveys, novels, letters, poems, travel accounts, architecture, popular songs, paintings, sculpture, landscape gardens, botanical specimens, diaries, scientific enquiries, moral philosophy, political economy – in short the entire nexus of culture, is brought within a gaze that might at one moment be focused through the techniques of close reading, at another through the technologies of visual studies, and at yet another through the complexities of narrative history. We take what we need from all these, and other, disciplinary formations in order to open up culture to a radically new optic, at the same time going beyond the traditional sources of information for analysing culture within any one or combination of the established disciplines.

The work of Michel Foucault had a deep impact on this enlargement of the field, not merely on account of his own choice of objects for study – the prison, political economy, grammar or the history of madness – but because of the power of his concept of discursive formation. Where heretofore 'history' had comprised people, events, edicts, bills of parliament, statistical surveys and so forth, now it became populated with 'discourses' that cut across or through, articulated or resisted these earlier historical entities, while at the same time finessing the epistemological problems that had traditionally vexed the study of how they were determined and related. Much of the scholarly work that began to treat history in this way may be said to have merely substituted the word 'discourse' for earlier terms – genre, ideology or *Weltanschauung* – so to some extent not much really changed. But in relation to the realm of culture, the articulation of Foucauldian discourse analysis with a parallel tradition of Marxist historiography and criticism led to far greater challenges. Although at the time few deliberately sought to mix the heady cocktail of Williams, Thompson and Foucault, in practice the conjunction of these three powerful figures prompted a complete redrawing of the map of culture.

It was not coincidental that such a combination of historical, literary-critical and visual inquiry, shot through with the methodologies of Marxist historiography and discourse analysis, took root in the study of the culture of the long eighteenth century. In a very significant sense, what we now recognize as 'culture' (in contradistinction from artistic production sponsored by royal, aristocratic or church patronage) came into being in this period, as a vehicle and product of Habermas's 'bourgeois public sphere'. In Britain there were no public art exhibitions before 1761, no musical performances in dedicated spaces before the 1740s. The late seventeenth and early eighteenth centuries saw the invention of the modern financial system, and (in 1707) of the modern British state, with all the appurtenances of its 'imagined community': newspapers, periodicals, reviews, theatres, museums, art exhibitions. Town planning took off, the postage system developed, and the modern law of contract came into being. The project of standardizing the English language (through dictionaries, grammars and lecture courses) simultaneously shaped the emergence of a new 'English' cultural canon and a vernacularist counter-movement which still lives and stirs today. In short the entire fabric of cultural production and its enabling institutions were first fully forged in compliance with or in reaction to the pressures and persuasions of the capitalist marketplace during the long eighteenth century. The study of this protean new phenomenon accordingly requires a multiplicity of techniques, a hetero-geneous sweep of material forms and a capacity to see beyond the borders of any single discipline.

Perhaps the most visible characteristic that emerges from this collection of essays in a new mode is a focalization through the aperture of what might be called 'the instance'. The histories, formations and effects of culture are read out from (as they were originally compressed into) a series of single entities (moments, events, texts, material objects) that have a specific historical or temporal locale. More materially embodied than the anecdote preferred by the practitioners of the new historicism, which may have a very dispersed physical-temporal locale or even none at all, the instance fixes and is fixed in a cultural array. And its very temporal specificity provides the multidisciplinary approach with a window onto the domain of culture *then*, at that moment, and *now*, in our present of enquiry. Tracking back and forth between these temporal locales stabilizes the object in the instance, even if, at a subsequent moment of enquiry, a different instance will be formed.

As multidisciplinary studies of this new long eighteenth century proliferate, there is already a sense that some particular frames of analysis reveal or enlighten more than others. Although the terms *Land, Nation, Culture*, signalled in the title to this volume are certainly not intended to be exhaustive, nor meant to delimit the range of issues covered by the individual essays here collected, they nevertheless highlight some productive lines of approach. Land, its history, representations and uses, has a profound bearing upon the terrain of culture; what might be called the 'manifold' of the land – its complex intermeshing of economy, society, rank, class and aesthetic sensibility – requires a range of disciplinary tools in order to understand it fully. Stephen Daniels shows how Turner's two images of Nottingham, produced over thirty years apart, infuse a local landscape with the national concerns of improvement and political reform. For David Simpson, Wordsworth's onomastic designs on his native Lakeland at least satirize and perhaps criticize Britain's colonial annexation of the land of others in an era of exploration and empire. David Solkin, in a suggestive response to John Barrell's study of the eclipse of the rural poor in British landscape painting, discusses the watercolorist Thomas Heaphy's contrary obsession with depicting the rural poor at their most threatening and licentious, reminding us again that the land is always imagined in the interstices of 'nature' and 'culture'. Perhaps the land, or the natural world, always provides a counterweight to the human no matter where we look in history, but at certain moments the fulcrum which balances nature and nurture, man and the world, has particular work to do. As Frances Ferguson shows us, the relations between naturalism, organicism and the human needs of society are particularly complex at the end of the eighteenth century.

Nation, a concept recently recuperated by historians after its relative eclipse in Marxist theory, takes on a new shape when planted in the rich soil of aesthetic representation – when two-way streets open between history, ideology and aesthetic forms. Nation now begins to operate as a *conceptual* category within which ideologies may be formed or discovered: as an 'imagined community' it provides the conceptual grounding for representations of self and other, much as those representations help maintain the ideologies of nationalism. T.J. Clark reminds us in his reading of David's *Rape of the Sabine*

*Women* that the *koinonia* or alliance enabling the transition from nature to the civil state is based on an act of gendered violence. From the salons of Paris to the beaches of the Pacific, the nature of this transition fascinated eighteenth-century thinkers. In David's painting the 'conjunctive' figure of Hersilia enacts the generation of law from 'the multiple alienations of kinship'; but this is also a linguistic turn of sorts, in the establishment of a new grammar of the nation state, whereby 'an almost uncontrollable heterogeneity becomes a single sentence'. Nigel Leask also pushes hard on the complexities of our language, its systems and social uses, politics and histories. In an essay devoted to linguistic standardization and vernacular resistance in consolidating the 1707 Union between England and Scotland, language, more than ever, is shown to provide the matrix for an 'imagined community'. Wordsworth's rejection of 'poetic diction' and his bid to imitate the 'real language of men' is inspired by Robert Burns and the poetry of the Scottish vernacular revival, but the poet is forced to imagine a non-regional *lingua communis* in reaching for a truly 'national' idiom. Anne Bermingham asks – via an analysis of Gainsborough's 'cottage door' paintings – what it means to conceive of the nation as a cottage family, or (by extension) of a cottage family in public terms as the nation.

But nation and nationhood are not only to be found in the places where one might most expect them – in state-sponsored history painting or music composed for state occasions – but also in the array of concepts which help build the cultural nexus: they appear in the determinants of value such as originality, transcendence or singularity; in the grounding of the notion of market and consumerism; in the very conceptual basis for the human subject. Peter de Bolla examines how the equivocal subjecthood of eighteenth-century actors – exemplified by 'Sheridan's Case' of 1747 – both threatened the gentlemanly model of person and influenced the legal definition of subjectivity, anticipating the modern 'divided' subject. And as with Burns' cultural challenge to 'standard English', the Irish setting of the Sheridan case highlights its importance as an 'act of union'. In her essay on the novels of Charlotte Smith, Harriet Guest argues that in the revolutionary aftermath, a network of spying and surveillance replaced the disinterested gentlemanly 'prospect view' as an important means of social regulation and control. Smith's later novels foreshadow the emergence of the largely female-authored genre of the 'national tale', which displaces the moral centrality of England to the Celtic and colonial peripheries and questions the centripetal certainties of the metropolitan 'spy'.

Our title's third term, *culture*, becomes an even more overdetermined concept once the protocols of multidisciplinarity are invoked. It at once contains the objects of the disciplines and is produced and reproduced by them, and it can seem hard to distinguish (as it may be inseparable from) the material and empirical phenomena of life which the disciplines severally investigate. In a sense all the essays here address the question of culture, but two in particular reach right to the heart of the matter. In a fine exemplar of 'the dog that didn't bark' analysis, Tom Crow speculates that Chardin's early still-life paintings *The White Tablecloth* and *The Ray* subtly encode a Jansenist protest against the contemporary celebration of the Eucharist. Yet he reminds us of the difficulty of relating artworks such as Chardin's still-lifes, concerned with the inwardness of the self, to the wider culture, considering (in this case) that Jansensist theology was itself concerned with the unbreachable privacy of the self, and the occult nature of God's manifestation in the object world. By contrast, John Brewer deals with an ostentatiously public instance, the murder of Martha Ray in Covent Garden in 1779 by her lover James Hackman, and the convoluted background to a tragedy which quite literally 'reads like a novel'. In an analysis of the exploitation novel *Love and Madness* (based on the murder) which Herbert Croft then published the following year, Brewer explores the eighteenth-century's view of the limits of fact and fiction, discovering in the discourse of sensibility a notion of 'irresistible impulse' common to forensic and aesthetic representations of Hackman's motivation. Both these essays exemplify the need to agitate a cultural instance, rocking it back and forth between its obvious and comfortable location and other, less immediately perceptible locales.

But it is the rider in our title – '*Thinking the Republic of Taste*' – which points towards the more cohesive bond that makes our essays into a collective enterprise. The phrase is an echo of the last words of an essay by John Barrell entitled 'The Birth of Pandora and the Origin of Painting', and we mean to signal by it a particular political inflection to the concept 'culture', and to route that concept through the discourse of aesthetics. It is here, in respect to a particular historical sensitivity to the aesthetic – by which we mean to include aesthetic forms (poetry, painting and so forth) as well as the architectonic which enables such forms to become visible precisely as *art* forms, the debates and discussions which comprise what the period termed 'philosophical criticism' – that a *multidisciplinary* approach seems most germane. Our reference to the *republic* signals the important influence upon our generation of an explicitly anti-Marxist intellectual historian: J.G.A. Pocock's work, especially his landmark book *The Machiavellian Moment* (1975), gave specific historical shape to a single (and in his view dominant) political ideal. Pocock showed how the classical republican language of virtue has not only shaped and determined social and political theory but also contributed to the DNA necessary for the generation of 'culture'. Of course *The Machiavellian Moment* describes a paradigm that was already 'anti-modern' in Renaissance Italy, where the civic humanist looked back to classical Rome, and was even more so in the eighteenth century, by which time any opposition to the developed capitalist economy risked looking like nostalgia. The civic humanist case against commerce, luxury and vested interest was thus open to various and unpredictable political uses between the radical and the reactionary. It is a language whose exact application to historical conditions may differ from its apparent claims. Pocock, writing as a political scientist and historian of ideas, did not fully explore the trajectory of civic virtue in all these different instances, and was indeed criticized for a failure to contextualize ideas: yet his task, marvellously performed, was to show the persistence of the civic humanist ideal as a guiding obsession of the republican tradition. Pocock's followers have been interested in the application of the paradigm to more specific occasions and local disciplines. One of the earliest and most sustained attempts to follow through this task was John Barrell's *The Political Theory of Painting from Reynolds to Hazlitt* but the same contours of enquiry can be found in the work of many of the scholars contributing to this volume – in the work of David Solkin, John Brewer, T.J. Clark and Stephen Daniels, for example. And if the standard civic humanist account of the fine arts has by now been challenged by rival accounts, it nevertheless remains the case that all such accounts are coloured by, even as they are in reaction to, the political inflection Pocock so forcefully presented. Marxist and liberal historiographies have been in fertile conflict around the pasts and presents of the republican tradition.

'Thinking the Republic of Taste' involves three, quite separate operations. It first requires us to probe the category of thinking itself. Where does the work of conceptual formation get done? Who does it? On behalf of whose interests? Wherein lies the authority to legislate, and who possesses the social credit to represent the social and cultural totality? Can a painter be as effective in this regard as a philosopher? Does a poet, say Wordsworth, engage in the business of re-mapping what it might be to think certain thoughts – what constitutes, protects or destroys vernacular language, or what it might mean to be at home in the world? Such questions might most easily be characterized as philosophical or conceptual, but they operate in and through instances, identifiable occasions and events.

Second, it asks us to remain constantly alert to the political, to the myriad ways in which a different culture in a period not our own asserts or denies the foundationalism of politics. And it asks us to do this in such a way that we become better equipped to identify what is and is not common to the period we study and the era we ourselves inhabit. Is the paradigm of the cottage in the late eighteenth century transferable to early twenty-first-century America? Does our own law in respect to crimes of passion depend upon or erase the legal code of the Enlightenment, and how might we tell the story of that code from our own perspective? What politics underpins such enquiry? Does the eighteenth-century 'republican' critique of commercial society still have resonance for modern democratic politics and cultural critique, or is it merely a 'fossilized' form of consciousness? What difference does our own post-colonial and devolutionary situation make to the way in which we understand eighteenth-century culture? How do overtly political concepts, such as class, exert differential pressure over time on the formation of culture: and what happens as and when these concepts themselves are subject to transformation or discarded? These questions, while manifestly embedded in our own senses of the political, are also deeply historical in nature, and therefore significantly present to our own moment of enquiry.

Third, and last, the word 'taste' sends us to another operation, to the assessment, appreciation and experience of aesthetic forms and to the ongoing work of understanding the theoretical basis for those forms, to the discourse of aesthetics. How does a painter, say David, *make* a painting, and what is it made out of? Is its materiality – the physical paint, canvas and so forth – capable of being extracted from the culture in which it was made, first seen, preserved, collected, or from the multiple meanings which accrue to it over time? Or how does a singular performance of a play become the prompt for an investigation and challenge to the laws in respect of the rights of person? How can its aesthetic material be reconciled to or dovetailed with its articulation in culture at large? These questions are primarily concerned with the different media and the protocols of investigation developed in respect to the various forms in which aesthetic objects come to us. They are at base questions of aesthetics in its widest sense.

Multidisciplinarity, as evidenced by the essays collected here, may not always move with ease from discipline to discipline: indeed the journey may itself cause friction or faultlines to appear. And it would seem to be inevitable that such work will not leave everything in its place, will not transform heretofore isolated forms of scholarly inquiry into new wholes leaving no remainder. Given that we are still trained in the scholarly protocols of our own particular disciplines, there is certainly a risk as well as a challenge to this new turn. But the benefit of such an approach, as we see it, is a more complex tool for understanding culture. Where before we may have been limited to a single coloured filter, albeit one whose colour may change in sequence, now we are beginning to understand how to operate a lattice-work of many colours, and to revolve, turn inside out or upside down the object of our scholarly gaze. In order to grasp the manifold that is culture we need to press hard on a number of fronts, to ask historical, conceptual and aesthetic questions – though perhaps not all at once, for that would be impossible. It is in this sense that the essays which follow set about thinking the republic of taste in honour of the work of John Barrell, to whom this volume is dedicated.

## Notes

1  E.P. Thompson, 'The Patricians and the Plebs', in *Customs in Common* (London: Merlin Press, 1991), p. 18.
2  Raymond Williams, *Culture and Society* (London: Chatto & Windus, 1960), p. xvi.
3  *Customs in Common*, p. 6.
4  John Barrell, *English Literature in History, 1730–80: An Equal, Wide Survey* (London: Hutchinson, 1983), p. 13.

# 1

# Reforming Landscape: Turner and Nottingham

*Stephen Daniels**

In *The Dark Side of the Landscape* John Barrell observes that the labourers in Turner's oil painting *Ploughing Up Turnips near Slough* (1809)

> slip between the two traditional ways of relating rustic figures to a landscape, and in doing so appear to us, not as Arcadians, nor automata, but as men. They are not in any way mere 'objects of colour' in the landscape; behind them looms the misty image of Windsor Castle, but nothing in the organisation of the picture encourages us to look through the figures in the foreground, to ignore them at first in favour of that sublime image behind them.[1]

The figures arrest our attention, in conjunction with the Castle, for the picture functions as a piece of patriotic theatre, framed by agrarian ideology of wartime, the country house of 'Farmer George' as a brilliant backdrop, the fieldworkers and livestock in the foreground, performing stages of the famous four-course rotation, if the men and women don't all dutifully toil in the shade on this autumn morning, but rest and talk and feel the cold, and one cow curiously sniffs a vaunted turnip.[2] If Turner's plebeian figures appear to follow their own inclinations in enacting larger themes and processes, so the patrician monuments in his pictures, castles, cathedrals and country houses are incorporated in scenes of present circumstances, placed firmly within a course of events.[3] In this essay I want to explore the conjunction of patrician monuments and plebeian figures in Turner's work further in the representation of urban landscape, in two pictures of Nottingham, focused on its castle and canal.

Between 1794 and 1840 Turner produced over 600 designs for prints: topographical views of places in Britain; from 1818 of places on the continent,

---

* I wish to thank Nicholas Alfrey, John Beckett and Sam Smiles for their comments on an earlier draft of this essay. Sheila Cooke, Clare Van Loenen and Suella Postles helped with illustrations.

in France, Holland, Germany, Switzerland and Italy; and from the 1830s literary vignettes, mainly illustrating scenes from English poetry and prose. Turner expanded the scope of topographical landscape as a genre: technically in watercolour drawing, and, through close supervision, in engraving; formally in compositional structures; and epistemologically in the range information and allusions represented. Apart from literary vignettes, and of scenes set in the eastern Mediterranean, most are views of sites Turner visited during extensive tours, usually following an established tourist track, selecting places marketable as prints.[4]

In the first sustained analysis of Turner's topographical style, in Volume 4 of *Modern Painters*, John Ruskin noted that once Turner had depicted a particular place, he seldom returned to prepare a new drawing: 'He never seems to have gone back to a place to look at it again, but, as he gained power, to have painted and repainted it as first seen, associating with it certain new thoughts or new knowledge, but never shaking the central pillar of the old image.' This remark is made in a comparison of Turner's two views of Nottingham, published 38 years apart, the first (Illustration 1.1) in 1795 one of his earliest, when Turner was 20, in *The Copper-Plate Magazine*, the second

NOTTINGHAM.

*Illustration 1.1*   J. Walker after J.M.W. Turner, *Nottingham* (1795), © British Museum

(Illustration 1.2) in 1833, as an established artist, in *Picturesque Views in England and Wales*. 'The one will be found to be merely the amplification and adornment of the other...The painter has returned to his boyish impression, and worked it out with his manly power.'[5]

In a 1979 book on the drawings for the *England and Wales* series Eric Shanes added that 'while Ruskin compares the two he fails to see *why* Turner chose to return to the subject'. A reason is evident in the letterpress to the later print, Nottingham's topical significance as a place in struggles over parliamentary reform, particularly a popular attack on its aristocratic landmark, Nottingham Castle: 'The drawing is a symbolic celebration of the passing of the Reform Bill'.[6] This essay develops the comparison between the pictures further, in terms of the cultural geographical contexts of the pictures. It positions the earlier picture within both local developments in landscape change and picture-making and the broader physical and ideological terrain of landscape improvement in Britain in the mid-1790s. It locates the later picture within Turner's representation of larger issues of historical-geographical change in the 1830s, in landscapes throughout Europe and literary illustration, including the life and work of Nottingham's best known European, Lord Byron.

*Illustration 1.2*   W.J. Cooke after J.M.W. Turner, *Nottingham, Nottinghamshire* (1833), © British Museum

# I

Issued from 1791–98, and depicting over 250 places, *The Copper-Plate Magazine, or Monthly Cabinet of Picturesque Prints*, 'consisting of sublime and interesting views of Great Britain and Ireland', proved to be a successful venture in topographical publishing in a period when the patriotic taste for British scenery was sharpened by the outbreak of war and restrictions on civilian continental travel. Published initially by Harrison and Co., who issued smaller topographical prints, including some after Turner, in *The Pocket Magazine*, *The Copper-Plate Magazine* was issued from its second volume by John Walker, the main engraver and a contributing draughtsman. Designs were commissioned from rising professional landscape artists such as Turner, Thomas Girtin and Humphry Repton, along with established names in the field such as Paul Sandby and Edward Dayes and some amateurs, notably the prolific John Nixon, city merchant and Secretary of the Beef-steak Club.[7] Views were to be made from studies on the spot. A number of artists were commissioned to depict sites in their home locality, others, like Turner, Girton and Nixon, undertook tours.[8]

The places depicted in *The Copper-Plate Magazine* are distributed throughout Britain, if four-fifths are in England.[9] A range of sites is represented: ports, parks, towns of varying kind, mansions, waterways, woodlands. Most prints focus on modern improvements, which, with the names of those respon-sible, are detailed in the accompanying letterpress. Views of country seats form fully half the plates of the first two volumes and were often issued with urban views in the monthly issue, priced one shilling, of two prints. Turner's view of Nottingham was paired with a print after E.J. Burney of Viscount Melbourne's Hertfordshire house Brockett Hall, showing the new mansion and bridge designed by James Paine and recent landscaping by Richard Woods; moreover, as a sign of the usefulness of such improvements, a man fetching fish from the lake and a woman milking a cow.[10] The print of Wiseton Hall, Nottinghamshire (after a drawing by 'Miss Acklom...the very ingenious and accomplished daughter of the present liberal possessor') shows the Chesterfield Canal, with laden barge, running through the park.[11] Repton's view of William Windham's Norfolk seat Felbrigg (possibly also a proposal for improvements on the ground) shows new tree-planting by the entrance.[12] The letterpress to another Repton view of a park in his home village, praising the landscape gardeners' 'taste in directing improvements of interesting scenery', was issued in May 1794 following the attack on his art by the picturesque connoisseurs Richard Payne Knight and Uvedale Price.[13] In its early volumes *The Copper-Plate Magazine* projects Britain broadly, as a prosperous country united in and through improvements, by professionals and amateurs, improvements in the art of depicting and designing landscape on paper as well as planning and managing it on the ground. Later volumes are more selective. After 1796, the proportion of country-house views drops dramatically, to less than one in five prints. The financial effects of the war were then reducing expenditure on architectural and parkland improvements, but this subject also presented a less public-spirited image. There is a concomitant rise in subjects like bridges, factories, forges, harbours and barracks, the infrastructure of a nation mobilized for war.

Sixteen prints after Turner were published in *The Copper-Plate Magazine*. The sites are scattered widely throughout Britain, but known to those with a modicum of geographical knowledge through touring or reading. In contrast to most of Turner's views published at the time in the polite miscellany *The Pocket Magazine*, interleaved with pages of moral essays, sentimental verse, practical tips and remarkable facts, are of familiar places in the south, Thameside views of the Tower of London, Staines, Windsor and Wallingford, also Oxford and Cambridge, Bristol and Bath.[14] Two Turner views in *The Copper-Plate Magazine* are panoramas of rapidly growing, conspicuously industrial centres, Birmingham and Sheffield, showing church spires in the city centre surrounded by extensive new residential and commercial development, reaching in *Birmingham*, in the form of a newly built canal, road and factories, to the foreground of the view.[15] Most other prints are of places with cathedrals or castles, which form an architectural focus for more picturesque compositions. The earliest, *Rochester*, published in May 1794, shows the castle across the Medway, with ships at full sail on the river and two anchored by a creek on the foreground shore. Two men are building a fence by the ships, appearing to be the first stage in converting a makeshift anchorage (complete with picturesque tree) into an orderly quay.[16]

*Nottingham* was the third print to be published, in February 1795.[17] Turner visited Nottingham on his tour of 1794, but there is no surviving sketch, nor worked-up drawing, for the print. The town is mentioned in preparatory notes in the sketchbook (perhaps taken from a guide book) listing routes, distances, and notable landmarks and architectural sights:

> Nottingham 3 Churches St Mary Gothic
> a large Castle romantic situated
> in the market Place one end Justice
> the other a Cross supported by Doric Columns
> a Bridge of 19 Arches ...[18]

The first two lines of these notes itemize the main focal points of Turner's design. The three churches, St Peter's, St Nicholas's and St Mary's, occupy elevated sites in the town, prominently the largest being St Mary's. Crowning the hill to the east of the city and rebuilt in the later fifteenth century, St Mary's displayed the spectacular, later gothic styling which appealed to picturesque tastes of the late eighteenth century. The 'large Castle romantic situated' is the mansion built for the Dukes of Newcastle on the clifftop site of a medieval castle, the main royal fortress in the midlands, if fallen into disrepair for much of its later history. Briefly refortified by Parliamentary forces during the Civil War, the old castle was then slighted and sold in 1660 to the first Duke of Newcastle. In a pun on the family name, repeated in subsequent accounts of the building, Robert Thoroton noted in *The Antiquities of Nottinghamshire* (1677) that 'this present year 1674, though he be above eighty years of age' the Duke had the foundations cleared to create 'a New Castle'.[19] Completed by the Second Duke, the new castle was designed as a fashionably Italianate urban palace with no concession to the appearance of the old castle, or to the style of English medieval architecture generally. 'The founder of this modern castle designed it to be one of the completest and best fitted in England' notes Charles Deering's *Nottinghamia Vetus et Nova* (1751), a book dedicated to the Newcastles and illustrated with a series of views of the Castle by Thomas Sandby.[20] By the end of the century, when the mansion had been abandoned as a family residence, the Castle's aesthetic reputation declined. In *Essays on the Picturesque*, Uvedale Price declared:

> The long unvaried line of the summit, and the dull uniformity of the whole mass, would not have embellished any style of landscape; but such a building, on such high ground, and its outline always distinctly opposed to the sky, gives an impression of ridicule and disgust. The hill and the town are absolutely flattened by it.[21]

In his new edition of Thoroton's *The Antiquities of Nottinghamshire* (1790–96), Robert Thoroton observed:

> If for a family residence its situation is no ways fitted for that purpose; as an object of admiration to the surrounding country, *in union with the rock on which it stands*, it falls very short of our wishes and expectation . . . Art should here have been in effect as bold as nature: a lofty and massy pile towering towards the heavens, with turrets and embattled walls, the taste of ages past, placed on its brow, instead of the present formal and squat edifice, would have created a scene of splendour.

As an object of admiration for the surrounding country, the Castle was no match for the gothic splendour of St Mary's church which 'stands on a bold eminence, and looks majestically on the south westwardly aspect'.[22]

Turner's print does not show the final landmark he lists, Trent Bridge, 'the bridge of nineteen arches', but he reworks the iconography of the river Trent in earlier views of Nottingham in showing the town from a new, modern waterway.[23] Sandby's *A South Prospect of the Town of Nottingham* (Illustration 1.3), from Deering's *Nottinghamia Vetus at Nova*, depicts the town from the Trent. In the left foreground, directly before the Castle on

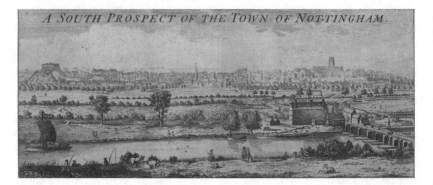

*Illustration 1.3*   After Thomas Sandby, *A South Prospect of the Town of Nottingham* (1751), Manuscripts and Special Collections, University of Nottingham

the horizon, a laden keel sails towards Trent Bridge at the right; the bridge carries the eye with the main road into town of Nottingham, lettered as such, crowned by its easterly landmark St Mary's church. In September 1793, 18 months before Turner's view was published, John Walker issued an engraving after a drawing by a Nottingham artist, J. Wigley *A South View of Nottingham* (Illustration 1.4). This was commissioned to illustrate Throsby's new edition of Thoroton's *The Antiquities of Nottinghamshire*, and sold separately before the book appeared. A more compressed view than Sandby's, this also shows a keel on the river and fishermen on the banks but is taken from a vantage point just to the east of Trent Bridge facing the site for the junction with new Nottingham Canal. Throsby noted that the celebrated Trent Bridge 'is now grown into disrepute, partly owing to its narrowness and its consequent insufficiency, as a passage, to convey the vast increase of passengers, and extended commerce to an from Nottingham, with ease and convenience'. The new 10-mile canal, bypassing Trent Bridge whose low arches impeded traffic, as well as the series of shallows above it, 'promises fair to be extremely useful to this place'.[24]

Planned by the country's leading canal engineer, William Jessop, responsible for the Grand Junction Canal as well as existing improvements to the Trent navigation, the Nottingham Canal proved an attractive financial proposition, quickly attracting £50,000 in £100 shares, and the promise of £25,000 more if necessary. The Bill authorizing the Canal received its Royal assent in May 1792, the news welcomed in the town by the ringing of church bells. It was formally opened in July the following year by the passage of three 'gaily decorated' boats laden with stone, the first carrying William Jessop with the regimental band of the Light Horse who played Rule Britannia at the filling of the first lock and other 'loyal and martial airs' including Hearts of Oak on their way into town. The canal brought castle and town closer by building

SOUTH VIEW OF NOTTINGHAM.

*Illustration 1.4*   J. Walker after J. Wigley, *South View of Nottingham* (1795), Manuscripts and Special Collections, University of Nottingham

the main lock and wharves below the castle, on the Duke of Newcastle's land, and opened up a new gateway for Nottingham.[25] The seal of the Canal Company (Illustration 1.5) is struck with an image showing a keel on the proposed canal below the Castle, above a motto, a quotation from Ovid, *Leve Fit Quod Bene Fertur Onus* ('The burden well borne becomes light').

As in the company seal, so in Turner's design, the canal occupies the traditional place of the river Trent in Nottingham iconography, and, as a prospectus, is evidently in the process of construction as well as being used. The canal was cut between the course of two streams, the river Leen running directly below the Castle in the middle distance, and Tinker's Leen in the foreground paralleling the waterway as an overflow channel. In the picture the relation between these waterways is not conclusively defined in what appears to be the construction of the basin around what became Castle Lock and the spurs to the Duke's Wharves, effectively the new port of Nottingham. The waterside scene is animated by various activities. Four figures shape a great log for the balance beam of a lock gate (the other of which has been completed). An empty cart is parked by the canal, another is drawn away. Two men operate the rigging of a keel. 'By means of canals', declares the letterpress, 'communication is opened across England, between the Humber

*Illustration 1.5*   Seal of the Nottingham Canal Company (1792), Nottingham Industrial Museum 1987–218

and the Mersey through the River Trent; which with several other canals, in various directions, increases the business of this place very considerably'. The letterpress notes that Nottingham Castle was only briefly and was now no longer a ducal residence, part being subdivided among tenants and the rest used as a military store. Turner's print offers a new and improved viewpoint of the Castle, rising dramatically on its rocky outcrop, as in views of palaces and villas around Rome and Naples, including those by John Robert Cozens, Turner copied in Monroe's Academy, an impression enhanced by the cyprus style trees to the right of the picture.[26] The Castle appears, as described in Turner's list, and against the views of its detractors, 'romantic situated'. The canal also offered a closer view of the expanding town. If not soaring so dramatically, as the archetypal City on a Hill on the company seal, Turner's print raises the town into view, highlighting its churches, notably St Mary's 'a noble structure' in the words of the letterpress. The landscape is dramatically lit in morning light, a new day in an improving era.

As it turned out, Turner's print was published precisely when confidence in the Nottingham canal slumped. After the first stretch, from near Trent Bridge to the town, was opened in July 1793, troubles multiplied, most seriously a steep rise in inflation and the appearance of immense fractures following a great flood in February 1795 . Calls on each £100 share reached £150 the following month, and the eventual cost escalated to £80,000, nearly twice the original estimate, with no dividends paid until 1804.[27] The Nottingham volume of *The Antiquities of Nottinghamshire* was issued three years after its illustration *South View of Nottingham*, and in a note in the text dated April 1795, Throsby observes of the canal: 'This work, like many others of this kind, projected in more favourable times, is in an unfinished state; it perhaps waits its completion from a return of peace and its concomitant blessings, plenteousness'. Such schemes would be completed only 'when gentlemen may turn their thoughts from war to local improvements'.[28] The full length of the canal was opened to boats in 1796, if work continued on side branches, bridges, wharves and warehouses for another six years.[29]

Turner's *Nottingham* was republished in 1799 when Walker retouched a hundred of the engravings from *The Copper Plate Magazine*, reprinting them on better paper in a volume entitled *The Itinerant* (1799). Virtually all are urban views, all Turner's prints are republished and he emerges as the predominant artist.[30] Turner's *Nottingham* shaped subsequent views of the city, in both and local and national publications. After the turn of the century, when the canal was a fully finished, paying proposition, and its towpath a frequented public walk, the view from below the Castle, showing boats gliding smoothly past polite spectators, became a standard pictorial image of Nottingham.[31]

## II

Turner revisited Nottingham as a subject for his *Picturesque Views in England and Wales*, a serial publication of 96 prints published by Charles Heath which ran from 1827 until 1838.[32] This series was the latest in a number by Turner since the turn of the century picturing the land and life of Britain, surveying its character and development. In contrast to Turner's topographical style of the 1790s, scenes are more populous, figures more dominant, the theatre more social.[33] Landscapes are more allegorical. When asked by a young engraver why he introduced a burst of light in a touched proof of *Wycliffe, near Rokeby* (1823), depicting the conjectural birthplace of the Bible's celebrated English translator, Turner replied, perhaps with a trace of self-parody, it was 'the light of the glorious Reformation' and that some large geese in the foregound 'are the old superstitions which the genius of the Reformation is driving away!'[34] Enhancing the range of sources, and raising the cultural ambition of topographical landscape as a genre, is an increased attention to poetry, including Turner's own fragmentary verse epic *The Fallacies of Hope*. The impression of literary landscapes is furthered by the deployment of devices like puns and rhymes. Views plot trains of associations from the here and now to wider worlds of historical and geographical change.[35] Exotic figures are transposed into English scenes, the French revolutionary figure Marianne appears in a Northampton election scene of 1830, figures in Greek national costume in a Hastings fishmarket scene of 1824.[36] There are topographical echoes of subjects from Turner's continental tours, with castles, rivers, lakes and canals resonating with, respectively, Rhenish, French, Swiss and Venetian scenes.

The largest proportion of subjects in *England and Wales*, over a third, are conventionally picturesque ones of castles, abbeys and cathedrals, and such medieval monuments also figure significantly in views which focus on natural features such as cliffs and lakes, and on modern developments such as harbours and canals. Over half the sites appear in Henry Boswell's *Historical Descriptions of Picturesque View of the Antiquities of England and Wales* (1786), the engravings for which the schoolboy Turner was employed to hand colour. In *England and Wales*, Turner surveys the condition of these medieval monuments, their various states of ruin, repair, rebuilding and refitting, and their place in the changing social and physical world which surrounds them. This is seldom a conventional opposition of old and new worlds. One nocturne dramatizes Robert Adam's improvements to the Duke of Northumberand's seat at Alnwick, the castle remodelled in gothic style as a fashionable residence, a full moon shining on large modern windows, its circumference rhyming with the reflected arch of Adam's gothic bridge; in another nocturne the ruined ramparts of Dudley Castle are silhouetted against a crescent moon, the castle commanding a luridly lit industrial canalside landscape which the absentee Earl of Dudley owned and controlled.[37] Some explorations of power in the land are focused on its redistributions in current arenas of social reform, in religion, politics, education, architecture, trade, transport, landed property, the armed services.[38] Motifs run through the series, notably clearing storms and disputing animals. Passages of regulation, such as a stretch of turnpike, troop of soldiers or coastguard patrol, counterpoint passages of abandon and disorder, including landslides, litter, wreckage and drunks. Pictures are cross-cut with contrasting trajectories and velocities, natural and human, avenues of rushing vehicles, placid arenas of grazing and fishing, vortices of wind and water.

The texts accompanying the pictures in *England and Wales*, in the catalogue entries for the exhibition of drawings, and in the letterpress to the engravings, gloss the pictures in various ways. The catalogue entries are anonymous, although the wording to some is replicated in the longer letterpress entries written by Hannibal Evans Lloyd, an author noted mainly as a translator of German travel texts. Presumably Turner was consulted on Lloyd's commission, but it is not clear if he collaborated in terms of content. The letterpress for *England and Wales* follows the pattern of Lloyd's entries for John Coney's *Architectural Beauties of Continental Europe* (1822): a historical description largely drawn from published sources, of the place and its principal buildings, including a few comments on current developments, some of which are not evident in published views.[39] The letterpress for *England and Wales* makes more of an engagement with the pictures, if only to indicate other possible views, for example in describing a vista from, not of, Dudley Castle, and in stating that although the vantage point of Turner's prospect of Coventry gives the impression that it is a 'place of great population and architectural importance...in this [a prospective visitor] will be disappointed; the approaches are mean the streets are narrow and ill-paved, and the domestic architecture is principally of an ancient character, with few traces of modern improvements'. While some human activities in a place are described, mainly of patricians, past and present, the texts are largely silent on the plebeian figures which predominate. Thus the letterpress for *St Mawes, Cornwall* (1822) struggles to say much of significance about the place, entirely overlooking the main activity, the dumping of fish on the beach in the foreground. This, Sam Smiles has shown, occurred during Turner's visit 11 years earlier, as a response to the closure of foreign markets for the pilchard catch during the Channel blockade. If the watercolour is a topical record of economic ruin, it is one occluded in the postwar issue of the print.[40]

The drawing for *Nottingham, Nottinghamshire* was probably made in the late summer or autumn of 1832 and issued the following year. Turner could have taken the opportunity to revisit the town on his Midlands tour of 1830 to sketch subjects for the series, including Northampton, Coventry and Dudley, but, characteristically, chose not to do so. The drawing was shown in London in June and July 1833, in the Moon, Boys and Groves gallery Pall Mall as part of an exhibition of watercolours for *England and Wales* mounted to boost subscriptions for the prints.[41] The entry in the exhibition catalogue and letterpress for the print identify the topicality of the subject, Nottingham's reputation as a centre in struggles for parliamentary representation, particularly the recent burning of the Castle by a crowd incensed at its owner's zealous opposition to the Reform Bill.

The Fourth Duke of Newcastle was a national figurehead of reaction, resisting reform, a word for him 'synonymous with revolution', in every sphere of civic life.[42] Newcastle's ultra Toryism made him a target of broad hostility, as a factional figure who abused his position and power to oppose a consensus over reform, and, at a time of insurrection in Europe, of unpatriotically provoking the very revolution he feared. In an editorial of September 1830, following his eviction of tenants for voting for a reformist candidate, *The Times* called Newcastle 'a modern man of business, and a capitalist in constitution-property'; in 'expel[lling] honest men from their habitations for exercising a constitutional right', he had 'perpetrated a *coup d'etat* against the people of England'.[43] Newcastle was assaulted in London and his mansion there attacked. When news reached Nottingham in October 1831 of the Lords' rejection of the second Reform Bill, a crowd gathered for a demonstration headed for the Castle (now empty and falling into disrepair), smashed the equestrian statue of the first Duke facing the town and set the building on fire (Illustration 1.6). The Castle was left a blackened shell. Blaming the violence on rowdies who had come into Nottingham for

SOUTH VIEW OF NOTTINGHAM CASTLE,
*As it appeared on the Evening of the 10th Oct.r 1831.*

*Illustration 1.6*   H. Dawe after R. Parker, *South View of Nottingham Castle as it appeared on the Evening of the 10th October 1831*, Nottingham City Council Leisure and Community Services (Local Studies)

the annual Goose Fair, *The Times* reporter described how the Castle 'blazed away in awful grandeur' lighting up the town in a lurid glare a 'terrible beacon to the surrounding country'. Only heavy rain that night 'prevented further mischief'. In the morning two charred corpses were found in the ruins and some of the crowd returned and 'gloated over the complete devastation'.[44] Despite the offer a £500 reward for information leading to prosecutions, only two men were arrested and they were released. When the Reform Bill was eventually passed, in June 1832, the town celebrated with banquets, illuminations and the ringing of church bells.[45] The Castle ruins quickly attracted visitors, some leaving graffiti mourning its fate: 'Call ye this Reform?', 'Doings of the Liberals', 'The work of ruin by Reformers done/ Should teach mankind their works to shun'.[46]

News of the destruction of the Castle occasioned accounts of its history. In its November issue following the event, the *Gentleman's Magazine* reissued Turner's 1795 print, now titled 'Castle and Town of Nottingham' with a detailed 'Description of Nottingham Castle' by editor John Gough Nichols. Drawing on Thoroton and Deering's accounts of the ancient and modern building as well as recent guide books and newspapers reports of the fire to chart the annals of the Castle, Nichols implied the fire was not an entirely tragic end for a building that was more 'a stately pavilion or garden temple than a mansion of residence'.[47] Newcastle's court action for compensation for the Castle's destruction prompted further enquiries on the Castle's cultural profile. The hearing was held at the summer Assize in August 1832, not in Nottingham, but in Leicester, where there would be 'no political feeling'. Newcastle's counsel Sir James Scarlett, a fellow reactionary and the country's most successful advocate, pressed for at least £30,000 to restore the Castle to its 'original strength, form and substance'. Under a recent Act, liability for 'injury by the violence of tumultuous mobs' fell on inhabitants of the hundred in which the property was situated. With evidence from old records, including royal Charters, pipe rolls and Domesday Book, and expert witnesses, including local residents, architects, surveyors and engineers, the hearing amounted to an inquiry on the place of the Castle, and its owners, in the past and future of Nottingham. This was literally so, for the defence for the hundred of Broxtowe (which stretched well beyond Nottingham) disputed, unsuccessfully, that the Castle occupied a legally identifiable location, 'may be some place that was between the town and county of Nottingham', Scarlett scoffed, 'or somewhere perhaps that was suspended between heaven and earth'. If the prosecution claimed the Castle was an 'inavaluable jewel', a noble mansion which should be restored to its 'external excellence and beauty' for future family members, the defence replied that Castle was just a 'lodging house'; surrounded by 'hovels, warehouses, steam engines and buildings of various description... nothing less than a speculation'. An architect called Jones in the employment of the Duke estimated at least £30,000 for the rebuilding, but town architect Henry Moses Wood, a witness for the defence, who thought the Castle had merits only as a villa, reckoned half that figure. The London builder and contractor engineer William Cubitt came up with a compromise figure of £21,000, the eventual award, and said for this price he would 'make the building stronger and better than it was'.[48] He estimated two years for the job, but if the rebuilding was projected in 1832, Newcastle pocketed the money without carrying it out, leaving the ruin as a rebuke to the town.

The catalogue entry to Turner's watercolour for *Nottingham, Nottinghamshire* identifies the town's waterway and castle as the principal features of the town:

> This town is situated on the river Trent, which is of very great service to the place in the transport of its manufacture, consisting chiefly of stockings, lace and shawls; it has also a considerable trade in coarse earthenware and ale, for which latter it is much celebrated. On the steep hill at the

west of the town formerly stood a castle of great antiquity; the castle which has lately been destroyed in a popular tumult, was a modern building, and occupied its site. The rock on which the town is built is of a soft sandy kind, out of which many of the vaults and cellars of the town are excavated.[49]

The letterpress to the print differs significantly from the wording and tone of this entry. It is more precise, noting that the town is located three-quarters of a mile from the 'noble river Trent' although not mentioning the canal. It cites the recent 1831 census to show that the population had greatly increased, to 30,000 (although the published figure was actually much higher, over 50,000), notes that trade and manufacture had expanded, and, as well as its three handsome parish churches there were now numerous meeting houses for dissenters (who controlled the corporation). While still one of 'the most pleasant and beautiful [towns] in England, from its pictur- esque situation, and the striking appearance of its buildings', its image had been tarnished by incendiary agitation over parliamentary reform. What is in the catalogue entry a 'popular tumult' visited on a 'modern building' which had 'occupied' the site of castle of 'great antiquity' has been transformed into a disruptive event:

The town is built on the ascent of hill, on the summit of which stands the castle, a very conspicuous object, and, when in its splendour, a great ornament to the town, but about two years since it was attacked and devastated by a lawless mob, out of spite to the noble owner, His Grace the Duke of Newcastle, whose political principles were obnoxious to the liberal population of the town, where parties have generally run very high. For this wanton devastation of his property, the Duke recovered of the county £30,000 damages.

The passage is interestingly inaccurate on some particulars – the castle, as the picture shows, is actually built on a separate hill to the town, and the compensation paid for devastating it was £21,000, not £30,000 (the amount claimed by Newcastle) – but these facts fit with its overall description of the event, which echoes the plaintiff's language in the hearing on Newcastle's action for damages.

How has Turner reworked his 1795 print of Nottingham for the 1833 design and what are the implications? While much of the content has been retained, the spatiality of the scene has been restructured. The topographical format of the earlier view has been transformed, principally through a cen- trifugal optic focused on the conglomeration of boats on the canal. This takes the form of a vignette, an elliptical, borderless, highly dynamic format, gyrating through the picture. Turner deployed vignettes extensively in the title pages and frontispieces of his illustrations to the works of contemporary poets as a way of making such images more than literal or decorative embellishments but inventive, expressive works in their own right, juxtaposing figures, landmarks, narratives and emblems, from varying sources, to illuminate, or rather re-vision, the texts.[50] The effect of the vignette form in *Nottingham, Nottinghamshire* is to increase the representational range of the subject, and to intensify its metaphorical register.

Compared to the 1795 view, Nottingham Castle has been cropped and pushed to the edge of the picture, making it more of a frame for a view along the canal to the town. But the Castle is still an arresting feature. In drawing closer to the canal, the castle looms higher, almost to the top edge of the picture, as in the castle-crowned crags of Turner's contemporary scenes of the Rhine and Loire. The landscape is now lit in a late afternoon sun, following a rain storm. The Castle is luminous. In the print, more than the watercolour, the building rises into a break in the storm clouds which form a backcloth to the town.[51] Far from showing signs of damage, let alone destruction, the Castle looks in pristine condition, with finely detailed brick and masonry work, its windows and balustrade shining in the sun. The viewing terrace, and bastion wall below, not apparent in the 1795 print, now jut out over the town. The fabrication perhaps alludes to plans for renovation, another 'New Castle'.

A less secure history is evident in the depiction of the Castle Rock. If on Turner's earlier print this appears a symmetrical base into which the Castle is fixed through a strong foundation, on the 1833 version it is presented as less stable structure, a sandstone cliff subject to forces of natural erosion and human excavation, showing gulleys, hollows, outcrops and walling. If shown with Turner's up-to-date knowledge of geology[52], it also recalls the representation of the castle rock in antiquarian images, such as the catacomb-like 'remarkable antient ruin' in Boswell's *Antiquities of England and Wales*. This focuses on the hollows cut into the rock, caves, hermitages and the 'long secret subterraneous passage' through which, the text informs us, a party of men supporting Edward III, the rightful heir to the English throne, entered the Castle in 1330 to overthrow Roger Mortimer, Earl of March, a usurper resented by 'the people he had too long tyrannized over'.[53] If the castle in Turner's 1833 print is not perched quite so precariously on the rock as in the view in Boswell's book, the brick foundations of his earlier view are obscured, by a plume of smoke. In an addition to the 1795 view, two figures are lighting a fire below the Castle; there is no routine reason for doing this on a precipitous slope, so this surely signifies the firing of the Castle (the cellars were torched), perhaps the two men arrested for arson.[54]

The canal scene is substantially recast. The scene is viewed from the towpath of the completed canal at The Duke's Wharves and Castle Lock. It is far more populous than the earlier view. Compared to the six figures there, little more than automata connected to canal construction, there are now 27 figures, expressively portrayed, in a series of groups, engaged in a variety of activities. Ruskin observed that the figures working in the earlier print are now removed to the distance where they are barely discernible, as if, we might add, the action is set back in time.[55] On the left bank of the canal men work around the wharves. On the water vessels are filled with boatmen and passengers. On the right bank the lock-keeper pushes open the gates. In front of him a group of anglers, taking advantage of the recent rain, have successfully hooked a fish, shown by a small splash in mid-stream. Conventional figures in river views, notably of the Trent, they confirm the waterway as now an established feature of Nottingham, even in 1833, with the opening of the first main railway line between Liverpool and Manchester, one passing into the national history of modern improvement. The vantage point is closer to the canal than the 1795 view, opening up the watersurface as a space for a virtuouso representation of reflections, not, as Ruskin noted, a duplicate image of what we see set back above the water, the golden summit of the Castle Rock, but 'an entirely new picture' of the canalside.[56] The view has been rotated to create a vista due east along the waterway. Through the opening lock gates St Mary's Church shines brilliantly against the storm clouds. There are remains of old boats, a dere-lict hull on the far bank (its weathered timbers echoing the eroded rock face above and rotting bank piles below), and on the near one an abandoned rudder. For an artist preoccupied with the struggles of steerage in his congested boat scenes, in difficult waters and among more highly powered vessels, the broken rudder takes on a natural symbolism to supplement its traditional image as an emblem of weak government and bad luck.[57]

Six, perhaps seven, vessels, of varying type, congregate. A narrowboat is anchored at the wharf, a keel in dock. A keel on the canal has its sail lowered, another has its sail hoisted, billowing in the wind, a rather reckless action at a lock. The sail appears to have an allegorical function, rhyming with the double rainbow over the town, a conventional symbol of hope. The scene is so elided that the sail appears to be attached to the principal vessel, a passenger boat. This new addition to the 1795 view is a puzzle to present canal historians. It may to be modelled on packet boats operating out of London's main canal port on the Grand Junction at Paddington, vessels which offered cheap and cheerful excursions, although it also recalls the long-distance packets in Turner's pictures of European river scenes.[58] A wherry with enough luggage for a long trip carries two women, making a farewell embrace, towards the packet; the one with her back towards the spectator is one of Turner's anachronistic figures, dressed in Tudor costume, perhaps a reference to the original period of the passing parliamentary system. There are at least five other women on the packet, one sitting on the roof of the cabin, looking up towards the castle. The helmsman wearing a Jack Tar costume, surrounded by female company, wielding his long pole, recalls the carnal role of sailors in Turner's coastal scenes.[59] All other named vessels in Turner's canal scenes indicate places – Lancaster, Dudley, Arundel, and Leeds. This one is named *FLY*. This may refer to its status as a so-called flyboat built for speed and given priority on the water especially at locks, but it also works as a pun in the picture: to fly also meant to set a sail and to hoist colours in triumph.[60] The mast is flying the blue and white striped flag of the newly independent nation state of Greece, a banner of freedom for liberal reformers throughout Europe.[61]

It is possible to discern a further, literary trail of allusion. Greece and Nottingham were associated with Byron, through his death at Missolonghi supporting the War of Independence and the transport of his body to his homeplace. The people turned out in their thousands, but not the local aristocracy who pointedly sent empty carriages.[62] Byron himself declared local loyalties, famously speaking in the Lords in 1812 in defence of the county's rioting framework knitters (likening their oppression to subjection under the Turks, which he thought well-timed for the impending publication of *Childe Harold*).[63] Byron never returned to Nottingham in his lifetime, fashioning himself a citizen of the world, but the association of the poet with his homeplace was strengthened after his death. Byron's former school friend, the radical Thomas Wildman, who purchased Byron's ancestral seat Newstead Abbey and refurbished it as a shrine to the poet, was a prominent figure at the funeral. Newcastle accused Wildman, in his capacity as a magistrate, of not taking adequate measures to quell the disturbance which led to the destruction of the Castle, and Wildman, in turn, led the campaign against compensation.[64] Byromania reached a new peak in 1830 with the publication of the first major biography authored by Thomas Moore (a friend of Turner a well as Byron). Turner himself contributed to the cult of the poet, exhibiting his most notable painting after Byron, *Childe Harold's Pilgrimage – Italy* at the Royal Academy in 1832, and designing title-page vignettes for a 17-volume pocket edition of Byron issued between 1832 and 1834, coupling Moore's Life with the poet's works.

Turner was the most distinguished of Byron's illustrators.[65] Like other artists of the time Turner responded to the pictorial quality of Byron's verse and the scenographic set-pieces in the longer poems. He followed in Byron's footsteps on some European tours and his choice of sites is influenced by specific passages. Turner is more attuned than most illustrators to Byron's searching vision of a place's history and geography, the juxtapositions of highbrow and lowbrow, epic and the everyday, the shifts in scale and viewpoint, the play of rhymes and puns. Turner focused on the places associated with Byron's life and work, if the references are oblique and elliptical.[66] Thus the frontispiece vignette to Volume 8 of Byron's works, which contained the whole of *Childe Harold's Pilgrimage*, is *Bacharach on the Rhine* (Illustration 1.7). While the poem is famous for its passage on the Rhineland in the third canto, Bacharach is not listed in the sequence of castles and

*Illustration 1.7*   E. Finden after J.M.W. Turner, *Bacharach on the Rhine* (1832), © The British Museum

river towns. Amalgamating pencil sketches he made on a tour of 1817, Turner shows features of Byron's Rhineland, the castled crag, the viticulture, represented by the barge laden with barrels for which Bacharach, 'Bacci ara' (the altar of Bacchus) had been famous since Roman times; also some land-marks absent from the poem, namely church spires and a ruined gothic chapel, and one that is implied in the poem's topographical sequence, the packet boat docking ashore.[67] The vignette connotes a longer, arguably more complex history of the Rhineland, than that presented in *Childe Harold*, one unfolding from the comings and goings of a working river town. As with old masters Turner addressed in his work, including Shakespeare and Rembrandt, there may well be an element of rivalry in Turner's engagement with Byron, an opportunity to reframe a figure who successfully projected and manipulated his own image. As Macaulay noted in his *Edinburgh Review* essay on Moore's biography: Byron 'was himself the beginning, the middle and the end, of all his own poetry –the hero of every tale – the chief object in every landscape'.[68] The biography confirms this conventional impression, eliding the figure of Byron with his most famous creation Childe Harold, the freedom-searching wanderer. A number of visual images prefigure this, famously Sanders' 1807–08 portrait published as a frontispiece for Moore's book, depicting the windswept young poet in nautical suit, about to be rowed to a waiting cutter.[69] Less flatteringly, George Cruikshank's 1816 broadside 'Fare Thee Well' shows Byron taking leave of his wife on the shore, the poet standing in a dinghy, fondled by three women, rowed to a waiting ship by a syphilitic Tar.[70]

With these embarkation images in mind, I'll venture a Byronic clue in *Nottingham*, as a further pun on the name of the packet boat, *FLY*. Flight, in its various connotations, is a defining conceit of *Childe Harold's Pilgrimage* and of the fashioning of Byron's life. The poem takes flight in one of those aeronautical excursions of long, liberal minded, topographical poems, if the hero's journey is not a conventional narrative of progress: 'There are no unities or time or place to fetter him', noted the *Edinburgh Review*, 'and we fly with him from hilltop to hilltop'.[71] At the start of the poem Childe Harold is described as a fly, hovering idly, one of a series of winged creatures animating a poem whose airspace is full of passing virtues: love, the soul, pleasure, freedom. Our hero is propelled from his homeplace on a sailing ship which assumes the fabled image of a flying vessel: 'The sails were fill'd, and fair the lights winds blew,/As glad to waft him from his native home'.[72] Moore's biography works the aerial image. Stanhope's words to the Greek Committee in London upon hearing of Byron's death are quoted at the end: 'The soul of Byron has taken its last flight. England has lost her brightest genius, Greece her noblest friend'.[73]

## III

At the beginning of this essay I quoted Ruskin's comments on Turner's reworking of his earlier view of Nottingham, 'associating it with certain new thoughts and knowledge, but never shaking the central pillar of the old image'. Even in terms of Ruskin's architectonic vision of landscape imagery – Volume 4 of *Modern Painters* is full of perpendicular images: pillars, towers, trunks, columns – the image has been shaken, or rather a new load-bearing structure, centring on the canal vessels, more pivot than pillar, has been put into place. Representing improvement in 1795, in 1833 Nottingham represented reform. Ruskin didn't draw the ideological associations about historic change, mainly social decline, that he did from some other Turner pictures of this period, but reform agitation in Nottingham would by the time of writing, a quarter of a century later, have lost its national currency. If Eric Shanes sees the design for the 1833 engraving as 'a symbolic celebration of the Reform Bill', the very publication of the print, with a letterpress hostile to reform, should prompt a more equivocal reading. The issue of reform represented by the print is part of a much wider cultural exploration of the cross-currents of historical and geographical change.[74]

*Nottingham, Nottinghamshire* was published towards the end of a flagging enterprise. Despite, or perhaps because of its inventiveness, *Picturesque Views of England and Wales* came to a premature end in 1838, 24 short of its planned total. The print market was now glutted with landscape views. An increasing number (including Turner's vignettes) were printed from harder-wearing steel plates which allowed much longer runs than from copper plates, in their thousands, not hundreds, selling more cheaply to a wider market. Turner himself compromised the luxury status of the *England and Wales* engravings by creaming off the best impressions for himself. Longman, who bore the losses of the bankrupt Charles Heath, tried to recoup by selling the entire stock, including copperplates and bound volumes, to H.G. Bohn a dealer in remainders and cheap prints. Declining his offer, they put the stock up for auction in 1839, and Turner purchased it at the reserve price of £3,000, about what he was paid, it total, for the drawings. Walking up to Bohn after the purchase, Turner said to him 'So, sir, you were going to buy my "England and Wales", to sell cheap I suppose – make umbrella prints of them, eh? – but I have taken care of that.'[75] After Turner's death the stock of engravings were auctioned off and the plates destroyed to preserve the market value of the prints. The watercolour drawing for Nottingham was originally purchased by John Knowles, proprietor of the Theatre Royal in Manchester, and copied in 1856 as an oil by his assistant scene painter Samuel Bough.[76] The view of the castle was reestablished as a promotional image of Nottingham when, after half a century in ruin, it was rebuilt as the nation's first municipal art gallery, opened in 1878, the same year the town's cigarette manufacturer John Player registered the image as a trademark for its 'Navy Cut' cigarettes.[77] Turner's drawing was purchased by the Corporation of Nottingham in 1940, with a contribution from the National Art Collections Fund, reflecting the renewed wartime taste for British topography, especially canal scenes.[78] As the Castle was a possible target for the Luftwaffe, the picture was put in storage with the rest of the art collection until after the war. The Castle escaped damage; the picture is there still.

## Notes

1   J. Barrell, *The Dark Side of the Landscape: The Rural Poor in English Painting 1730–1840* (Cambridge: Cambridge University Press, 1980), pp. 153–4.

2   C. Payne, *Toil and Plenty: Images of Agricultural Landscape in England 1780–1890* (London and New Haven: Yale University Press, 1993), pp. 87–9.

3   S. Daniels, *Fields of Vision: Landscape Imagery and National Identity in England and the United States* (Cambridge: Polity Press, 1993), p. 114.

4   S. Smiles, *J.M.W. Turner* (London: Tate Publishing, 2000); E. Shanes, *Turner's Human Landscape* (London: Heinemann, 1990); J. Gage, *J.M.W. Turner: A Wonderful Range of Mind* (New Haven and London: Yale University Press, 1987).

5   J. Ruskin, *Modern Painters Volume IV Of Mountain Beauty* Second edition (London: George Allen, 1898), pp. 30–1.

6   E. Shanes, *Turner's Picturesque Views of England and Wales 1825–1838* (New York: Harper & Row, 1979), pp. 59–60.

7   M.H. Grant, *A Dictionary of British Landscape Artists* (Leigh-on-Sea: F. Lewis, 1952), p. 138.

8   If the independently wealthy Nixon could well afford to tour, probably as part of a holiday, Turner's and Girtin's costs of getting to a site at this time often exceeded their payment for a drawing. Turner is said to have received some travelling expenses from *The Copper-Plate Magazine* as well as a two guinea fee. L. Herrmann, *Turner's Prints: The Engraved Work of J.M.W. Turner* (Oxford: Phaidon,1990), pp. 10–11; M. Clarke, *The Tempting Prospect: A Social History of English Watercolours* (London: British Museum Publications, 1978) p. 51.

9   The most represented county is Yorkshire, the largest, if also perhaps favoured by Walker whose family home was in Thirsk. The 33 sites in Yorkshire and 11 in neighbouring Lincolnshire, not a popularly scenic county, contrast with much lower frequencies in the patrician sector of Buckinghamshire (eight), Berkshire (seven) and Oxfordshire (five) and the paucity in the farming country of East Anglia and the tourist country of Lakeland and North Wales.

10  *The Copper-Plate Magazine, or Monthly Cabinet of Picturesque Prints* Vol. 2 (London: Harrison & Co and J. Walker), Plate 76.

11  *Ibid.*, Vol. 1, Plate 5.

12  *Ibid.*, Vol. 1, Plate 40.

13  *Ibid.*, Vol. 2, Plate 66. On the controversy between Repton and Price and Knight see S. Daniels, *Humphry Repton: Landscape Gardening and the Geography of Georgian England* (New Haven and London: Yale University Press, 1999), pp. 103–30.

14  Hermann, *Turner's Prints*, p. 260.

15  *The Copper-Plate Magazine* Vol. 2, Plate 91; Vol. 4, Plate 157. On the discourses of urban development informing the view of Birmingham see M. Berg, 'Representations of industrial towns: Turner and his contemporaries', in M. Rosenthal, C. Payne and S. Wilcox (eds), *Prospects for the Nation: Recent Essays on British Landscape 1750–1850* (New Haven and London: Yale University Press), 115–32.

16  *The Copper-Plate Magazine* Vol. 2, Plate 55.

17  *Ibid.*, Vol. 2, Plate 75.

18  'Matlock' sketchbook [Finberg XIX] D00211, Clore Galley for the Turner Bequest, London.

19  R. Thoroton, *The Antiquities of Nottinghamshire* (London: Henry Morlock, 1677), p. 490; T. Foulds, ' "This Great House, so Lately Begun", and all of Freestone: William Cavendish's Italianate *Palazzo* called Nottingham Castle', *Transactions of the Thoroton Society* 106 (2002), pp. 82–101.

20  C. Deering, *Nottingamia Vetus et Nova, or an Historical Account of the Ancient and Present State of the Town of Nottingham* (Nottingham: George Ayscough and Thomas Willington, 1751), p. 186.

21  U. Price, *Essays on the Picturesque* Vol. 2 (Hereford: D. Walker, 1798), p. 250n. In this note Price is making a comparison with nearby Wollaton Hall, 'a house, which for the riches of its ornaments in the near view, and the grandeur of its masses from every point, yields to few, if any, in the kingdom'. It is interesting that Turner's only surviving sketches in the neighbourhood of Nottingham from his 1790 tour are of Wollaton Hall ('Matlock' sketchbook, D00246–7) but they were not worked up into designs for publication.

22   J. Throsby, *Thoroton's History of Nottinghamshire, Republished with Large Additions* Vol. 2 (Nottingham: Burbage, Tupman, Wilson and Gray, 1790), pp. 25, 82.

23   On the iconography of the river, see N. Alfrey (ed.), *Trentside* (Nottingham: The Djangoly Art Gallery, University of Nottingham, 2001).

24   Throsby, *Thoroton's History* pp. 128–9.

25   J.F. Sutton, *The Date-Book of Remarkable and Memorable Eevents Connected with Nottingham and its neighbourhood 1750–1850* (London: Simkin and Marshall, 1852); C. Hadfield, *The Canals of the East Midlands* (Newton Abbot: David and Charles, 1966), pp. 54–6; S. Zaleski, *The Nottingham Canal, Past and Present* (Nottingham: Local History Press in Association with Nottingham City Council, 2001), pp. 5–8.

26   A. Wilton, *The Art of Alexander and John Robert Cozens* (New Haven: Yale Centre for British Art, 1980), pp. 41–62.

27   Hadfield, *The Canals of the East Midlands*, p. 57.

28   Throsby, *Thoroton's History of Nottinghamshire*, pp. 129, 128.

29   Zaleski, *The Nottingham Canal*, p. 7.

30   *The Itinerant: A Select Collection of Interesting and Picturesque Views in Great Britain and Ireland* (London: John Walker, 1799).

31   For example, after T. Barber, *View of Nottingham Castle*, frontispiece to *The History, Amtiquities and Present State of Nottingham* (Nottingham: J. Dunn, 1807); Edward Finden after William Westall, *Nottingham Castle, South West View*, in *Great Britain Illustrated* (London: Charles Tillet, 1830), p. 25. An unsigned early nineteenth-century oil painting based on Turner's view, with additional figures, boats and trees, presently hangs in The University of Nottingham's Personnel Department.

32   Shanes, *Turner's Picturesque Views*, pp. 10–15.

33   S. Smiles, *Eyewitness: Artists and Visual Documentation in Britain 1770–1830* (Aldershot: Ashgate, 2000), pp. 147–78.

34   Quoted in W.G. Rawlinson, *The Engraved Work of J.M.W. Turner* (London: Macmillan, 1908), p. 35.

35   S. Daniels, 'The Implications of Industry: Turner and Leeds', *Turner Studies* 6, 1 (1986), pp. 10–17.

36   Gage, *J.M.W. Turner*, p. 217; Smiles, *J.M.W. Turner*, p. 59; Shanes, *Turner's Picturesque Views*, pp. 38–9.

37   Shanes, *Turner's Picturesque Views*, pp. 32,43; W.S. Rodner, *J.M.W. Turner: Romantic Painter of the Industrial Revolution* (Berkeley and Los Angeles: University of California Press, 1997), pp. 107–13.

38   Shanes, *Turner's Picturesque Views*, pp. 18–23; E. Helsinger, 'Turner and the Representation of England', in W.J.T. Mitchell (ed.), *Landscape and Power* (Chicago, IL: University of Chicago Press, 1994), pp. 103–26.

39   J. Coney, *Architectural Beauties of Continental Europe in a Series of Views of Remarkable Ancient Edifices, Civil and Ecclesiastical, in France, the Low Countries, Germany and Italy* (London: J. Harding, 1826).

40   S. Smiles, 'Picture Notes', *Turner Studies* 8, 1 (1988), pp. 53–9.

41   Shanes, *Turner's Picturesque Views*, p. 13.

42   Newcastle, Henry Pelham Fiennes, Duke of, *An Address to All Classes and Conditions of Englishmen* (London T. & W. Boone, 1832).

43   *The Times*, 29 September 1832.

44   *The Times*, 13 October 1831.

45   R.A. Gaunt, 'The political activities and opinions of the Fourth Duke of Newcastle 1785–1851', unpublished PhD thesis University of Nottingham, 2000, pp. 154–216;

J. Beckett, 'The Nottingham Reform Bill Riots of 1831', *Parliamentary History Supplement*, October 2005, in press. My thanks to Professor Beckett for allowing me to see this before publication.

46  J. Hicklin, *The History of Nottingham Castle, from the Danish Invasion to its Destruction by Rioters in 1831* (London: Hamilton, Adams,1831), p. 196.

47  JGN [John Gough Nichols], 'Description of Nottingham Castle', *Gentleman's Magazine* new series, vol. 101, part 2 (1831), pp. 393–6.

48  The hearing is reprinted as an appendix to Hicklin, *The History of Nottingham Castle*; reported in *The Times*, 11 August 1832.

49  *A Descriptive Catalogue of Drawings by J.M.W. Turner for Views in England and Wales and also for Sir Walter Scott's Poetical Works* (London: J. Moyes, 1833), no. 60.

50  I owe this insight to Nicholas Alfrey, who, in a commentary on an early draft of this chapter, showed how the vignette structure accounted for many of the changes I described. See his account of Turner's vignettes in N. Alfrey, 'A Voyage Pittoresque: Byron, Turner and Childe Harold', *Renaissance and Modern Studies* 32 (1988), pp. 80–96. Also J. Pigott, *Turner's Vignettes* (London: Tate Gallery, 1993).

51  The colours of the drawing may have faded. In a note on a touched proof, Turner told the engraver to 'get the sky right'. Rawlinson, *The Engraved Work of J.M.W. Turner*, p. 154.

52  Gage, *J.M.W. Turner* pp. 218–24.

53  H. Boswell, *Views and Representations of the Antiquities of England and Wales* (London: Alexander Hogg, 1786), np.

54  Shanes is surely right to identify this as arson, but not, also, on a precipitous rock face, as 'stubble-burning', *Turner's Picturesque Views*, p. 40.

55  Ruskin, *Modern Painters*, Vol. 4, p. 31.

56  John Ruskin, *Modern Painters*, Vol. I, *Of General Principles, and of Truth*, new edition (London: George Allen, 1897), pp. 381–2.

57  Along with her wheel, a broken rudder is one of Fortuna's emblems. For the use of a rudder as an image of the tiller of the ship of state see Repton's vignette, reproduced in Daniels, *Humphry Repton*, p. 22. Even allowing for Turner's transpositions, it is surely too far-fetched for Shanes to say the rudder 'exactly resembles a butcher's cleaver...complete with blood red handle', *Turner's Picturesque Views*, p. 41.

58  Hadfield, *The Canals of the East Midlands*, pp. 120–2; M. Denney, *Historic Waterways Scenes: London and South-East England* (Ashbourne: Moorland, 1980), no. 143. I am grateful to Sheila Cooke, Shardlow Heritage Trust, Denny Plowman, Nottingham Castle Museum, and P.J. Sillitoe, National Waterways Museum, for information on this.

59  See for example the phallic helmsman in *Gosport, Entrance to Portsmouth Harbour* published in 1831 singled out by Shanes in *Turner's Picturesque Views* p. 34.

60  See the meanings listed in the *Compact Edition of the Oxford English Dictionary* (London: Book Club Associates, 1979), pp. 1036–7.

61  This was first noted by Eric Shanes in *Turner's England 1810–1838* (London: Cassell, 1996), p. 229.

62  *The Times*, 19 July 1824.

63  T. Moore, *Letters and Journals of Lord Byron, with a Memoir of his Life*, 2 vols (London: John Murray, 1830), Vol. 1, pp. 337–9.

64  J.V. Beckett with S. Aley, *Byron and Newstead: the Aristocrat and the Abbey* (Newark NJ and London: University of Delaware Press and Associated University Press, 2001), p. 280.

65   D.B. Brown, *Turner and Byron* (London: Tate Gallery, 1992).

66   Alfrey, 'A Voyage Pittoresque'; 'Reading into Turner', the 2000 Kurt Pantzer Memorial Lecture, *Turner Society Newsletter*, no. 85, 2000, pp. 6–10.

67   The details of the picture are described in C. Powell, *Turner's Rivers of Europe: The Rhine, Meuse and Mosel* (London: Tate Gallery, 1991), pp. 112–13.

68   Quoted Alfrey, 'A Voyage Pittoresque', p. 123.

69   A. Peach, 'Portraits of Byron', *The Walpole Society* (2000), pp. 1–144 (27–33); C. Kenyon Jones, 'Fantasy and transfiguration: Byron and his portraits', in F.Wilson (ed.), *Byromania* (Basingstoke: Palgrave Macmillan, 1999), pp. 109–36.

70   R.A. Voyler, *The Graphic Work of George Cruikshank* (New York: Dover Publications, 1979), p. 2.

71   Alfrey, 'A Voyage Pittoresque', p. 113.

72   'Childe Harold's Pilgrimage' Canto I, lines 29, pp. 101–2, 116; Canto II, line 653, Canto III, line 874, in J.J. McGann (ed.), *Byron* (Oxford: Oxford University Press).

73   Moore, *Letters and Journals of Lord Byron*, Vol. 2, pp. 3–4, 351, 669, 773.

74   The politics of Turner's landscapes have always proved hard to pin down as a symbolic point of view; scenes of ploughing in 1809, woollen manufacture in 1815, canal transport in 1833, or a steam express train in 1844, signal the distributions of power in the land, in widening fields of vision. Daniels, *Fields of Vision*, pp. 112–45.

75   Shanes, *Turner's Picturesque Views*, p. 15. Umbrella prints were illustrations torn from books and magazines before disposal for pulping and sold cheaply, for a penny or less, in the street pinned to the inside of umbrellas.

76   Private communication from the picture's owner. Bough was a member of the Royal Society of Artists and exhibited in London until the 1870s.

77   Foulds, ' "This Great House" ', p. 81.

78   On the 1940 purchase *National-Art Collections Fund Thirty-Seventh Annual Report 1940* (London: NACF 1941), p. 9. The cost, for the time and the city, was a substantial £230, to which the NACF contributed £50. That same year Turner's 1802 drawing *Edinburgh from the Water of Leith* was purchased by the fund, out of the Cochrane Trust, for £315 and presented to the National Gallery of Scotland, Edinburgh. In 1940 Nottingham also purchased, for £15, Paul Sandby's watercolour *East View of Nottingham Castle* (1777). My thanks to Michael Cooper for discussing with me relevant material in the files of the Nottingham Castle Museum.

# 2
# The Simple Life: Cottages and Gainsborough's Cottage Doors

*Ann Bermingham*

In quest of the simple life we find ourselves at the cottage. Embowered by trees, covered in flowering vines, roofed in thatch, and walled with timbers, brick and roughcast, the cottage stands in eighteenth-century thought as the natural domain of domestic peace and happiness. In romantic Britain the cottage was an alternative to all that was cold, formal and forbidding. For as one cottage enthusiast, the architect and drawing master James Malton, declared in comparing the cottage to the manor house:

> The matured eye, palled with gaudy magnificence, turns disgusted from the gorgeous structure, fair sloping lawn, well turned canal, regular fence, and formal rows of trees; and regards, with unspeakable delight, the simple cottage, the rugged common, rude pond, wild hedgerows, and irregular plantations. Happy he! Who early sees that true happiness is distinct from noise, from bustle, and from ceremony; who looks for it, chiefly, in his properly discharging his domestic duties, and by early planting with parental tenderness, the seeds of content in his rising offspring, reaps the glad harvest in autumnal age.[1]

Inseparable from 'true happiness' is the cottage's remoteness; nestled in an unimproved landscape far from the life of the city and the pomp of the great house, the cottage figures as a space of rural retreat and retirement. Add to this, the cottage's intimate scale, which presumably made familial closeness unavoidable, and one has a veritable blueprint of domestic bliss.

Cottages were, of course, the habitat of the rural poor, humble dwellings bordering the dark side of the landscape where too often multiple generations were confined to one or two small, dank, fetid rooms. Nevertheless, the conspicuous fantasy of the cottage embodied in Malton's description deserves our attention precisely for its fantastic elements. In it the cottage and the rustic landscape offer refuge from the city and from a domestic life marked by ceremony rather than by intimacy and affection. In a sense, the traditional themes of the classical literature of retirement which viewed pastoral scenes as escapes from the treacheries of the court and disillusionment with the *vita activa* are now transposed onto the middle-class registers of urban life and the home.

Malton's book was one of many treatises and pattern books published between the last decade of the eighteenth century and the first two decades of the nineteenth century that described the joys of cottage life and offered the means to attain them. Their sheer number indicates that the fantasy described by Malton was shared by many of his contemporaries. One can, without exaggeration, speak of this period's romance with the cottage as a kind of 'cult' which manifested itself in everything from architectural design to Staffordshire tea-pots, and which found expression too in the poetry and literature of the time. I want to look at this cult of the cottage and, in particular, at the cottage as both a fantasy and physical embodiment of new ideas of privacy and domesticity that emerged in the later part of the eighteenth century. I believe these ideas are not only rehearsed in the literature on cottage architecture but anticipated in the series of paintings produced by Thomas Gainsborough which take for their subject a family gathered before a cottage door. Gainsborough's cottage-door paintings have been the subject of extensive discussion which has focused largely on their possible meanings for the artist. Instead, I want to examine the meanings these works may have had for the late eighteenth and early nineteenth centuries as harbingers of a new and emerging discourse of nationhood and private life, and as indices of the contradictory ideas and desires this discourse harbored. To do so I wish to begin by turning to the architectural literature of the cottage – that is to say to the many treatises and pattern books in which these new ideas were voiced and given physical form.

## Cottage architecture

Archeological evidence reveals that cottages existed in England in Roman times, and it is likely that they date as far back as the earliest Bronze Age when cultivation first began on the chalk downs and high moors. Men shared these primitive one-room rural habitations with their domesticated beasts. Simple cottages of this type – half house and half barn – survived into the eighteenth century and were associated with the unimproved landscape and with the peasant life of open fields and commons.[2]

The antiquity of the cottage made it close cousin to the 'primitive hut', that mythic structure beloved of neo-classical architectural theorists (Illustration 2.1). Described in Vitruvius as the origin of architecture, the primitive hut was revived in the eighteenth-century architectural literature by the French architect Marc Antoine Laugier. In his *Essai sur l'architecture* (1753), Laugier argued that all architectural forms had their basis in 'simple nature', and were first expressed in the rude 'rustic hut' built by savages from tree branches.[3] Since the primitive hut was composed of columns, entablature and pediment, all other structural forms such as the vault, door,

*Illustration 2.1* Frontispiece from Marc-Antoine Laugier's *Essai sur l'architecture*, 1753, engraved by Charles Eisen. Courtesy of Davidson Library, University of California, Santa Barbara

window and pedestal were not essential to architecture and were evidence of civilization and refinement. Laugier's Rousseauian treatise on architecture was translated into English in 1755 and was discussed by British architects such as Isaac Ware (*Complete Body of Architecture*, 1756) Sir William Chambers (*Treatise on Civil Architecture*, 1759), and Sir John Soane (*Lectures on Architecture delivered to the students of the Royal Academy between 1809–1839*, 1929).[4] While his ideas about essential architectural form were subject to debate and criticism, Laugier's notion of the primitive hut as the originary architectural structure was accepted without question.

Peasant cottages were often viewed as throwbacks to the Vitruvian primitive hut. As Charles Middleton in his *Picturesque and Architectural Views for Cottages, Farm Houses, and Country Villas* (1793) explained, 'Cottages are inhabited by the poorer sort of country people, and are chiefly built of slight materials, and frequently by their own skill and labour: – they are the work of necessity, for which no rules can be given.'[5] By contrast, Middleton's cottages were not to be confused with primitive huts. Nevertheless, the term 'cottage architecture' employed by Middleton and others to describe their designs was something of an oxymoron, for in the eighteenth-century cottages, like the Vitruvian primitive hut, were not strictly architecture. Architecture, as the picturesque theorist Uvedale Price explained, was 'the divinity that raises the porches of cottages, and the rude posts that support them, into porticoes and colonnades'.[6] This formal sophistication came at a price for, 'while it refines and ennobles, it [architecture] necessarily takes off from that quickly-changing variety and intricacy of form, and that correspondent light and shadow, which are so striking in picturesque buildings'.[7] Cottages were picturesque, and because of this not really architecture.

In his *Essay on the Picturesque* (1794), Price set the standard for the true picturesque cottage when he wrote approvingly of the cottages painted and etched by the seventeenth-century Dutch master Adrian van Ostade:

> The outside of [Ostade's] cottages are no less distinguished for their variety and intricacy. Their outline against the sky, is generally composed of forms of unequal heights, thrown into many different degrees of perspective; the sides are varied by projecting windows and doors by sheds supported by brackets, with flower-pots on them; by the light, airy, and detached appearance of cages hung out from the wall; by porches and trellises of various constructions, often covered with vine or ivy: these, and many other picturesque objects, are so happily grouped with each other and with trees, that the bare outline would prove how much the eye may be pleased ... There is an idea of rural simplicity annexed to a thatched cottage, which is very much in favour of that covering; and indeed the appearance of new thatch, both from its neatness and color, is remarkably pleasing. It is no less picturesque, when mossy, ragged, and sunk in among

the rafters in decay; a species of that character, however, which the keenest lover of it, would rather see on another's property than his own.[8]

Price singled out variety, intricacy, irregularity in the form of the cottage, and decorative details such as twining vines, flower pots, bird cages and thatch as the essential ingredients of the picturesque cottage. He also made plain, in his remarks on the picturesque beauty of decaying thatch, that picturesqueness was not only at odds with 'architecture' but also with modern notions of comfort and agricultural improvement.

As one might expect, the authors of books on cottage architecture were less extreme in their views, and saw no tension between the cottage and modern architectural design. Indeed, it was the picturesque, they argued, that permitted cottages to be thought of as architecture. In his preface to *Hints for Picturesque Improvements in Ornamental Cottages*...(1804) Edmund Bartell claimed, 'Among the various objects of picturesque beauty, the cottage, whether ornamented or not, has been but slightly noticed; and I do not recollect to have seen any attempt to lay down rules for the management of such buildings upon picturesque principles.'[9] Like picturesque nature, cottage architecture could now be made subject to the rules of design and the laws of taste. Moreover, while striving to maintain the cottage's picturesque qualities, cottage architects were determined to build clean, modern, habitable dwellings. Their mission was to assure readers that cottages, those ancient peasant habitations, could also be made into suitable, practical and picturesque residences for the gentry. To this end they set out a wide range of designs and floor plans for cottages and analysed the different local materials that might be most appropriate for their construction.

The pattern books' promotion of the cottage challenges the assumption that consumption is stimulated by a desire to emulate one's social betters.[10] According to these terms taste flows down from the elite to the middle classes to finally the working classes. In this downward spiral quality filters away so that by the time the object of emulation reaches the lower classes it has become an inferior debased version of the original. The cult of the cottage suggests that this is not necessarily so. Cottage architecture is a striking example of taste bubbling upwards and it poses a question we will want to consider: how is it that a lowly form, traditionally associated with peasant life, could become the effervescent object of middle-class desire?

In part this desire was created by the architects. Claiming the title 'architecture' for modest buildings like cottages was the work of a young and growing profession that sought commissions not just from the elite but from those of the middling ranks as well.[11] Their promotion of cottage architecture benefited from a new nationalism stimulated by the wars with France. Derived, as it was, from local and vernacular forms of building, cottage architecture, the designers boasted, was a truly 'English' style. Unlike the Palladian and Gothic styles, cottage architecture did not demand too much in the way of professional training or extended study. The building methods and materials were familiar to most carpenters. In addition, with its origins in the picturesque taste for variety, cottage architecture was not based on orders but on relatively free-form designs. Such freedom permitted the client and the architect extensive leeway in devising individual stylistic expressions. Cottage architecture was a way for this expanding body of architectural professionals to reach out to a new group of clients offering them a range of imaginative designs and levels of comfort. It provided architects with a means to show off their talents while accommodating every taste and pocketbook.[12]

Books on cottage architecture insist on the necessity of a picturesque appearance that harmonizes with the rural setting. This criterion derives from the fact that the first inhabited ornamented cottages evolved from authentic cottages, but also from garden follies intended to enhance the picturesque effect of the landscape garden. Examples of such structures would be the 'root house' designed by Thomas Wright at Badminton (*c.* 1746), or the Convent in the Woods at Stourhead (*c.* 1760–70). Evolving as it did from garden follies such as these to modest residences for grounds-keepers, romantic cottage architecture maintained a connection to the overall landscaping of the estate. In his *Views for Cottages, Farm Houses, and Country Villas* (1793) Charles Middleton notes that:

> Cottages which are built at an entrance, or in different parts of the park or pleasure grounds … may serve the twofold purpose of use and ornament. They are generally inhabited by persons in the service of the family on whose estate they are erected; and situated near or at a distance from the mansion, according to the employments they hold, and should be so planned and distributed as to allow that admission of a family. The cottage built at the entrance of a park will form a convenient lodge. At a small distance from the mansion, the dairy, larder, bath, &c., may assume that characteristic form of a Cottage.[13]

One of the first such residential cottages was designed (but never built) by Humphry Repton in 1789 for the water-porter and his family at Holkham Hall. Intended for a clearing by the lake, it had a thatched roof and brick nogging – elements Repton claimed to have borrowed from fisherman's huts he had seen in the West country.[14] Repton got to build his first residential cottage in 1797 when he constructed a woodman's cottage at Blaise Castle. Such 'rural fabricks', Malton argued, should be proper habitations and not simply

> Those tasty little dwellings in noblemen's and gentlemen's pleasure grounds, often making the Porter's Lodge, adorned with handsome Gothic windows, and glazed with painted glass. Alike distant from both is the genuine British Cottage, which equally rejects the wretched poverty of the one and the frippery of the other.[15]

Neither poverty nor frippery had any place in the genuine 'British Cottage'.

As a result of these rather playful beginnings, cottage architecture was elastic enough to include a wide range of styles such as Gothic priories and Swiss chalets. Nevertheless, most cottage architects would agree with Malton when he declared that:

> When mention is made of the kind of dwelling called a Cottage, I figure in my imagination a small house in the country; of odd irregular form, with various, harmonious colouring, the effect of weather, time and accident; the whole environed with smiling verdure, having a contented, cheerful, inviting aspect, and door on the latch, ready to receive the gossip neighbor, or weary exhausted traveler. There are many indescribable somethings that must necessarily combine to give a dwelling this distinguishing character. A porch at entrance; irregular breaks in the direction of the walls; one part higher than the other; various roofing of different materials, thatch particularly, boldly projecting; front partly built of walls of brick, partly weather boarded, and partly brick-noggin dashed; casement window lights, are all conductive, and constitute its features.[16]

As this suggests, the vast majority of the cottage architecture books favoured the look of an irregular cottage built in loose imitation of sixteenth- and seventeenth-century English models with local materials, and featuring decorative touches such as thatched roofs, curly barge boards, leaded windows and, of course, porch pillars made from rough tree trunks in homage to the Vitruvian primitive hut. Such a look was codified by John Nash at Blaise Hamlet, Bristol (1811), when he designed a cluster of thatched cottages for the Quaker banker John Harford for his retired servants.

Cottage architecture books begin appearing regularly in the 1790s. From the start they had a dual audience and a dual purpose. On one the hand they were directed at the great landowner who wished to improve housing for his estate labourers, and on the other they addressed the upper- and middle-class householder seeking a modest rural retreat. While some books contain only designs for labourers' cottages or for middle- and upper-class residences, many present a combination of the two. They begin with the simplest plans for labourers' cottages and evolve into more complex plans for substantial middle- and upper-class residences. In reviewing the literature on cottage architecture it is important therefore to take a moment to distinguish between these two types of cottages.

## The labourer's cottage

In the second half of the eighteenth-century the deteriorated state of labourers' cottages was a matter of social concern. Books with designs for such cottages appealed to the improving landlord's feelings of sympathy and paternalistic responsibility, while also proposing how such improvements would result in economic and political benefits. Thus, in 1775, Nathaniel Kent in his *Hints to Gentlemen of Landed Property* pleaded that improving landlords refurbish their labourers' cottages and allow each cottage half an acre of land for pasturage and a small garden. A clean, dry cottage and the small subsistence provided by a cow, pig, fruit and vegetables, Kent believed, 'would be of great use and ornament to the country, and a real credit to every man's residence'.[17] While manufacturing towns were 'destructive both to morals and health, the country', Kent declared, 'must be the place; and cottages, and small farms the chief nurseries, which support the population'.[18] Thus the condition of the cottage reflected the benevolence of the improving landlord, and improved cottages, those nurseries of the labouring classes, would ultimately help preserve the morals of the nation.

In his introduction to *A Series of Plans for Cottages or Habitations of the Labourer* (1781), John Wood noted that the 'ruinous state of the cottages of this kingdom' have become 'offensive both to decency and humanity' and that this is a 'matter worthy the attention of every man of property'.[19] Once he began to study cottages, Wood confessed that he found it impossible to confine himself to the rural habitations of farm laborers, but he had to broaden his study to include those of 'the workmen and artificers in the cloathing and other manufacturing counties'.[20] As a result, his final designs are intended to be suitable for both rural laborers in the country and industrial workers in towns.

In a similar spirit of civic minded reform, William Atkinson began his essay on *Cottage Architecture* (1805) by announcing that:

> The building of Cottages for the labouring classes of society, and the keeping of them in good repair, are objects of the first national importance; as it is from the active exertions of the industrious labourers, that the other classes derive the greater part of those benefits which they enjoy...for by introducing improvement on these objects [cottages], they [men of property] may add to their pleasure, by producing the most picturesque scenery; and at the same time, add to the comfort and happiness of their fellow creatures.[21]

In Atkinson's mind, support for the poor and aesthetic pleasure for the rich could be united in improved cottage architecture.

Edmund Bartell announced that:

> Beneath the rugged features and russet garb of humble life are, not unfrequently, found feelings the most exquisite, and sentiments that would reflect honour upon the highest situations in life. With a view to

cherish these tender and delicate plants, this Essay takes into consideration the dwellings of the laboring poor; not only as a source of ornament, but with a view also of pointing out what appears to be an easy means of bettering the conditions and morals of a considerable body of that useful and highly important class of people.[22]

The assumptions underpinning such arguments are that the poor are naturally disposed to goodness, but that it is the responsibility of men of property to foster this predisposition through improved housing and design.

The domestic engineering implicit in the reform of labourers' cottages maps onto a wider cultural preoccupation with improving 'domestic economy'. Domestic economy was household management, and as Anne K. Mellor and others have explained, in the later eighteenth-century the management of the home was equated by social reformers with the management of the nation.[23] As Hannah More argued in her *Strictures on the Modern System of Female Education* (1799), 'your private exertions may at this moment be contributing to the future happiness, your domestic neglect, to the future ruin, of your country'.[24] The emphasis on domesticity as the foundation of nationhood not only placed women at the center of a civic project to refashion the nation along the lines of a middle-class Christian home, but in doing so it eroded the distinction between private life and the more broadly defined public sphere.

The diagnoses and design solutions of the cottage reformers to the problem of working-class housing are grounded in ideals of benevolence, community and sensibility. Atkinson, for instance, was determined to build cottages with fireplaces that would conserve the cottagers' precious supply of fuel for he observed that 'cottagers are always more intelligent, and industrious, where fuel is cheap'.[25] The moral state of cottagers thus depended on their having a comfortable fireside which 'promotes social mirth and instructive conversation'.[26] Significantly, Atkinson's image of cottage life is not of a private retreat but rather of a communal space, a sort of public sphere of the fireside.

John Wood was convinced of the need to make cottages that were cheerful, clean and morally decent. Nevertheless, rather than simply impose his design solutions, he interviewed cottagers as to their needs and desires. 'It was necessary', Wood explained, 'for me to feel as the cottager himself; for I have always held it as a maxim...that no architect can form a convenient plan, unless he ideally places himself in the situation of the person for whom he designs'.[27] To that end, Wood claims that he visited with cottagers to observe their way of living and to listen to their complaints. Architecture, Wood insists, is an art in which sensibility, that is the ability to put oneself in the place of another and to feel with him, is an essential requirement.

Typically, Atkinson's and Wood's plans show modest one- or two-room dwellings. In Wood's plan one-room cottages are designed with at least one window, a fireplace and a sheltered doorway, a pantry or shed, and a water-closet or privy. Atkinson's designs are more elaborate (Illustration 2.2); his cottages have two floors. The ground floor is made up of a kitchen with a fireplace and scullery sink, a pantry and a privy. Stairs lead to sleeping quarters under the roof which contain two bedrooms. For convenience a cowshed, piggery and dairy are attached to the cottage. This addition of a barn-like space to the cottage is typical of all Atkinson's designs and it derives from the old tradition of quartering farm animals with the family.

## The cottage ornée

In contrast to the books by reformers, the architectural pattern books associated with the 'ornamented cottage' or the 'cottage ornée' are addressed to the gentry. In his *Rural Residences* (1818), John Papworth declared that the cottage ornée is not 'the habitation of the labourious, but of the affluent, of the man of study, of science, or of leisure; it is often the rallying point of domestic comfort'.[28] These books imagined the cottage as a rural retreat for those in search of the simple pleasures of retirement. Recalling, it would seem, Marie Antionett's Hameau, Thomas Dearn observed that even those who find themselves in reduced circumstances could now 'under the sanction of fashion' enjoy the frugal comforts of a cottage without any shame for indeed 'we have seen even royalty become the inmate and inhabitant of a cottage'.[29]

Much of the rationale for the cottage ornée derived from the pastoral tradition that envisioned upper-class life as burdensome. The taste for cottages, Thomas Malton claimed, 'prevails in all ranks of people', yet he noted it was 'more fervent in those whose elevated sphere of life has excluded from the likelihood of ever tasting, but whose nice sensibility could give conception to those pleasurable sensations that are the offspring of moderate enjoyment'.[30] A refined sensibility coupled with a never to be requited longing were the prerequisites for cottage love. Thus Robert Ferrars could enthuse to Elinor Dashwood, whose reduced circumstances meant residing with her mother and sister at Barton Cottage, that 'I am excessively fond of a cottage; there is always so much comfort, so much elegance about them'.[31] As Austen makes clear, the danger of Robert Ferrars ever having to live in a cottage was so remote that its ever-receding image could glow all the more warmly in his imagination.

Robert Ferrars' idealization of the cottage and cottage life is echoed by Malton when he notes that, 'the greatly affluent in sumptuous equipage, as they pass the cheerful dwelling of the careless rustic or unambitious man, who prefers agrestic pleasures to the boisterous clamour of cities, involuntarily sigh as they behold the modest care-excluding mansions of the lowly contented'.[32] Rather than a guarantee of personal liberty, wealth becomes in this scenario – enslavement. The great, Malton notes, are burdened by the

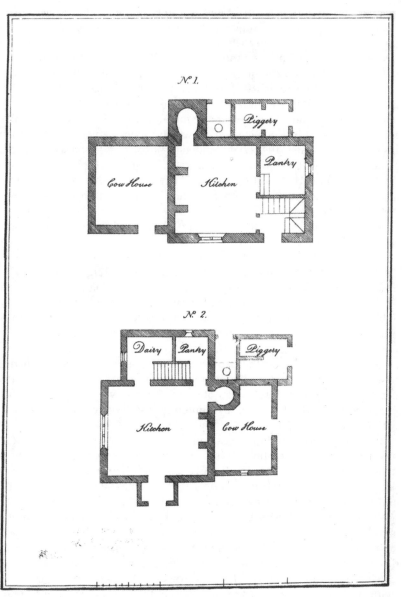

*Illustration 2.2* Plate 1, from William Atkinson's *Cottage Architecture, Including Perspective Views and Plans of Labourers Cottages, and Small Farm Houses,* 1805. Courtesy of Davidson Library, University of California, Santa Barbara

need always to appear great; 'When considering the master as mere man', Malton opines, 'there is found no consistency between the possessor and the thing possessed: the immensity of his demands, the attentions he must necessarily exact of others, and a continual reliance upon them for the support of his dignity, more immediately renders him dependent, rather than the lord of his servants'.[33] Greatness is thus contingent on others. The great man's freedom is curtailed by a complex network of social exchanges. Rather than a private retreat where he might be free to express his intimate self, the mansion is a public space in which the great man must maintain his image. Conversely, the cottage embodies a happiness that rests on privacy, personal liberty, and wealth regulated by simple necessity, not public display. Despite the burdens of wealth it appears that few great men actually retired to cottages to pursue the 'agrestic pleasures' of the 'lowly contented'. Those who did, like Richard Payne Knight, chose cottages on their own estates where, when necessary, they could flee their picturesque inconveniences.

Clearly the cult of the cottage depended on creating an image of upper-class life that is the antithesis of domestic happiness. Jürgen Habermas has described the ideal eighteenth-century middle-class home as a space that is imagined to be one of 'psychological emancipation' where 'intimacy apparently set free from the constraint of society' allows individuals to be themselves.[34] Such autonomy appeared 'to be established voluntarily and by free individuals and to be maintained without coercion; it seemed to rest on a community of love on the part of the two spouses; it seemed to permit that non-instrumental development of all faculties that marks the cultivated personality'.[35] Home, Habermas notes, was a place where family members imagined themselves as capable of entering into 'purely human' relations with one another.[36]

Given this vision of middle-class domesticity, the floor plans of the cottage ornée deserve our attention. While their exterior designs are at pains to maintain the look of the simple rustic cottage, the interior plans feature parlours, drawing rooms, dining rooms, libraries, music rooms, conservatories and servants' quarters. Fireplaces and windows are found in nearly every room, and conveniences such as pantries, store rooms, sculleries and privies are common features. Just as there were a range of plans for how poor labourers might live, plans for the cottage ornée suggest there was a great deal of latitude in determining how simple the simple life might be.

While peasant cottages did not distinguish between rooms for eating, living and sleeping, since it was not unusual for all these functions to take place in one room, the ornamented cottages of Malton, Middleton, Dearn, Bartell, Papworth and others assign various domestic functions to separate rooms. Curiously, however, there appears to have been some uncertainty as to where, given their functions, the kitchen and privy might be placed in the overall plan of the cottage ornée. While most place the bedroom – for quiet and decency's sake – apart from the main living rooms, there is no conformity about the placement of the kitchen and the privy.

In peasant cottages the kitchen was the main room of the house and served as dining room, living room and even bedroom. As architects like Atkinson observed, it was the kitchen hearth around which all family socializing took place. In middle-class cottages, or cottage ornées, the kitchen occasionally retains some of this central importance. Rather than being relegated to the back of the house with the servants quarters, it is often found in the front of the house and can even be the room on to which the front door opens.

For instance in Charles Middelton's designs for simple cottages, one enters the cottage through the kitchen which leads to the parlour (Illustration 2.3). A favourite design solution, one used by Dearn, Papworth and others, was to have the front door open to a main hall from which visitors can either turn left to the living room or right into the kitchen.

Like the kitchen, the placement of the privy appears to have been open to different interpretations. Dearn shows it in the hall alongside the staircase, while others such as Atkinson place it in the back of the house (Illustration 2.4). Only rarely does it appear next to the bedrooms.

This uncertainty about the proper place of the kitchen and the privy suggests an uncertainty as to what role they should play in the life of the home. Is the kitchen the centre of family life, or a service area to be hidden away? Is the indoor privy a novel and welcome convenience for arriving guests, or a necessary but an unpalatable utility to be exiled to the back of the house? No doubt the answers to these questions have practical as well as ideological dimensions. Depending on their technologies, kitchens and especially privies could be unpleasant places that one might well want them separate from the main living quarters of the house. Yet all things being equal, the fact that these rooms move around in the floor plans for cottages seems indicative of an uncertainly as to whether they were public or private rooms, luxuries or necessities, central or peripheral, important or trivial to the life of the cottage. While the bedroom had by this time been locked into place by middle-class notions of sexual propriety, kitchens and privies were complex enough in their associations and possibilities to occupy a number of different domestic locations. Just as the addition of drawing rooms and music rooms to the cottage ornée bespeaks an uncertainty as to how much upper-class elegance and refinement was needed to maintain the middle-class home as a place of cultivation, so too the indeterminate placement of the kitchen and the privy reflects a confusion of class interests and identities.

Cottage architecture could serve the needs of both the labouring rural poor and the leisured middle classes. Its dual nature is reflected in the fact that so many of the cottage books include designs both for middle-class cottage ornées and for small-scale dwellings for the labouring poor. Often in

50

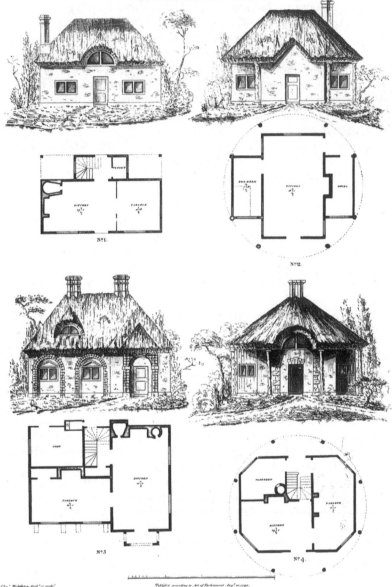

*Illustration 2.3*  Plate 1, from Charles Middleton's *Picturesque and Architectural Views for Cottages, Farm Houses and Country Villas*, 1793. Courtesy of Davidson Library, University of California, Santa Barbara

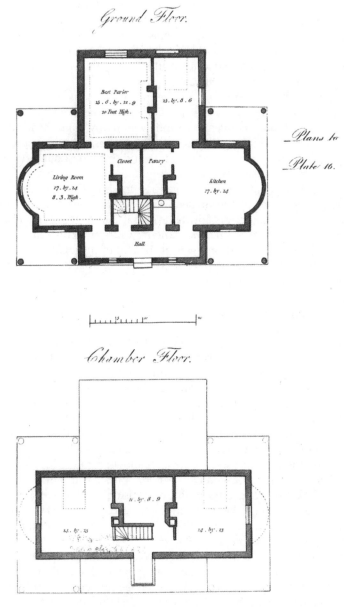

*Ground Floor.*

*Chamber Floor.*

*Plans to Plate 16.*

*Illustration 2.4* Plate 15, from T.D.W. Dearn's *Sketches in Architecture, Consisting of Designs for Cottages and Rural Dwellings, Suitable to Persons of Moderate Fortune, and for Convenient Retirement,* 1807. Courtesy of Davidson Library, University of California, Santa Barbara

these books it is difficult to distinguish between cottages intended for the poor and those for the gentry, other than by the number and complexity of the rooms, and in some cases there appears to have been an intentional blending of the two types. In these books, working-class cottages often partake of conveniences that one would expect to see in middle-class cottages. Atkinson, for instance, insists on privies for all his labourers' cottages. This suggests that the question for architects and designers was how distinct should middle-class and working-class domesticity be from one another? For instance, how much convenience and even luxury might be introduced into the labourers' cottages without running the risk of raising the social expectations of the poor too high? Or, on the other hand, should the cottage ornée reflect rustic sociability and the communality of peasant life, or the more retired and private life of the gentry? In short, how much peasant conviviality represented by the kitchen was relevant to middle-class domestic happiness and how much was antithetical to it and to the genteel privacy and refinement represented by the parlour? Cottage architecture demonstrates how open these questions were at the end of the eighteenth century and how uncertain architects were as to what might add or detract from a stable class hierarchy and from middle-class domestic happiness.

## Gainsborough's *cottage doors*

Writing to his friend William Jackson from Bath, Gainsborough complained 'I am sick of portraits and wish very much to take my Viol da Gam and walk off to some sweet Village where I can paint Landskips and enjoy the fag End of life in quietness and ease.'[37] To Sir William Chambers he wrote, 'If I can pick pockets...in the portrait way two or three years longer I intend to sneak into a cot & turn a serious fellow.'[38] These oft-quoted remarks have served as evidence of Gainsborough's fondness for landscape, music and the pastoral dream of rural retirement to a cottage.[39] Such assumptions are supported by the fact that some time after moving from Bath to London, Gainsborough purchased a cottage near Richmond Hill. Other accounts, such as Walter Armstrong's, have him purchasing a cottage at Kew, while J.T. Smith wrote that he had lodgings in Hampstead. Finally there is a drawing by Thomas Rowlandson of a cottage in Essex, which Rowlandson identifies as belonging to Gainsborough.

In her important recent book, *Gainsborough in Bath*, Susan Sloman observes that notions of rural retreat were popular among Gainsborough's Bath friends, many of whom like Ann Ford and her husband Phillip Thicknesse were Tories and even Jacobite sympathizers.[40] Jacobite sociability, so evident in Gainsborough's Bath circle, 'centered on an image of genteel separation, seclusion or retirement, that lasted well in to the 1760s and beyond'.[41] The Marquess of Grandby, later the Duke of Rutland, who purchased the first cottage door, *The Woodcutter's Return*, was, though a Whig himself, married to Lady Isabella Somerset, the sister of the fifth Duke of Beaufort, a family with deep Jacobite attachments. Gainsborough's wife, Margaret Burr, was, as Sloman has shown, the third Duke of Beaufort's natural daughter. If I were to push this evidence uncovered by Solman further, I would suggest that the cottage doors' theme of rural retirement owes a great deal to Gainsborough's Tory friendships and his wife and friends' cultural Jacobitism.

Gainsborough's fondness for the countryside extended to its poorest inhabitants. Uvedale Price recalled that when Gainsborough came upon 'cottage or village scenes, to groups of children, to any objects of that kind which struck his fancy, I have often remarked in his countenance an expression of particular gentleness and complacency'.[42] If all this were not enough to convince us of Gainsborough's fondness for the rural pastoral, we have the pictorial evidence of the cottage door paintings themselves.

The first of the cottage doors, *The Woodcutter's Return*, dates from Gainsborough's late Bath period, *c.* 1772–74, and the last was finished a few months before his death in August of 1788 (Illustration 2.5). All together there are four large-scale cottage doors that survive, five if one counts Mrs Scudamore's painting now at Ipswich. However, from the 1760s onwards one can find similar scenes of cottagers outside their cottages in smaller landscapes, or used as *staffage* and tucked into larger landscape compositions.[43] Three of the cottage doors are vertical in format and concentrate on figures clustered in a pyramidal group at the door of a cottage, and two are horizontal and depict figures spilling down the cottage steps horizontally onto the landscape (Illustration 2.6). All are marked by the Rubens-like color and handling of Gainsborough's later style. As John Hayes has noted, Gainsborough cottage doors are the first significant treatment of the theme of cottage life in British art.[44]

The Cincinnati and the Huntington paintings were exhibited at the Academy in 1778 and 1780 respectively. However, it seems that the others were not entirely unknown. A eulogy by 'D.W.' entitled 'On Seeing Mr. Gainsborough's Pictures at Bath', which appeared in the *Gentleman's Magazine* in December 1773, describes the Rutland *Woodcutter's Return* as a 'scene of beauty and domestic love'.[45] Similar words of praise greeted the exhibited works. A writer for the *Morning Chronicle* called the Huntington *Cottage Door* a 'beautiful scene where serenity and pleasure dwell in every spot, and the lovely figures composed in the finest rural style, their situation worthy of them, forms a scene of happiness that may truly be called Adam's paradise'.[46] The reputation of the cottage doors continued into the nineteenth century. Thomas Hearn noted that Gainsborough's 'representations of simple life are given with such taste as to delight and never offend. He is never coarse; His Peasant in rags has no filth; no idea of dirt & wretchedness is excited.' J.M.W. Turner called the Huntington *Cottage Door* a scene of 'pure and artless innocence', and John Constable, speaking of Gainsborough's landscapes generally, told a London audience that 'the landscape of Gainsborough is

*Illustration 2.5*  Thomas Gainsborough, *The Woodcutter's House, c.* 1772–73 (58 × 48 inches), The Duke of Rutland, Belvoir Castle, Leicestershire/Bridgeman Art Library

soothing, tender and affecting... On looking at them, we find tears in our eyes, and know not what brings them.'[47]

The major cottage door compositions all show young, refined-looking women and cherubic children clustered at the door of the cottage. The children feed themselves from bowls or are suckled at the breast. In several compositions (Cincinnati, UCLA and Rutland) single male figures either return home

*Illustration 2.6*   Thomas Gainsborough, *Cottage Door with Children Playing*, RA 1778 (48 1/4 × 58 3/4 inches), Cincinnati Art Museum, Cincinnati, Ohio

from gathering wood or take their ease before the cottage.[48] In all the compositions, the cottage melts imperceptibly into its landscape setting; its roughcast blends with the soil and rocks of the landscape, its thatch seems an extension of the leafy tree branches that shelter it, and in the case of the Rutland painting a tree appears to spring up from the doorstep where the women and children gather, becoming a virtual structural element in the cottage's design. In these paintings the cottage is not just an extension of nature into culture but a remaking of nature as culture. It is a nature made wholly domestic, a nature made home. The cottage seems like nature but not like any nature that we know exists. Other aspects of the cottage doors call attention to the compositions' fantastic reconfigurations of our relationships to our surroundings. The placement of the women at the door of the cottage links them to its recessed interior while the labouring man suggests the wider world beyond. The powerful maternal presence in the cottage doors, so powerful that the young women attending the children number three in the Rutland and Cincinnati versions, and the emphasis on nourishment (food) and comfort (fuel) suggests the Freudian notion of the 'heimlich'; that is to say the home with all its connotations of shelter, comfort, intimacy, safety, quiet content and the inevitable association of these qualities with the maternal body.[49] The power of the cottage door image is precisely its ability to displace fantasies of maternal succor and security from the body of the mother onto an image of a cottage. The cottage thus becomes a powerfully charged trope of infantile desire.

In rather different terms, John Barrell has discussed Gainsborough's cottage doors as fantasies of a rural England or 'Happy Britannia' that never was.[50] With their combined scenes of industry and domestic peace, the cottage doors idealize an England of independent, happy peasantry. Nevertheless, when viewed in the historical context of rural poverty exacerbated by enclosures and the loss of common land, the *cottage doors* are also implicated in what was a national debate over support for the displaced and impoverished rural poor.[51] Gainsborough's 'taste', described by Hearn, created images of the deserving poor, of cottagers who are clean, naturally refined, domestic and, if one includes the woodman, industrious and hard-working. While such idealized figures may be out of place in scenes of rural life, they were, as Barrell points out, precisely the image of the rural labourer that the Poor Law reformers envisioned as the worthy recipients of nation's largesse.

Barrell's analysis helps us to see how the cottage doors are not only of their time but of ours. Moreover, it rounds out a psychoanalytic reading such as the one I have proposed by suggesting the wider political and cultural engine that drove this fantasy of home and made it resonate for Gainsborough and his contemporaries. It suggests that the cottage doors pose questions about private pleasure and social responsibility in much the same way as the literature on cottage architecture partakes in a national debate about class, rural poverty and the private, civic and even national responsibility to relieve it. What we find in the cottage doors and the literature on cottage architecture is a commingling of ideas of privacy, individualism, domestic comfort and happiness on the one hand with notions of community, nation and social responsibility on the other. What does it mean to conceive of the nation in private terms as a cottage family, or to conceive of the cottage family in public terms as the nation? Just as the paintings convert the image of nature into the cottage and the cottage into an icon of infantile desire for comfort and security, they also invite us to view the cottage family as the embodiment of the nation, and to see their security and well being as both a natural state and a natural right.

'Cottage architecture' is both the origin of *private* middle-class suburban-tract housing and the ancestor of *public* council housing. Inevitably, the questions posed by Gainsborough's cottage doors point on the one hand to possessive individualism, and on the other to social welfare. And these contradictory impulses coexist in Gainsborough's cottage doors just as they do in the cottage architecture books. They signify a larger national uncertainty about individual responsibility and social responsibility, about what is owed to the self and what is owed to others. Such questions are basic to a bourgeois democracy, and in eighteenth-century Britain they could not be resolved in art because they were unresolved in the culture at large.

The term that mediated between these two contradictory impulses was 'sensibility'. Let's return for a moment to those tears Constable says that we find in our eyes when we gaze at Gainsborough's rustic scenes. What are they if not the power of sympathy to feel with another while remaining exquisitely aware of one's own private emotions. Sensibility motivated the cottage reformers, it softened Gainsborough's countenance into an 'expression of particular gentleness and complacency', and it brought tears to Constable's eyes when he gazed on those scenes of rural life by Gainsborough's brush. As a mode of feeling, and feeling with, sensibility attempted to solve the dilemma of what was due to the self and what was due to the other, of what belonged to the individual through his own enterprise and what belonged to others by nature of their humanity and their fellowship in the nation. The answer posed by sensibility was not self *or* other, but self *and* other. Precisely because one was a sensate being, an individual, one also recognized oneself as a part of the larger fellowship of nation and humankind.

Like the treatises on cottage architecture, Gainsborough's cottage-door paintings recast the nation as a humble domestic space. In doing so they posit the welfare of the poor to be a national as well as private responsibility. Their idealization of the cottager strikes a chord for it allows their middle-class viewers to project themselves into their pastoral visions of domesticity and to take pleasure in their rural protagonists' simple life. We can fault the sentimentality of such images, but in doing so we should not overlook their powerful appeal to sensibility and their potential to embody in visual terms a new, and as of yet, politically inchoate rationale for the care of the nation.

The questions posed by the treatises and paintings are relevant today, for once again it seems we are living a fantasy of the cottage. Even before September 11, when Americans supposedly traded in their frequent flyer miles for the pleasures of hearth and home, magazines like *Cottage Life* and artists like Thomas Kinkade were doing brisk business. For instance, in the year 2000, the Media Arts Group, a group that produces Kinkade's various art-based products such as jigsaw puzzles, calendars and night-lights, reported $132 million in revenues. Since 1994, stock in Media Arts Group has been traded on the New York Stock exchange.[52] Kinkade's fame rests on his cottage scenes, which typically feature thatched cottages covered in blooming vines, cloaked in twilight and set in rustic picturesque landscapes that for reasons presumably having to do with his moniker, 'painter of light', are often incongruously illuminated by a glowing lamppost (Illustration 2.7). The phosphorescent light emanating from the lamp, the cottage windows and the distant sunset brilliantly illuminate the flowering shrubs and vines turning them into vibrant, psychedelic visions. A housing development based on his cottage scenes has been built in El Segundo California.

*Illustration 2.7*   Thomas Kinkade, *Moonlight Cottage* (*September*) from *Thomas Kinkade: Painter of Light*, 2003 Calendar

Kinkade describes himself as a 'Christian' and he believes that Christian family values are the inspiration behind his paintings.

To what do we owe this cottage revival? If the previous cult of the cottage is any guide, I believe that Americans are living at a time when our obligations as to what we owe to ourselves and what we own to others are open to national debate. While the previous response to the questions posed by the cottage was to side with those who urged benevolence and social responsibility culminating ultimately in a version of the socialist welfare state in the United Kingdom and in federal programmes like the New Deal and Great Society in the United States, I am not optimistic that anything so sweeping or enlightened will result this time. Kinkade's cottages, I fear, represent a retreat from political and civic responsibility into a private world of possessive individualism. They are about wealth, not care of the poor. Such images emerged in the 1980s at a time of new economic growth, and peaked in the 1990s during the height of the dot.com boom. This growth in national wealth has come at a time when the taxation of the very rich is at its lowest point since the institution of the income tax.[53] In a period of great wealth Kinkade's images recall a simpler more modest existence; they encourage viewers to see 'Christian family values', embodied in a visual fantasy of simple cottage life, as coexisting in harmony with affluence and governmentally sanctioned greed. They encourage a belief that as a nation we have not lost our moral compass. At best, they indicate a nagging discomfort with wealth, an embarrassment with its materialism and a need to transmute it into something less base. At worst they encourage viewers to salve their consciences with private domestic comforts swaddled in moral platitudes rather than to see wealth put to something larger like the welfare of others.

But even if the recent cottage revival signals a shrinking of the public sphere, the idea of the cottage is, as we have seen, necessarily ambivalent and thus it contains within it the potential for another, more civic, kind of meaning. As much as it can resonate with the values of conservative possessive individualism, the cottage, and the promise of the simple life it holds, still asks us to consider how much we need to possess in order to be happy, and whether the small man's pursuit of happiness should not be as much a priority as the great man's. Moreover, because they embody eighteenth-century fantasies of rural pastoralism and paternalism, Gainsborough's cottage doors still have the ability to ask us to consider the possibility that the cottage is the nation, and that the security of small stakeholders must therefore be a shared, national responsibility.

## Notes

1  James Malton, *An Essay on British Cottage Architecture* (London: Hookham & Carpenter, 1798), pp. 6–7.
2  Helpful architectural histories of the cottage include: Olive Cook, *English Cottages and Farmhouses* (London: Thames & Hudson, 1982); John E. Crowley's 'Picturesque Comfort: The Cottage', in his *The Invention of Comfort: Sensibilities and Design in Early Modern Britain and Early America* (Baltimore and London: Johns Hopkins University Press, 2000), pp. 203–29; Tony Evans and Lycett Green, *English Cottages* (New York: The Viking Press, 1983); Sutherland Lyall, *Dream Cottages: From Cottage Orneé to Stockbroker Tudor* (London, Robert Hale Ltd, 1988). The cult of the cottage has been explored by John Dixon Hunt, 'The Cult of the Cottage', *The Lake District: A Sort of National Property* (London: Victoria and Albert Museum, 1988), pp. 71–84. On the 'simple life' see Maren-Sofie Røstvig, *The Happy Man: Studies in the Metamorphoses of a Classical Ideal*, 2 vols (Oslo: Norwegian Universities Press, 1954).
3  Marc-Antoine Laugier, *Essay on Architecture* (Los Angeles, CA: Hennessey & Ingalls, Inc., 1977), p. 12.
4  Wolfgang Herrmann, *Laugier and Eighteenth-Century French Theory* (London: A. Zwemmer, Ltd., 1962), pp. 173–84. See, too, Joseph Rykwert, *On Adam's House in Paradise: The Idea of the Primitive Hut in Architectural History* (Cambridge, MA: MIT Press, 1981).
5  Charles Middleton, *Picturesque and Architectural Views for Cottages, Farm Houses and Country Villas* (London: Edward Jeffery, 1793), p. 1.

6   Uvedale Price, *Sir Uvedale Price, On the Picturesque, with an Essay On the Origin of Taste, by Sir Thomas Dick Lauder, bart., and sixty illustrations, designed and drawn on the wood by Montagu Stanley, R.S.A.* (Edinburgh: Caldwell, Lloyd, 1842), p. 393.
7   Price, p. 393.
8   *Ibid.*, pp. 392–3, 397–8.
9   Edmund Bartell, *Hints for Picturesque Improvements in Ornamental Cottages and Their Scenery: Including some Observations on the Labourer and His Cottage. In Three Essays* (London: J. Taylor, [1800], 1804), p. vii.
10  The classic formulation of emulation is Thorstein Veblen's *Theory of the Leisure Class* (1899); more recently Neil McKendrick has used this model to describe the marketing successes of Josiah Wedgwood (see N. McKendrick, J. Brewer and J.H. Plumb, *The Birth of Consumer Society: The Commercialization of Eighteenth-Century England*, 1982).
11  Lyall, pp. 22–7.
12  *Ibid.*, pp. 21–2.
13  Middleton, p. 1.
14  Stephen Daniels, *Humphry Repton: Landscape Gardening and the Geography of Georgian England* (New Haven and London: Yale University Press, 1999), pp. 82–4.
15  Malton, p. 4.
16  *Ibid.*, p. 5.
17  Nathaniel Kent, *Hints to Gentlemen of Landed Property* (London: J. Dodsley, 1775), p. 238.
18  Kent, p. 231.
19  John Wood, *A Series of Plans for Cottage or Habitations of the Labourer* (London: J. Taylor, 1806, first edition 1781), p. 3.
20  *Ibid.*
21  William Atkinson, *Cottage Architecture, Including Perspective Views and Plans of Labourers Cottages, and Small Farm Houses* (London: J. Barfield, 1805), pp. v–vi.
22  Bartell, p. x.
23  Anne K. Mellor, *Mothers of the Nation* (Bloomington and Indianapolis, IN: Indiana University Press, 2000), pp. 25–32.
24  Hannah More, *Strictures on the Modern System of Female Education*, in *The Works of Hannah More* (London: H. Fisher, R. Fisher & P. Jackson, 1834) III: 44.
25  Atkinson, p. viii.
26  *Ibid.*
27  Wood, p. 3.
28  John B. Papworth, *Rural Residences, Consisting of a Series of Designs for Cottages, Decorated Cottages, Small Villas and Other Ornamental Buildings* (London: R. Ackerman, 1818), p. 25.
29  T.D.W. Dean, *Sketches in Architecture Consisting of Original Designs for Cottages and Rural Dwellings, Suitable to Persons of Moderate Fortune, and for Comfort and Retirement* (London: J. Taylor, 1807), p. 5.
30  Malton, p. 5.
31  Jane Austen, *Sense and Sensibility*, ed. R.W. Chapman, 5 vols (Oxford and New York: Oxford University Press, 1982) I: 251.
32  Malton, p. 6.
33  *Ibid.*, p. 8.
34  Jürgen Habermas, *The Structural Transformation of the Public Sphere: An Inquiry into a Category of Bourgeois Society* (Cambridge, MA: MIT Press, 1989), p. 46.

35  *Ibid.*
36  *Ibid.*, p. 48.
37  John Hayes, ed., *The Letters of Thomas Gainsborough* (New Haven and London: Yale University Press, 2001), p. 68.
38  *Ibid.*, p. 152.
39  See Marcia Pointon, 'Gainsborough and the Landscape of Retirement', *Art History*, 2 (December 1979), pp. 441–55; John Hayes, *The Landscape Paintings of Thomas Gainsborough*, 2 vols (Ithaca, NY: Cornell University Press, 1983) I, pp. 149–56; Michael Rosenthal, *The Art of Thomas Gainsborough: 'A Little Business for the Eye'*, (New Haven and London: Yale University Press, 1999), pp. 204–11.
40  Susan Sloman, *Gainsborough in Bath* (New Haven and London: Yale University Press, 2002), pp. 112–17, 179.
41  *Ibid.*, p. 112.
42  Price, p. 408.
43  The four large cottage doors are: *The Woodcutter's Return*, Belvoir Castle, c. 1772–73 (58 × 48 inches); *Cottage Door with Children Playing*, Cincinnati Museum, RA 1778 (48 1/4 × 58 3/4 inches); *The Cottage Door*, Huntington Museum, RA 1780 (58 × 47 inches); *Peasant Smoking at Cottage Door*, University of California, Los Angeles, Spring 1788 (77 × 62 inches). The Scudemore painting, *Cottage Door with Woman Sweeping and Girl with Pigs* (38 3/4 × 48 3/4 inches), is now in the Ipswich Museum. A copy of *The Woodcutter's Return* (Belvoir Castle), made by Gainsborough, is the Fuji collection in Japan.
44  Hayes, *The Landscape Paintings of Thomas Gainsborough*, I, p. 150.
45  *Ibid.*, p. 151.
46  Quoted in Robyn Asleson and Shelley Bennett, *British Paintings at the Huntington* (New Haven and London: Yale University Press, 2001), p. 112.
47  Asleson and Bennett, p. 112, and John Constable, *John Constable's Discourses*, ed. R.B. Beckett (Ipswich: Suffolk Records Society, 1970), p. 67.
48  The only variation from this formula is the Scudemore *Cottage Door with Women Sweeping and Girl with Pigs* (Ipswich) which shows a dejected young girl seated at the steps of a cottage observing a pig while a woman stands at the door with a broom.
49  Sigmund Freud, *The Uncanny* (1919), in *Collected Papers*, ed. Joan Reviere, 4 Vol. (New York: Basic Books, 1959) IV, pp. 376–7, 399, 403.
50  See his 'Gainsborough's Rural Vision', *The Listener*, 12 May 1977, pp. 615–16, and *The Dark Side of the Landscape: The Rural Poor in English Painting 1730–1840* (Cambridge, London, New York, New Rochelle, Melbourne, Sidney: Cambridge University Press, 1980), pp. 65–77.
51  Barrell, *The Dark Side of the Landscape*, pp. 70–7 and 'Gainsborough's Rural Vision', pp. 615–6.
52  On Kinkade's commercial empire see Susan Orlean, 'Art for Everybody: How Thomas Kinkade turned Painting into Big Business', *The New Yorker* (15 October 2001), pp. 124–31.
53  In short, the tax burden in the United States has been shifting steadily downwards so that those classes least able to afford to pay taxes and those most in need of what taxes can secure are one and the same. Meanwhile corporations and the upper 10% of householders who currently hold more than 96% of the nation's wealth pay less that 10% of the nation's income tax. Thus the middle and lower classes, who bear an inordinate tax burden because of these gross

inequalities, come to resent a tax system which has become increasingly oppressive. For this reason, the right-wing agenda to dismantle the federal and state tax systems continues to enjoy popular support. On this subject see, among other political analysts, Paul Krugeman, *The Great Unraveling: Losing Our Way in the New Century* (New York: W.W. Norton & Co., 2003).

# 3

# The Other Half of the Landscape: Thomas Heaphy's Watercolour Nasties

*David H. Solkin*

> It is indeed commonly affirmed, that truth well painted will cer-
> tainly please the imagination; but it is sometimes convenient not
> to discover the whole truth, but that part which only is delightful.
> We must sometimes show only half an image to the fancy; which if
> we display in a lively manner, the mind is so dexterously deluded,
> that it doth not readily perceive that the other half is concealed.
> Thus in writing Pastorals, let the tranquillity of that life appear full
> and plain, but hide the meanness of it; represent its simplicity as
> clear as you please, but cover its misery.
>
> (Thomas Tickell [?], *The Guardian*, no. 22, 6 April 1713)

In *The Dark Side of the Landscape*, John Barrell uses *The Guardian*'s prescription
for pastoral poetry by way of introducing his classic study of 'the constraints –
often apparently aesthetic but in fact moral and social – that determined
how the poor could, or rather how they could not be represented' in English
eighteenth- and early nineteenth-century art.[1] His book puts forward a persuasive argument that the painters of rural life had to balance the demand
for a mythic portrayal of 'delightful' contentment and social harmony
against the equally pressing requirement for sufficient realism, if they were
to succeed in 'deluding' and thereby satisfying contemporary viewers. Of all
the painters whom Barrell examines, only George Morland (1762/3–1804)
seems to have offered any resistance to this imperative – and he did so only
rarely, in a small number of exceptional works that 'offer a comment on the
attitude of the rich to the poor which might almost be made on behalf of
the poor themselves'.[2] On these occasions Morland may have hinted that
the rural poor were neither as happy nor as industrious as most pastoral art
(including the vast majority of his own pictures) supposed them to be; but if
the results perturbed some of his early biographers, their unease was as
nothing compared to that provoked by the genre scenes of Thomas Heaphy

(1775–1835), who sprang into prominence a few years after Morland's death.

Starting in 1807, but especially between 1808 and 1811, Heaphy dominated the annual exhibitions of the Society of Painters in Water Colours (henceforward SPWC) with a succession of large, highly finished narrative pictures of the vices and virtues of the poor. His portrayals of rustic criminality in particular attracted an enormous amount of public and critical attention, which helped push up the prices for his work to levels far higher than any that watercolours had ever before been able to command.[3] Although Heaphy's success with buyers proved crucial to the very survival of the SPWC in its early years, from the outset his popularity was dogged with controversy. Even as late as 1824 his fellow watercolourist William Henry Pyne could not speak of his achievements without marked ambivalence:

> We have a distinct recollection of the favourable impression which the works of this artist wrought upon admirers of water-colour paintings. For, not only on the first opening of the [SPWC] exhibition in Brook Street [in 1805], but for three or four more seasons, the high prices which were paid for his novel designs, were sufficient proofs of public approbation – though not entirely complimentary to public taste; for many of the compositions of his ingenious hand, represented scenes in low life, or rather vulgar life, which, although depicted with great observance of character and truth of expression, yet being destitute of that moral point which characterise [*sic*] the works of the incomparable Hogarth, they were disgusting to good feeling, and repulsive to delicate sentiment. Even the fastidious can admire those ragged vagabonds of the wild heath, the tawny gypsies, for their picturesque fitness to the scene; or the ferocious banditti, scarcely better clad, inhabitants of rocks and caverns, for their savage grandeur. Yet, what satisfaction can arise from the contemplation of villainy depicted in ragged, cadaverous groups of juvenile inmates of a night-cellar, with robbery and incipient murder, marked on every brow.[4]

That seems a reasonable question for us to ask as well. Even before we look at any of Heaphy's pictures, Pyne's almost hysterical invocation of a nightmare image of vulgar criminality is enough to tell us that we'll be dealing with scenes that stand far apart from the mainstream of the English genre tradition – perhaps even further apart (if such things can be measured) than the half-dozen or so paintings by George Morland to which I've alluded above. Barrell contends that Morland 'exposed the limits of what was acceptable' in a well-established pictorial mode which was normally dedicated to admitting only enough actuality into an ideal image of the rural poor as was required to conceal the disjunction between the two. In Heaphy's case, on the other hand, it was universally conceded that he had in fact stepped well beyond those limits, abandoning the ideal altogether in favour of exposing 'repulsive' realities that were no less palatable for being so truth-fully described. The striking appearance of his large compositions, as well as their remarkable technical virtuosity, doubtless helps to account for their sensational impact at the annual exhibitions, as well as their popularity with early nineteenth-century collectors; but a host of other factors will need to be brought into play before we are in a position to explain either the reception or production of a sizeable body of imagery that so blatantly defied 'the constraints which governed how the . . . poor could be portrayed so as to be an acceptable part of the *décor* of the drawing rooms of the polite'.[5]

After a decade working as a portraitist, during which time he managed to secure an official appointment in this capacity to the Princess of Wales, in 1807 Heaphy struck out onto hitherto uncharted territory by exhibiting his first two pictures of the evils of rural life: one of these, *Young Gamblers*, has been lost, but its companion-piece, entitled *Robbing a Market Girl* (Illustration 3.1) was purchased by the 8th Lord Kinnaird for 35 guineas and is now in the Yale Centre for British Art.[6] Although considerably faded after decades of exposure to light – finished paintings in watercolour were always intended to be shown framed and glazed – the work still retains a powerful visual gestalt, thanks in part to its considerable size (it is just under two feet in height) but above all to the frankly appalling nature of the action represented. In disturbing proximity to us, we witness a pair of louts brutally assaulting a young countrywoman (the swell of her breasts tells us that she is more than a mere girl). The actions and attitudes of her two assailants suggest that each may have his own agenda. Short of stature but heavily thickset, his impassive pig-like face half-obscured by shadow, the nearer of the robbers appears to be contemplating a rape (though contemplating may well be the wrong word): while it is impossible to tell whether his left hand has actually gripped his victim's dress, the confrontation's sexual overtones are heightened by the ominous shadow he casts on the girl's upper torso, which echoes the outlines of her cleavage just beneath. In the meantime the more finely-featured thief at left reaches out to lay his fingers on the duck that she carries in her basket, while gently lifting the covering cloth. Caught between two criminal types – feminized slyness on the left, masculine brutality on the right – with her goods and her person simultaneously under threat, the girl's powers of resistance seem extremely limited, though for the moment she remains undaunted. Her stalwart efforts to push away the youth blocking her path are matched by a facial expression of intense deter-mination which tells us that she has no intention of giving up without a fight. There is no doubt, however, as to who will ultimately triumph; the only uncertainty is how much the girl will lose. Her exposed situation is underlined by the distant figure of an old man walking with the aid of a stick: clearly he doesn't see what is going on, and even if he did, he would be too far off and too frail to intervene. Beyond him to the left, and even further away, a church steeple stands out silhouetted against the sunlit sky – a marker

*Illustration 3.1*  Thomas Heaphy, *Robbing a Market Girl*, watercolour, 1807; Yale Center for British Art, Paul Mellon Collection, New Haven, Connecticut. Photo: © Yale Center for British Art, Paul Mellon Collection

of Christianity and community, entirely at odds with the godless violence in the foreground. Here in a muddy and barren English heath, the only man-made structure is a signpost for Epsom, a place famous for horse-racing and gambling; hanging over and partially hiding the sign itself is a blossoming convolvulus, an attractive but deadly weed which chokes the life out of more useful plants. As emblems of good and evil respectively, the church tower and the signpost suggest the possibility of a Hogarthian moral framework for the narrative unfolding between them, which in itself would not have been out of place in *The Four Stages of Cruelty*; but whereas Hogarth's Tom Nero inevitably pays for his crimes, no such fate, or at least none that we can see, awaits Heaphy's 'ferocious banditti'. On the contrary, all the indicators are that they will get away scot-free. No wonder that Pyne and others objected that such works were 'destitute' of any clear 'moral point' – a failing only partially redeemed by their extraordinary 'truth' to nature.

That claim to truth was in part founded on Heaphy's critical engagement with the established conventions of pastoral art, and most obviously with its well-worn narratives of love. In the case of *Robbing a Market Girl*, his specific point of reference seems to have been a print of 1788 after Francis Wheatley (1747–1810), entitled *The Recruiting Officer*, showing a pretty rustic maid coyly trying to ward off the unwanted advances of a handsome young soldier (Illustration 3.2); but even while retaining some of his model's basic postures and accoutrements, Heaphy has transformed Wheatley's depiction of mildly erotic foreplay into a tableau of crude sexual violence. The same process also describes his brutal refashioning of the late eighteenth-century fancy picture, from which Heaphy borrowed his childlike cast of characters and the basic format of their landscape setting: it's as though we're seeing one of Thomas Gainsborough's melancholic cottagers being mugged by a couple of hardened juvenile delinquents. Like the appealing young countrywoman in Wheatley's *Recruiting Officer*,[7] Gainsborough's *Peasant Girl Gathering Faggots* (Manchester City Art Gallery) belongs to that species of feminine virtue in distress which played a central role in the culture of sensibility – whereas the equivalent figure in Heaphy's image is neither unambiguously virtuous, nor indeed correctly feminine.

Contemporary viewers would have been well-aware that any young woman travelling alone along a public thoroughfare, and displaying a considerable expanse of bare flesh, put herself in an exposed position, and not just visually; as Jane Rendell has observed, 'Walking in the public streets...and wearing revealing or conspicuous clothes, was suggestive of a woman's immorality'.[8] By way of strengthening this implication, Heaphy has given his lone female a mallard to carry, which reveals that she belongs to the widespread network of illegal trafficking in wild game. Though more directly derived from Wheatley, the same detail may also have reminded knowledgeable spectators of the first plate of *A Harlot's Progress*, where a dead goose with its head hanging out over the edge of a straw basket accompanies a buxom country lass as she foolishly embarks on a career of vice. Like Hogarth's Moll Hackabout, Heaphy's market girl cannot be regarded as entirely blameless for the peril in which she finds herself – and thus she cannot command the sympathy that a 'sensible' audience would normally have expected to

*Illustration 3.2*  Stanier after Francis Wheatley, *The Recruiting Officer*, stipple engraving, 1788. Photo: Courtesy of the Witt Library, Courtauld Institute of Art, University of London

extend to a poor young woman in distress. The hardened expression on her face further inhibits the operation of our benevolent impulses; among British moral philosophers it was an article of faith that one could only feel for a suffering individual who showed signs of feeling for themselves, which this figure – notwithstanding her evident youthfulness and the 'weakness' of her sex – stoically refuses to display (here the contrast with the Wheatley could hardly be more dramatic). One paradoxical consequence of this refusal is that it heightens the resemblance between her and her attackers. Indeed with her hair tied back, and her resolute look of concentration – even her raised left eyebrow speaks of muscular engagement – the girl appears positively boyish, and certainly no less masculine than the thief just behind her, whose flowing hair and softer facial features (are there signs of sympathy in his glance?) seem at odds with his role in the narrative. This confusion of gender boundaries is reinforced by the contrast between their gestures: his, tentative to the point of delicacy, hers a rough push and pull of strength. The aggressive nature of the girl's response, coupled with the clear evidence of her sexual maturity, speaks for an emphatic physicality entirely at odds with the norms of 'proper' femininity; thus in struggling to free herself from the clutches of the robbers, she takes on a character no less brute-like than theirs. In short, she altogether fails to meet the criteria of helpless victimhood required to appeal to the benevolence of her social superiors, as Wheatley's farmgirl or Gainsborough's meek and vulnerable cottage children were so much better equipped to do. Having engaged with the culture of sensibility, Heaphy then ruthlessly denied its satisfactions.

*Robbing a Market Girl* likewise deliberately snubbed its audience's most cherished aesthetic expectations. Early nineteenth-century English viewers could normally count on native artists to depict rustic scenes in accordance with the dictates of picturesque taste, and were prepared to respond accordingly; 'even the fastidious', as Pyne said, could 'admire those ragged vagabonds of the wild heath . . . or the ferocious banditti, scarcely better clad'. In his *Analytical Inquiry* of 1805, Richard Payne Knight put it as a general rule of thumb that, 'The dirty and tattered garments, the disheveled hair, and general wild appearances of gypsies and beggar girls are often picturesque.'[9] They are not always so, however: while the ragged clothes and lumpen forms of the idle poor may look attractive at a distance, when seen from close up they can be anything but appealing; witness the large shapeless grey posterior of the boy on the right of Heaphy's composition. For picturesque theorists, Gary Harrison has noted, 'gypsies, itinerant vagrants and banditti arouse interest only as objects fixed in a stabilizing aesthetic classification. Any non-aesthetic grasp or apprehension of [such figures] . . . would disgust, or would involve the viewer in a face-to-face encounter that would quickly turn the pleasing, picturesque experience into a moment of fear that might anticipate the sublime.'[10] But *Robbing a Market Girl* presents too immediate and too menacing a prospect to permit us to transcend our fear; when Pyne and so many others spoke of their 'disgust' with Heaphy's pictures, in effect they were saying that for them his imagery lay beyond the pale of aesthetics altogether.

What must have made the robbery scene all the more revolting was its refusal to offer the attractions of nature as a compensation for the hideousness of its squalid human narrative. On this open stretch of heath nothing grows apart from the occasional weed and patch of grass or shrubbery, which do little or nothing to disrupt the muddy sameness of the whole. 'The ugliest ground', wrote Uvedale Price, 'is that which has neither the beauty of smoothness, nor the picturesqueness of bold and sudden breaks, and varied tints of soil'[11] – none of which can be found here. What makes this ground even uglier is the monstrous specimens of humanity whom it has spawned, and who personify its worst aspects. A spokesman for the late eighteenth-century Philanthropic Society likened the unemployed children of the idle poor to 'a tract of land...productive of noxious herbs, and generating poisonous reptiles...which produces rapine, murder, theft, prostitution, disease, fatal punishments, and lingering miseries'.[12] A more repellent prospect would be difficult to imagine.

Moreover, evils like rape and robbery were usually regarded as urban vices – as features that defined the sinful and chaotic city against the wholesome tranquillity of the countryside, and which were not meant to spread from one realm to the other. Nor were scenes of this sort deemed acceptable for inclusion in pictorial representations of rural life. As the watercolourist Edward Dayes wrote in 1805:

> The universal affection for landscape painting does not arise from the love of imitation only; the pastoral scenes of the Dutch delight from other motives, and principally because familiar to every imagination; they exhibit a life of peace, leisure, and innocence, with joy, plenty, and contentment; blessings not to be found in the bustling scenes of active life. One rule we are obliged to observe in the pastoral; that is, not to represent scenes of wretchedness, or such objects as may disgust.[13]

Heaphy could hardly have broken this rule in more dramatic fashion. Even his choice of locale is significant in this regard: Epsom was not only a problematic site in its own right, but it also lay close to London, and thus within the orbit of its corrupting moral influence. This liminal area just beyond the borders of the metropolis was notorious as the haunt of criminals who preyed on coaches and individual travellers; 'The fields near London', wrote the farming expert John Middleton, 'are never free from men strolling about in pilfering pursuits by day, and committing greater crimes by night'.[14] In this virtually lawless no-man's land there was no safety to be found even in broad daylight, or at least this is what Heaphy's picture invites us to surmise. If proximity to the capital was one factor contributing to the problematic character of his landscape, another was its removal from the productive scenes of agriculture. Uncultivated common land – for this is what we are seeing – caused considerable anxiety not only because it was idle and wild, but also because it was believed to foster the same sort of behaviour among its inhabitants. Middleton condemned such unenclosed territory as the 'constant rendezvous of Gypsies, Strollers, and other loose persons... The women and children beg and pilfer, and the men commit greater acts of dishonesty. In short, the Commons of this Country are well known to be the constant resort of footpads and highwaymen, and are literally and proverbially a public nuisance.'[15] Here was one writer who had no tolerance whatsoever for those nostalgic pastoralists who idealised England's unfenced fields and open forests as some sort of Arcadian paradise. Nor, apparently, did Heaphy, whose *Robbing a Market Girl* no less stridently rejected that elegaic vision of a rustic Golden Age so beloved of Gainsborough, Wheatley, and other late eighteenth-century British artists.

Having completed this initial act of ideological demolition, Heaphy then set about targeting his critical focus onto other conventional forms of English pastoral art. In 1808 the Society of Painters in Water Colours exhibited no fewer than 13 of his works (compared to just six the year before), of which nine appear to have depicted the follies and worse of the English lower classes.[16] Writing in the *Examiner*, Robert Hunt noted that Heaphy stood out at the exhibition 'for his subjects of low character';[17] meanwhile the critic for the *Monthly Magazine* was moved to complain of 'a tendency to excessive vulgarity, which it is to be wished Mr Heaphy would correct'.[18] One of the pictures that made reviewers so uncomfortable was *Inattention* (Illustration 3.3), a reworking – 'unworking' might be more apt – of the *cottage door* scene, one of the best-loved items in the entire repertoire of English genre painting.

Actually, as Greg Smith has pointed out, *Inattention* unites the *cottage door* with the *Cries of London* tradition, to mutually explosive effect. Whereas the first had traditionally 'functioned as a symbol of domestic virtue and security', and 'the door-to-door seller as a picturesque representative of the world of bounteous commerce',[19] Heaphy combined the two into a hybrid image of immoral conduct on both sides: at the moment when the servant girl is lost in contemplation of a ballad that has been offered to her for sale, her purse lies temporarily forgotten on the threshold beside her. Taking advantage of her distraction, one of the salesmen stoops stealthily down to capture this unexpected find, while his confederate squints anxiously at the caged magpie – a species notorious for thieving – hoping that it will refrain from squawking until the other pedlar has pocketed his prize. In its overall format – though not in its specific narrative content – *Inattention* once again closely derives from the imagery of Francis Wheatley, whose highly popular genre scenes of the 1780s and 1790s had taken Gainsborough's sentimental pastoralism to new heights of artifice. As early as 1794, Wheatley had come in for criticism for making 'the character of our village Daphnes... so prodigiously fine at the expense of truth',[20] in works such as *Rustic Benevolence*, one of his typically cleaned-up and morally uplifting *cottage door* compositions.[21] Although Heaphy must have been familiar with pictures like this, his principal target was the celebrated *Cries of London*, exhibited (as oils) at the Royal

*Illustration 3.3*   Thomas Heaphy, *Inattention*, watercolour, 1808; Yale Center for British Art, Paul Mellon Collection, New Haven, Connecticut. Photo: © Yale Center for British Art, Paul Mellon Collection

Academy between 1792 and 1795, and published as stipple engravings from 1793 to 1797 (Illustration 3.4).

Wheatley's *Cries* transformed what had hitherto been an emphatically urban imagery of street commerce into a species of pastoral art. The majority

Painted by F. Wheatley R.A.

Engraved by Vendramini

Old Chairs to mend

CRIES
of
LONDON.
Plate 10.ᵗʰ

Vieilles chaises à raccomoder

London Pub.ᵈ as the Act directs Sep.ᵗ 1ˢᵗ 1795 by Colnaghi & Cᵒ N.º 132 Pall Mall

*Illustration 3.4* Giovanni Vendramini after Francis Wheatley, *Cries of London Plate 10th. Old Chairs to Mend,* stipple engraving, 1795. Photo: Paul Mellon Centre for Studies in British Art, London

of his hawkers are pretty young countrywomen, who, as Sean Shesgreen has remarked, 'personify an idealized rural sensibility characterized by love of children, animals, the meek and the deserving poor'.[22] Even where the sellers are male, the ambience tends to be overwhelmingly rustic; but whereas Wheatley invokes the country as a means of idealizing the city, Heaphy blends the two realms in order to puncture the balloon of pastoral simplicity. Crime, it appears, can be found even where one least expects it, together with the folly – here the fatal lack of attention – that any miscreant will be all too ready to exploit. In the cottage's very picturesqueness we can read the signs of material and moral neglect: in the warped gate that threatens to come off its hinges, the moss growing on the canopy above the doorway, the ivy that partially blocks one of the windows, the cracks on the walls. And even if the young woman has learned how to read, her example teaches us that a little knowledge, in the wrong hands, can leave the door – a cottage door, no less – open to corruption.

Active vice on this occasion takes the form of two pedlars, of whom one appears to be a poacher, judging by his fur cap and the game (ducks and rabbits) spilling out of his basket; he holds another mallard out for inspection. Though often claimed by the poor as their customary right – and precisely because of the frequency of such claims – poaching was widely castigated as the first step on the road to far more serious transgressions. In the words of a clergyman-cum-magistrate in one of Hannah More's *Cheap Repository Tracts*:

> With poaching much moral evil is connected; a habit of nightly depradation; a custom of prowling in the dark for prey produces in time a disrelish for honest labour... He who begins with robbing orchards, rabbit-warrens, and fish-ponds, will probably end with horse stealing or highway robbery. Poaching is a regular apprenticeship to bolder crimes.[23]

Heaphy's poacher, whose shadowed face suggests both his nocturnal activities and the darkness of his character, is caught at the moment of transition from one form of larceny to another. His partner in crime makes an even more arresting figure: with his face screwed up in an attempt at non-verbal communication, and his hand scratching dog-like at his head, he seems the very picture of bestial humanity. Although he has come bearing a number of useful items for sale – tapers, a candle snuffer, spoons and other household implements – here his role is to tempt the girl with a frivolous commodity that will keep her from noticing the poacher's furtive downward advance. Heaphy's viewers would have known full well that hawkers were notorious as agents of corruption, who were all too prepared to take criminal advantage of their customers' gullibility. Thus the reforming judge Patrick Colquhoun warned his respectable readership to beware of 'Sharpers and Swindlers who obtain Licences to be Hawkers and Pedlars; under the cover of which every species of villainy is practised upon the country people, as well as upon the unwary in the Metropolis, and all the great towns in the Kingdom'.[24]

One such 'species of villainy' involved the sale of popular literature: in an era when there was enormous anxiety about what the lower orders were reading – and considerable disagreement among the governing classes as to whether they should be taught to read at all – repeated efforts were made to suppress the 'vile publications'[25] sold by hawkers, though to little avail. The printed matter they peddled consisted mainly of broadsides and slips carrying ballads, ribald or obscene stories, accounts of executions, public funerals and the like, as well as criminals' last dying speeches; from the tiny but amazingly legible inscriptions in *Inattention*, we can see that Heaphy's squinting rogue is carrying stock of precisely this sort. The two broadsheets hanging over the side of his basket are a [DE]ATH of/[B]RAVENELSON and a hanged man's final words; but the girl shows no interest in patriotism or moral instruction. Though it's impossible to tell exactly what she is reading, we are given a pretty clear idea by the broadside that the hawker holds in his hand; its title – 'TOM[true?]LOVE' – and the crude headpiece showing a man and a woman are typical of the popular romantic ballads that were widely held responsible for corrupting the minds of susceptible country girls.[26] In this instance the consequences are plain to see: an improper printed tale has distracted its reader to the point where she has dropped both her purse and her guard, leaving her small savings and (by implication) the cottage and its virtues exposed to the pedlars' vicious proclivities. She looks set to pay a high price for her lack of vigilance.

Thus as in the case of *Robbing a Market Girl*, *Inattention* refuses to draw any hard and fast distinctions between the perpetrators of crime and their victim. Instead of staging a confrontation between endangered rustic virtue and predatory urban vice, Heaphy described only different shades of culpability; he has taken away the comforting myth of pastoral innocence and left nothing in its place, apart from the vision of a modern world where the laws of morality (and of society) seem conspicuous only by their very absence. In so doing he was following a cultural path that, if not exactly well trodden, was certainly familiar to contemporary viewers of art and readers of poetry. Thomas Rowlandson, for instance, had in 1799 lampooned Wheatley's 'meretricious and theatrical' pictures of street-sellers with a comic series of *London Cries*, full of crime, deceit and overtones of lewd sexuality.[27] But much closer in tone to Heaphy's vice-ridden genre scenes is the poetry of the Rev. George Crabbe, who in *The Village* of 1783 had stated his ambition to

> ... paint the Cot,
> As Truth will paint it, and as Bards will not[28]

As John Barrell has argued, Crabbe aimed to attack the poetic image of the leisured poor, particularly as expressed by Oliver Goldsmith in *The Deserted*

*Village* (1770), 'as an idealising falsification'; in its place he offered the more repressive vision of a suffering rural populace, who could only relieve their plight by means of their own assiduous labour.[29] By curious coincidence – and I very much doubt if there was any direct connection – Heaphy's move into anti-pastoral genre precisely coincided with the appearance of *The Borough* (also 1807), Crabbe's first major attempt to revisit 'the dark side of the land-scape'[30] since his initial foray almost a quarter-century before. A critical furore ensued. Like Heaphy, Crabbe was admired for his descriptive precision (the reviewer who spoke of his 'Dutch minuteness'[31] was only one of several who compared his verses to seventeenth-century Netherlandish paintings of common life), while also being roundly condemned for the 'disgusting' nature of his representations.[32] In these and other important respects, the artist and the poet can be described as kindred spirits; but whereas Crabbe (like William Cowper and Gainsborough) rejected the mythology of pastoral ease in favour of an ostensibly truthful but in fact prescriptive image of Georgic industry, in the pictures that forged his reputation (though not in all his works) Heaphy offered the far more disturbing prospect of an English countryside in the unrelieved grip of idleness and criminality.

At a time when residual anxieties about lower-class radicalism coupled with the demands of the Napoleonic Wars had given rise to acute anxieties about the state and character of the poor, to pretend that the masses were more virtuous than was actually the case could seem not only delusive, but dangerously naïve. One pointed reminder of the gap between cultural myth and social reality came from the portraitist and Royal Academician Martin Archer Shee, in his *Elements of Art* of 1809:

> It may suit the purposes of Utopian theorists, and poetical philosophers, to represent the country as an Arcadia, and every clown a Corydon; to make every hamlet the abode of happiness and peace, and describe its inhabitants as the purest models of beauty and virtue: but a little experi-ence quickly dissipates these delusions. A peep into this paradise of enthusiasts, discovers the serpent, even there, lurking amidst the flowers. We soon find that vice can pervade the cottage as well as the palace, and that it is very possible to be ignorant and awkward, without being innocent or picturesque.[33]

But it was one thing to discover the serpent in theory, and quite another to put this discovery into artistic practice, as Heaphy had already learned to his cost.

In 1808 (and to a lesser extent in 1809), discussions of his novel anti-pastoral images dominated press coverage of the exhibitions of the Society of Painters in Water-Colours; and while most reviewers were quick to express their admiration for Heaphy's virtuoso handling of his medium, none could bring himself to sanction the artist's choice of subjects, or at least not without considerable misgivings. Among the first wave of critics, the engraver John Landseer was probably the most sympathetic; certainly no other early nineteenth-century writer made a more serious or sustained attempt to legitimize a form of artistic behaviour that struck most contemporary commentators as not just unusual, but downright perverse. Landseer begins by praising Heaphy as 'THE painter of *Comedy*' according to the rules set down by Aristotle and du Bos: it 'being not less in painting than in stage performances, the office and business of Comedy to hold the mirror up to nature *as it is*, in order to its becoming what it *ought to be*'. How this works in Heaphy's case he then illustrates by means of a motif-by-motif account of *Credulity*, a scene set in a cottage interior (Illustration 3.5):

> It represents a young servant maid, sufficiently handsome for the sentiment of the picture, whose countenance is lit up with a degree of wild delight, occasioned by a letter which she has just received from her lover, and which, in her whisking round to attend to a gipsey [*sic*] who appears at the kitchen window, has fallen to the ground, but has fallen so, that by lucky accident, the spectator may read it...
>
> The attention of the girl being thus attracted by the appearance of the fortune-teller, while her head and heart are bewildered with the content of her lover's epistle, she is as heedless of the surrounding mischief, as she is unconscious of the lurking danger; a dish of mutton-chops falls unperceived from her lap; the cat steals a fish and knocks down the crockery unobserved; and the cuckow bawls unheard from the clock, that the hour of twelve is arrived; while a thief, who may be supposed to be a confederate of the gypsey, and who has stolen in at the kitchen door, is handing something from the cupboard. Meanwhile the observer sees, that, though the scene is laid in the country, no preparations are yet made for dinner, and all the morning business of a servant is yet to do; the rabbit is not skinned, the pigeon is yet to pluck, and the potatoes and cabbage lie untouched; in short, the whole performance fully answers to the couplet which Mr Heaphy has inserted in the catalogue.
>
> When Love's epistle its sweet tale explains,
> Time flies untold, and wild confusion reigns.

For Landseer the only problem with such 'exquisite comic scenes' – though perhaps not this particular example – was that Heaphy's imagery 'sometimes tends a little too much toward farce, and in the broadness of his mirth, loses its morality'.[34] If viewers were inspired to laugh at vice, then they might easily forget their duty to condemn it; the legitimate role of comedy was to instruct, and not merely to amuse.

Prior to the early nineteenth century, such seriousness of purpose had not normally been demanded of genre scenes done in watercolour, which

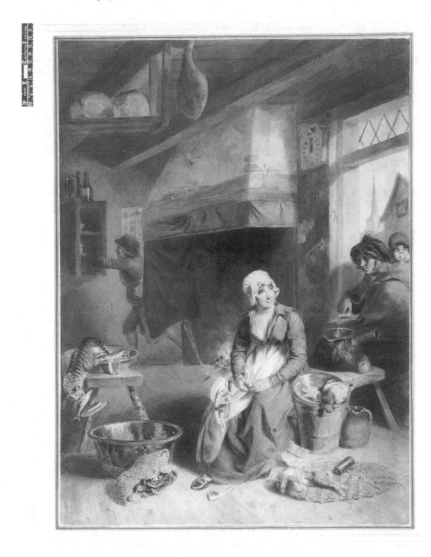

*Illustration 3.5*   Thomas Heaphy, *Credulity*, watercolour, 1808; The British Museum, London. Copyright © The British Museum

enjoyed the status of an informal medium, one that could license the suspension of moral judgment in favour of irresponsible private delight. Thomas Rowlandson's contemporary comic drawings of the transgressive poor, as Barrell has observed, need to be understood in this light. But for the new generation of 'painters in watercolour', among whom Heaphy was a leading light, theirs was an unequivocally public art-form, and as such had to be answerable to a set of prescriptive terms: Barrell lists these as including ' "decent" or serious', along with 'the "stable", the "permanent", the "responsible", and the "moral" '.[35] These criteria normally entailed the depiction of the poor as happily domesticated, industrious and therefore deserving of the benevolent sympathies of their social superiors – though not in Heaphy's case. Here the disjunction between the undeniable seriousness of his executive precision (we shall have more to say about this below) and the obviously improper nature of his subject-matter seems to have resulted in a curious sort of semantic stalemate, which raised the disturbing prospect of an artist who simply portrayed whatever he saw, whether good or evil, with the same unflinching objectivity. In 1809 the writer for *Le Beau Monde*, taking up where Landseer had left off the year before, had difficulty deciding whether he was bothered more by the artist's chosen themes or by the sheer consistency of his realism:

> Mr Heaphy maintains his station as the water-colour painter of *Comedy*, though he sometimes degenerates into Farce, and is at others (in his choice of subjects) vulgar, without being humorous, or moral. To tell such truths as he has accidentally seen, or sought for, and found, and been able to combine, and to repeat accurately with all their circumstantial details, appears to be his constant purpose. He seems to care little for the *kind* of truth: he paints a detail of wickedness, or a detail of virtue, with the same interest, or the same apathy.[36]

Meanwhile other critics urged Heaphy to apply his talents to less offensive themes. It was the considered opinion of the *Repository of Arts*, 'that the human figure and the human mind are not the walks in which he is likely to excel. Subjects such as the Dutch painters indulged in, markets, in which the commodity offered for sale (whether fish, vegetables, poultry, or game), formed the leading feature of the picture, and where the venders [*sic*] are secondary and subordinate, seem much better calculated for his genius than any he has yet chosen'. The same reviewer was perfectly prepared to admit that 'Heaphy has carried high-finishing and minute detail as far as it will go; but that he would apply his powers to some better purpose than painting squinting blackguards [as in *Inattention*, presumably] ... "is devoutly to be wished".'[37] Similarly the *Literary Panorama* insisted that 'Labours such as his are thrown away, unless the composition be of some respectability as well as interest',[38] while Robert Hunt castigated Heaphy for 'delight[ing] in disgust and depravity'.[39] Two years later William Henry Pyne was still harping on the same theme:

> We observe no alteration in the performances of Mr Heaphy, nor can we perceive that he has advanced one step towards a more refined taste. His characters, although judiciously varied, are too coarse, his view of human

nature too low, and the scenes he exhibits are deficient in that moral effect which alone can excuse the representation of vulgarity. It is to be hoped, that an artist, who has shewn such extraordinary talent in the department of art which he has chosen, will in future pay more attention to the quality which is its primary recommendation. With the example of Hogarth before him, he may learn the art of exhibiting an impressive moral lesson, or a poignant satire. He will not then mistake the means for the end, and content himself with the credit of wasting his skill on the delineation of brutish character and manners.[40]

The contemporary critical response to Heaphy's work is not just remarkable for what it says – I can think of no other British artist of the early nineteenth century whose efforts were so harshly judged – but equally so for what it leaves out. Whereas it was normal and expected practice for contemporary reviewers to draw reassuring moral lessons from narrative scenes of everyday life, in Heaphy's case most found this an extraordinarily difficult task, despite all of the artist's best efforts to facilitate their endeavours. In 1809, for instance, he exhibited a watercolour of *Gamblers* (unfortunately now lost), showing six youths playing dice amid the ruins of a country church. The theme must have reminded his more knowledgeable viewers of *The Idle 'Prentice at Play in the Church Yard during Divine Service*, plate III of Hogarth's *Industry and Idleness*; and Heaphy's point in linking lower-class corruption with evidence of modern spiritual decline could hardly have been easier to plumb. The picture's basic message certainly posed no problem for the critic for *Le Beau Monde*, who lost no time in drawing his readers' attention to an appropriate passage from the Bible: 'My house shall be called the house of prayer, but ye have made it a den of thieves' (Matthew 21:13). Yet even after successfully decoding the picture's religious meaning, he was only prepared to justify Heaphy's procedure in the most tentative and qualified terms:

> Perhaps, in arguing for the morality of his practice, he may say with the poet [i.e. Alexander Pope],
>    'Vice is a matter of so frightful mien,
>    That to be dreaded need only be seen.'
> At least this is the best apology we can make for him, when he lavishes the riches of his art upon thieves and gamblers, and boys blowing flour in the eyes of an innocent girl, that they may purloin her pastry with impunity.[41]

The final clauses refer to *Return from the Baker's* of 1808 (Illustration 3.6), a more light-hearted but no less distasteful variation on the theme of *Robbing a Market Girl*. As the passage we've just cited makes clear, subjects like these should have been the stuff of Hogarthian graphic satire – but no satirist

*Illustration 3.6*  Thomas Heaphy, *Return from the Baker's*, watercolour, 1808; London art market. Photo: courtesy Sotheby's

worthy of the name would have portrayed crime without reference to punishment, or treated the dregs of humanity with such 'lavish' concern for detail.

Had he steered clear of the vices of the lower orders, Heaphy would undoubtedly have enjoyed a much easier ride. The euphoric reception given to David Wilkie's genre scenes from 1806 onwards shows that in this period English art critics were able and willing to lend their enthusiastic support to painters who catalogued the 'truths' of everyday life down to the smallest minutiae. But whereas Wilkie's realism was mitigated by his obvious indebtedness to seventeenth-century Netherlandish art, and by liberal doses of humour, picturesqueness and heart-warming sentiment, Heaphy's watercolours offered none of these compensations, nor (and most important of all) did they provide a subject-matter free from the taint of 'low' Dutch vulgarity. Instead of refining on the works of his predecessors by judiciously selecting from common nature, as Wilkie was often hailed for doing, Heaphy appeared to have taken the opposite path, leading to baser truths that could only disgust.

According to the principles of Reynoldsian academic theory which remained the main touchstone of value for early nineteenth-century art critics, such representations were not just lacking in moral value, but could even endanger the virtue of unsophisticated viewers. Edward Dayes put this case with characteristic forthrightness:

A well-ordered picture becomes a lesson of polite education, by which our manners are amended; on the contrary, dirty ragged ruffians, accompanied with trash and common-place objects, are not only beneath the dignity of painting, but may corrupt young minds; nay, may not rudeness be justified by a reference to pictures exhibiting clownish and hoggish examples, or people the most base and corrupt of humanity?[42]

The same anxiety underlay John Landseer's uncomfortable reaction to *Return from the Baker's*, perhaps prompted in particular by the man shown grinning at the foreground action from within the bakery doorway at far left: if Heaphy 'continues to paint the crafty and mischievous tricks of evil disposed boys', Landseer insisted, 'he should paint them so as to excite our decided displeasure. He should not make us laugh at a successful piece of roguery, and laugh *with* the rogues, or *at* the distress of an innocent girl.'[43]

This scene also drove *Le Beau Monde*'s critic to warn the artist to

reflect that there is much *energy* displayed in these occasions, and if what a modern philosopher has asserted is true, that whatever calls forth voluntary energy, must give delight; and that hence mankind are led to sympathise rather with the general energy of an impassioned character, than against the particular passion by which he may be actuated. God knows how easily the tide of mind when it is once attracted, flows into the channels that example has hollowed out for it! or, to speak without metaphor, how easily we are seduced by the passion, when we have once allowed ourselves to sympathise with the energy displayed on any given occasion.[44]

This fascinating passage raises the entirely credible possibility that the portrayal of a violent crime might, by virtue of its 'impassioned character', lead us to sympathize with the perpetrator, and not the victim – a terrifying prospect indeed, and one which further helps us understand why most of Heaphy's critics simply could not see any moral content in his depictions of the vices of the poor.

Though the negative press coverage evidently proved no obstacle to potential buyers – Heaphy sold 12 of his 13 exhibited works, to the value of over £650, in 1808 alone, making him by far the highest-paid watercolourist of the period – the artist himself seems to have taken the reviewers' words to heart, and to have altered his strategy accordingly. Despite the enormous impact he had made at the SPWC in 1808 – or precisely because of the nature of that impact – in the years that followed Heaphy beat a steady retreat from his by-now notorious interest in low criminality in favour of depicting a range of altogether more conventional – that is to say, virtuous – themes of humble life. Of the eight works he displayed in 1809, only one – the lost *Gamblers* referred to above – featured the sort of subject-matter that had caused such a furore at the previous exhibition, and which did so yet again. Otherwise he stayed on safer ground, with two still-lives, a large and complex view of the fish market at Hastings,[45] a gleaning scene dominated by a pretty peasant girl (Hereford Art Gallery), a sentimental image of two *Fisher Children*, and *The Family Doctress*, a cottage interior with an old woman attending to a farmer's wounded leg (both these watercolours are in the V & A). Yet notwithstanding this shift in thematic direction, on the whole Heaphy's critics remained fixated with the problematic aspects of his imagery, and proved reluctant to give him their unqualified approval. In a deliberate effort to mollify them he may even have tried to make up for past misjudgments with his final exhibit of 1809: entitled *The Offer Accepted* (unlocated), the SPWC catalogue identified this as the companion-piece to the previous year's much-discussed *Credulity* (see Illustration 3.5 above) – so despite the kitchenmaid's neglect of her duties in favour of reading love letters and listening to gipsy fortune-tellers, viewers were now able to assume that she did return to the straight and narrow, and marry her sweetheart in the end.

Heaphy's decision to incorporate one of his 'problem pictures' into a serial narrative balancing evil against good suggests that he was now trying to tread a more Hogarthian path, as several commentators had urged him to do. The expansion of his thematic repertoire also gave at least one buyer the opportunity to create his own pairing of morally antithetical images: the London merchant George Hibbert who had purchased *Return from the Baker's* at the SPWC in 1808 returned two years later to pay the same price of 80 guineas for *The Mother's Prayer* (Illustration 3.7), a Madonna-like scene of fecundity, Christian devotion and maternal bliss.[46] Though only this and one other of Heaphy's exhibits of 1810 can now be traced, the two survivors

*Illustration 3.7*   Thomas Heaphy, *A Mother's Prayer*, watercolour, 1809; formerly London art market. Photo: courtesy Sotheby's

and the titles of the rest confirm his thorough conversion to an overtly virtuous subject-matter. Indeed one would be hard put to think of a more harmonious image of lower-class life than *Domestic Happiness* (Illustration 3.8), which the *Morning Herald* admired as,

*Illustration 3.8* Thomas Heaphy, *Domestic Happiness*, watercolour, 1810; Laing Art Gallery, Newcastle. Photo: © Tyne and Wear Museums Service

one of the best pieces of domestic history, in water colours, that we have ever seen: the character of the husband is bold and manly, and conveys a very adequate idea of an English yeoman, seated with delight in the bosom of his family. The features of the wife are amiable, and the infant in her arms is fabby [*sic* – flabby?] and playful. The other parts of the grouping are well managed, and we have no doubt but this artist, as he is sedulous, will reflect credit upon his country, as well as his profession.[47]

Heaphy could hardly have put more distance, it seems, between the painter he had now become and the watercolourist responsible for those digusting scenes of human depravity who had achieved so much notoriety just a few short years before. But in fact the distance was no greater than that between one side of a coin and the other.

While the early nineteenth-century English were generally agreed that representations of exemplary conduct could promote the cause of virtue, it was no less universally understood that depictions of human evils could also serve the same laudable end. Indeed a number of Heaphy's critics were prepared to concede as much; here we may recall Alexander Pope's poetic dictum, slightly misquoted in *Le Beau Monde*, that:

Vice is a monster of so frightful mien,
As, to be hated, needs but to be seen.

But to be seen in what form, where, and by whom? The contemporary reactions to Heaphy's works suggest several answers to these questions. First of all, a clear sense emerges that there could be no justification for highlighting the vicious behaviour of the vulgar populace in any art more serious or more elevated than graphic satire, and only then provided that there could be no mistaking the artist's critical intent; secondly, there were aesthetic rules – Barrell justly calls them 'constraints' – that governed the visual representation of the poor in high, public art (including paintings in watercolour) – a largely unspoken code which Heaphy had wilfully transgressed; and last but certainly not least, the purpose of those constraints was to produce an imagery of 'low' social life suitable for consumption by a polite audience. Exhibited genre paintings which disobeyed these rules posed a dual threat to polite subjectivities: for not only did they confront their public with unpalatable evidence of social disorder, but they also asked the same viewers to take aesthetic pleasure in scenes that individuals of refined sensibilities were not even meant to see, never mind enjoy.

There is no reason whatsoever to suppose that Heaphy ever meant to cause offence; on the contrary his rapid retreat onto safer thematic territory following the trouble he'd caused at the SPWC exhibition of 1808 suggests a strong compulsion to amend his conduct, even if this meant jeopardizing his continued financial success (as in fact proved to be the case).[48] To explain that compulsion for change, and the artistic strategy that had landed him in so much trouble in the first place, we need to consider another, personal factor: Heaphy's Christian beliefs.

'We have heard that Mr Heaphy is a man of a religious turn of mind',[49] in 1809 the reviewer for *Le Beau Monde* reported in a significant aside. Since this sort of information hardly ever figured in the art criticism of the period, one presumes that the writer felt that the idiosyncratic nature of Heaphy's genre scenes demanded recourse to an exceptional form of explanation, which in this case I believe was fundamentally correct.[50] The evidence provided by the watercolours themselves points to a more specific conclusion: that their author was a devout Evangelical Christian, who aimed to use his art as a vehicle for his faith.

In Donna Andrew's useful summary, the Evangelical variety of Anglicanism 'both acknowledged the utter depravity of man and the ubiquity of palpable evil and misery, and the necessity for individual moral reform and conversion before social improvement could take place'.[51] One of the *Reports of the Society for Bettering the Condition and Increasing the Comforts of the Poor* phrased this doctrine as follows:

> Our creator has made *moral and natural evil* the instrument of his operations in this world; and the means of awakening the energy, and invigorating the virtues of those rational creatures, which he has imbued with sufficient wisdom and strength to be virtuous, and *as far as their nature admitted,* happy.[52]

Whereas spokesmen for polite culture tended to distrust representations of evil conduct as potential invitations to moral corruption – we've seen that such certainly was the opinion of Edward Dayes – Evangelical ideologues took precisely the opposite point of view – though usually, albeit, with a less than polite audience in mind. When put into practice as a cultural pro-gramme, their thinking gave rise to a host of depictions of lower-class vice ostensibly addressed to the poor themselves, and designed to function as instruments of their moral and spiritual salvation. Perhaps the most celebrated products of this reformist agenda – which was also designed to curb the seditious political tendencies of the lower orders in the wake of the French Revolution – were Hannah More's *Cheap Repository Tracts*, which circulated in great numbers throughout the 1790s and beyond.

The links between More's *Tracts* and Heaphy's genre scenes are close and multi-layered. The two share the same emphasis on vividly observed detail, which in both cases helps to create the impression that they are treating their poor subjects as distinct individuals inhabiting particular environments all of their own. In their respective media, furthermore, neither shows any reluctance to deal with what in polite circles would normally have been regarded as unacceptably vulgar subject-matter, or indecorous narrative situations. Numerous other thematic connections can be made. In 'Tawny Rachel; or, the Fortune Teller', for instance, More describes how her protagonist 'was continually practising on the *credulity* of silly girls [my emphasis]; and took advantage of their ignorance to cheat and deceive them. Many an innocent servant has she caused to be suspected of a robbery, while she herself, perhaps, was in league with the thief'.[53] Elsewhere she writes of the evils of Black Giles the Poacher, and of the sins committed by hawkers of dangerous goods; the *Tracts* contain repeated warnings to avoid ballad sellers, who in More's eyes posed a particular threat to the Christian way of life she was trying to promote. If this reminds us of Heaphy's *Inattention*, so, too, does 'Parley the Porter. An Allegory. Shewing how Robbers without can never get into an House, unless there are Traitors within'. Here, in the story of a servant who allows himself to be persuaded to let thieves into his master's castle, More uses the 'House' to stand for the world that men temporarily inhabit before they rise to God's heavenly dominions. During their brief time on earth, they must remember to live by the proverb, 'Happy is he that feareth always' – for the forces of evil are always lying in wait outside each human soul, in hopes that a fatal lapse in vigilance will allow them to enter and carry out their work of destruction.[54] Another tract features a poor but hard-working shepherd who tells a genteel visitor that 'Christians, you know, sir, must be doubly watchful; or they will not only bring disgrace upon themselves, but what is much worse, on that holy name by which they are called'.[55]

These pious words may serve to remind us that More told improving tales of virtue as well as vice, as of course did Thomas Heaphy; even if the pater-familias of his *Domestic Happiness* happens to be a fisherman, in all other respects his circumstances might just as well be those described in 'The Shepherd of Salisbury Plain', the most celebrated of all the *Cheap Repository Tracts*. Its protagonist's cottage, we are told, showed

nothing but the most perfect neatness. The trenchers on which they were eating were almost as white as their linen; and notwithstanding the number [eight] and smallness of the children, there was not the least appearance of dirt or litter. The furniture was very simple and poor, hardly indeed amounting to bare necessaries. It consisted of four brown wooden chairs, which, by constant rubbing, were become as bright as a looking glass; an iron pot and kettle; a poor old grate, which scarcely held a handful of coal, and out of which the little fire that had been in it appeared to have been taken, as soon as it had answered the end for which it had been lighted – that of boiling their potatoes. Over the chimney stood an old fashioned broad bright candlestick, and a still brighter spit; it was pretty clear that this last was kept rather for ornament than for use. An old carved elbow chair, and a chest of the same date which stood in the corner, were considered as the most valuable part of the Shepherd's goods, having been in his family for three generations. But all these were lightly esteemed by him, in comparison with another possession, which, added to the above, made up the whole of what he had inherited from his father...a large old bible, which lay on the window seat, neatly covered with brown cloth, variously patched... On the clean white walls was pasted a hymn on the Crucifixion of our Saviour, a print of the Prodigal Son, the Shepherd's Hymn, and Patient Joe, or the Newcastle Collier [a *Cheap Repository Tract*].[56]

I've quoted this passage at such length in order to highlight the enormous care that More devotes to her descriptions of the poor and their humble surroundings, and how she treats each telling visual detail as a sign of moral value – for this was Heaphy's procedure in a nutshell.[57] Not only does each of his watercolours painstakingly catalogue a plethora of minutiae, but there is hardly a detail in his pictures that cannot be plumbed for its significance to the narrative; of all the exegeses I have cited, John Landseer's close account of *Credulity* probably best demonstrates the sort of patient reading that was demanded and the pleasurable knowledge that it could yield. One object omitted from Landseer's description is the woodcut 'hymn on the Crucifixion of our Saviour' pasted on the wall beyond the fireplace – only one of many motifs in Heaphy's genre scenes that might have been lifted directly from the *Cheap Repository Tracts* or other writings of the same ilk. Another case in point is the family Bible in the lower left-hand corner of *Domestic Happiness*; it is shown open at Isaiah LIII, with the first word of v.1 (WHO) clearly visible. The heading 'Christ's sufferings' presumably refers to vv.3ff ('He is despised and rejected...'), implying that the fisherman and his brood have found contentment in their mean condition by keeping in mind of the Saviour's hardships, and His sacrifice for their sins. Doubtless as a consequence of pious overuse, the Bible has come away from its boards; stuck inside the back cover is a sheet of paper inscribed with important events in the family's recent history. The writing, now much faded, records that John [*****hope? born?] married Mary Smith on May[?] 1, 1795; in the intervening 15 years she has given birth to seven children, of whom at least five appear to have survived, along with their aged grandmother. Like More, Heaphy represents the worthy and the unworthy poor with the same degree of scrupulous precision, as certain critics recognized, but found so hard to understand. We may recall that *Le Beau Monde* took this equality of treatment as a sign of the artist's moral 'apathy'; but such a conclusion, we now realize, could hardly have been further from the truth.

Why, it seems more than fair to ask, was Heaphy so badly misjudged, when More's writings were so universally admired? The answer centres on the 'fit', or rather the lack thereof, between subject-matter, medium and audience. Hannah More could be praised for writing in a simple, descriptive manner about the transgressions of the rural poor – it is worth emphasizing that she, too, harbours no illusions about pastoral innocence – because she packaged her narratives of everyday life as inexpensive, 'popular' tracts expressly designed for the edification of a lower-class readership. Heaphy's pictures of vulgar depravity, by contrast, came in the costly and culturally prestigious form of paintings in watercolours, which were directed to a different audience altogether. He may have tried to shape their reading of his works by inserting occasional maxims in the catalogue: a lost picture of *The Poacher Alarmed*, for instance, was accompanied by 'The trembling of a leaf alarms the guilty mind'.[58] Yet with the possible exception of an Evangelically-minded minority, the affluent visitors to London's annual art exhibitions came unprepared for anything other than a pleasurable aesthetic experience, and most of them evidently failed to appreciate the improving lessons that Heaphy meant to impart. Because in this context viewers were unable to see how his depictions of '*moral and natural evil*' could possess any didactic value for themselves – this is where Landseer's invocation of comedy breaks down – instead of taking them to heart the metropolitan art public appears to have responded with laughter, or expressions of disgust. It was this ignoble, visceral reaction, as much as any of the features within Heaphy's works themselves, which the critics found so deeply disturbing, raising as it did the unhealthy prospect of a polite audience approaching all too closely to the character of the 'low'. I suspect that no one was more horrified by the viewers' responses than the artist himself.

What rescued Heaphy from all-out condemnation was the astounding precision of execution that was such a distinctive feature of his imagery. Reviewers could hardly say enough in praise of his 'high-finishing and minute detail',[59] which produced a fidelity to nature unsurpassed by anything previously seen in the watercolour medium:

> With respect to intimate knowledge of the localities of nature, and accuracy of representation of individual objects, both animate and inanimate, we conceive it to be hardly possible to carry water-colour painting further than Mr Heaphy has carried it.[60]

There can be no doubt but that these sentiments were shared by those affluent aficionados of watercolour painting who were willing to spend such enormous sums on the artist's work; what is harder to determine is whether they also subscribed to or even recognized his particular brand of Christian faith. Another strong possibility is that (as was certainly the case with Wilkie) they derived pleasure from the contrast between the refinement of his execution and the vulgarity of his subject-matter. In any event, the unstinting admiration for Heaphy's technical skill was inseparable from an awestruck amazement at the sheer amount of labour that had gone into the production of his pictures. After visiting the SPWC in 1810, David Wilkie – no slouch himself when it came to 'high-finishing' – privately recorded his own feelings of inadequacy when confronted by Heaphy's art:

Went to the Exhibition in the evening. I looked at and liked the drawings of Varley, De Wint and Heaphy. The industry of the latter is beyond all example. When I think of the number of highly finished objects which he has in these pictures of his, and compare them with what I myself have done in the same time, my labour seems idleness. I must exert myself more.[61]

Although he may not have known it, what Wilkie was responding to was further evidence of Heaphy's religious beliefs – for in Evangelical thought no virtue was more highly prized than industriousness, which was to be 'seen as doing God's duty in the world'.[62] Whether he was depicting scenes of evil or good, Heaphy consistently embraced the same Christian values, as expressed through his emphatically laborious craft.

The fact that reviewers were united in their praise for Heaphy's industry, even if they felt it had been too often wasted on improper subjects, shows that here we are dealing with one aspect of Evangelical thought which held equal importance for the English early nineteenth-century cultural mainstream. This was a relatively recent development, as Barrell has observed in *The Dark Side of the Landscape*:

In 1700, industriousness was not an important virtue; in 1800, it is the chief, and often seems to be the only virtue. We are right to understand this change broadly in terms of a change from a paternalist to a capitalist economy; industriousness is the prime and self-contained virtue of the capitalist entrepreneur; but we should also notice in this connection that the change of emphasis from wise passiveness to wise activity involves a change, too, in whose virtue and whose wisdom is in question. Virtue is passive in 1700 because it is the virtue of the gentleman that is of most concern, and of the retired gentleman that is most praised; it is active in 1800, because the poor labourer is now at once the model of the industrious, and so of the virtuous life, and the man on whom the wisdom and necessity of continuous industry must be more and more urgently and oppressively enjoined, if the outlay of the entrepreneur is to find its proper reward.[63]

With one or two exceptions, however, including the *Gleaners* scene mentioned above, Heaphy eschews the direct portrayal of agricultural labour. An important clue as to why he showed so little interest in what might have seemed such an obvious vehicle for his talents comes from the passage of text that accompanied his (now unlocated) *Woman with Cabbage Nets* when it appeared at the SPWC in 1807:

Industry, oh, couldst not thou provide for old age?
Ah no! deep poverty marks her footsteps, and follows her to the grave.[64]

Evangelical thinkers refrained from fully embracing the Georgic because it held out the delusive prospect that labour might provide a means of relieving the miseries of poverty, whereas the paupers' Christian duty was to embrace suffering as their lot, and to find contentment in doing so; this, as we've seen, was the point of the biblical reference in Heaphy's *Domestic Happiness*. But in his version of anti-pastoralism, though the poor are always implicitly urged to resist their natural inclination to idleness and vice, they are only rarely portrayed as models of industriousness; instead virtue is located first and foremost in the assiduous efforts of the artist, and of active middle-class citizens like himself. If the unfortunate truth is that poverty goes hand-in-hand with criminality, then it is the responsible man's Christian duty to try and eradicate the seeds of evil, either by persuading the poor to accept the inevitability of their oppressed condition, or by devising means of keeping their vicious tendencies under the strictest possible control. Whether the lower orders were to be governed from within or without, the key to their effective regulation lay not in the benevolent exercise of aristocratic paternalism, but rather in a regime of close surveillance operated by a laborious and self-disciplined bourgeoisie.

While the growing demand in Britain at the turn of the nineteenth century for detailed knowledge about the nation's dangerous classes may have found its best-known expression in Benthamite panopticism, the same impulse also registered its presence in the contemporaneous turn to the particular in visual representations of the poor – a shift that in turn went hand-in-hand with an increasingly critical examination of the disjunction between the image of happy rustic innocence conveyed by pastoral art, and what could actually be observed of the darker realities of the contemporary British countryside. Thomas Heaphy was far from alone in rejecting the conventions of pastoralism, or in his concomitant refusal to subscribe to the cult of sensibility or the picturesque. But his determination to adhere to the tenets of his strong Evangelical faith led him further than any other painter of rural life into the 'other half' of the landscape, the half that artists were not supposed to depict, and that viewers were not meant to see. Here Heaphy found worldly fame and material wealth, but only at the cost of a widespread miscomprehension of the moral and spiritual lessons that he had set out to convey. Having broken through one set of constraints, he simply discovered more obstacles that he was helpless to overcome: the constraints – moral, social, as well as aesthetic – imposed by art itself.

### Notes

1 John Barrell, *The Dark Side of the Landscape: the rural poor in English painting 1730–1840* (Cambridge: Cambridge University Press, 1981), p. 1.
2 *Ibid.*, p. 128.
3 Heaphy's *Fish Market* (SPWC 1809; private collection) sold for £400; the 42 works he exhibited at the Society between 1807 and 1811 were valued at over £4,200, and prior

to 1811, when his market seems to have dried up, all but a few of these were sold. See Greg Smith, *The Emergence of the Professional Watercolourist: Contentions and alliances in the artistic domain, 1760–1824* (Aldershot: Ashgate, 2002), pp. 143–5; further information on Heaphy can be found in Smith's 'The watercolour as commodity: the exhibitions of the Society of Painters in Water Colours', in Andrew Hemingway and William Vaughan (eds), *Art in Bourgeois Society* (Cambridge: Cambridge University Press, 1998), pp. 45–62. I would like to thank Dr Smith for bringing Heaphy's art to my attention, and for his unstinting practical help and intellectual generosity.

4  'Ephraim Hardcastle' [pseud. for William Henry Pyne], 'The Rise and Progress of Water-Colour Painting in England', *Somerset House Gazette; or, Weekly Miscellany of Fine Arts, Antiquities, and Literary Chit Chat*, I, no. 13 (1824), p. 194. I have found no record of Heaphy ever producing an image of young criminals carousing in the basement of a tavern, so this description may be the product of Pyne's still troubled imagination. For an exemplary discussion of his own very different portrayals of the working classes, see John Barrell, 'Visualising the Division of Labour: William Pyne's *Microcosm*', in *The Birth of Pandora and the Division of Knowledge* (London: Macmillan, 1992), pp. 89–118.

5  Barrell, *Dark Side*, pp. 128, 5.

6  Heaphy's *Young Gamblers* was sold to a Mr W. Peters (possibly the artist Matthew William Peters?) for a similar price. Most of my information on the details of Heaphy's career comes from William T. Whitley, *Thomas Heaphy (1775–1835), First President of the Society of British Artists*, Royal Society of British Artists' Art Club Publications no. 1 (London 1933). This short monograph remains the most comprehensive study of the artist and his work. Charles, 8th Lord Kinnaird (1780–1826) also purchased Heaphy's *Inattention* (Illustration 3.3) from the SPWC exhibition of 1808. Although 35 gns. was a relatively high price for a watercolour, here it may be worth recalling that in April 1807 Kinnaird bought Titian's *Bacchus and Ariadne* (National Gallery, London) for 3,000 guineas.

7  R. Stanier's stipple engraving after Wheatley's picture bears the following caption:

> O Tempt me not kind Sir I pray,
> Or wish to lead an innocent astray,
> To ruin first, You are inclin'd,
> And then Desert the injur'd mind,
> In virtues path I wish to move,
> A stranger to ungenerous love.

The Gainsborough is reproduced in Barrell, *Dark Side of the Landscape*, p. 83.

8  Jane Rendell, ' "Serpentine allurements:" disorderly bodies/disorderly spaces', in Iain Borden and Jane Rendell, eds, *InterSections: Architectural Histories and Critical Theories* (London and New York: Routledge, 2000), p. 255.

9  Richard Payne Knight, *An Analytical Inquiry into the Principles of Taste* (London, 1805), p. 194.

10  Gary Harrison, *Wordsworth's Vagrant Muse: Poetry, Poverty and Power* (Detroit, MI: Wayne State University Press, 1994), p. 64.

11  Uvedale Price, *An Essay on the Picturesque, as Compared with the Sublime and the Beautiful*, 2 vols (Hereford, 1794–98), I (1794), p. 166.

12  *First Report of the Philanthropic Society. Instituted in London, September 1788, for the Prevention of Crimes*, 2nd edn (London, 1790), p. 21.

13   Edward Dayes, *The Works of Edward Dayes* (London, 1805), p. 199.
14   John Middleton, *View of the Agriculture of Middlesex* (1798), q. Patrick Colquhoun, *A Treatise on the Police of the Metropolis*, 6th edn (London, 1800), p. 87.
15   *Ibid.*, p. 84.
16   The catalogue of the 1808 Society of Painters in Water-Colours exhibition identifies the nine genre scenes in question as follows: *Disappointment, or the lease refused* (catalogue no. 26); *The Poacher Alarmed* (no. 100); *Boys disputing over their day's sport* (no. 174); *Inattention* (no. 183; Illus. 3.3, Yale Centre for British Art, Paul Mellon Collection); *Return from the Baker's* (no. 206; Illus. 3.6; London art market, 2003); *Tired Pedlar* (no. 214); *Chiding the Favourite* (no. 241); *Credulity* (no. 255; Illust. 3.5; British Museum); and *The Lout's Reward* (no. 290). Of these only the three works for which I have provided locations now appear to be extant.
17   [Robert Hunt], *Examiner* 19 June 1808, p. 398.
18   *Monthly Magazine* XXV (May 1808), p. 398.
19   Smith, *Emergence of the Professional Watercolourist*, p. 144.
20   Anthony Pasquin [pseudonym for John Williams], *A Liberal Critique of the Exhibition of the Royal Academy* (London, 1794), pp. 31–2.
21   Wheatley's *Rustic Benevolence* is reproduced in Mary Webster, *Francis Wheatley* (London: Routledge, 1970), p. 182.
22   Sean Shesgreen, *Images of the Outcast: The Urban Poor in the Cries of London* (Manchester: Manchester University Press, 2002), p. 179.
23   Hannah More, 'Black Giles the Poacher', in *The Works of Hannah More* (London, 1801), V, pp. 416–7.
24   Colquhoun, *Treatise on the Police*, p. 116.
25   This phrase, taken from an unattributed source of 1805, is quoted in R.K. Webb, *The British Working Class Reader* (London: Allen & Unwin, 1955), p. 26.
26   See, for example, Hannah More, 'The Sunday School', in *Works*, IV, p. 379. Presumably the broadsheet held by the hawker was a popular version of the song *Tom Truelove's Knell*, from Charles Dibdin's entertainment *Great News, or a Trip to the Antipodes*, first performed in 1794. Here Tom Truelove figures as a sailor whose sweetheart dies; Tom finds consolation in thinking that he still has a best friend, but he, too, comes to an early end. Then Tom himself is killed in battle, and names his lost love with his dying breath. All the details can be found in an undated bound volume of Dibdin's *Songs*, BL G.382.1–73. I am grateful to Scott Wilcox for his help in deciphering the inscriptions in *Inattention*.
27   The condemnation of Wheatley's *Cries of London* as 'meretricious and theatrical' comes from Edward Edwards, *Anecdotes of Painters who have resided or been born in England* (London, 1808), p. 269. For the best discussion of Rowlandson's series, and for the issue of anti-pastoralism in *Cries* imagery, see Shesgreen, *Images of the Outcast*, pp. 136–48, 173–95.
28   George Crabbe, *The Village* (London, 1783), I, lines ll. 33–4.
29   Barrell, *Dark Side of the Landscape*, pp. 14, 87, and *passim*.
30   This phrase comes from an anonymous review of Crabbe's *The Village* in *The Gentleman's Magazine*, LIII (Dec. 1783), p. 1041.
31   *Critical Review*, XX (July 1810), q. Arthur Pollard, ed., *George Crabbe – The Critical Heritage* (London and New York: Routledge, 1995), p. 108.
32   See, for example, [Francis Jeffrey], *Edinburgh Review*, XVI, no. 31 (April 1810), pp. 34–8.

33 Martin Archer Shee, *Elements of Art, A Poem; in Six Cantos* (London 1809), p. 53n.
34 [John Landseer], *Review of the Publications of Art*, no. 2 (1808), pp. 186–8.
35 John Barrell, 'The Private Comedy of Thomas Rowlandson', in *The Birth of Pandora and the Division of Knowledge* (Manchester: Manchester University Press, 1992), pp. 15–16.
36 *Le Beau Monde, and Monthly Register*, n.s. I (July 1809), pp. 338–9.
37 *Repository of Arts*, I (June 1809), p. 492. This was probably written by William Henry Pyne; see note 40 below.
38 *Literary Panorama*, VI (1809), p. 547.
39 [Robert Hunt] 'State of British Art as Evinced by our late Exhibitions', *Examiner* (2 July 1809), p. 426.
40 *Repository of Arts*, V (June 1811), p. 345. On Pyne's extensive involvement in Ackermann's art publications, see Smith, *Emergence of the Professional Watercolourist*, p. 162.
41 *Le Beau Monde, and Monthly Register* n.s. I (July 1809), p. 341. The couplet is an inaccurately remembered quotation from Alexander Pope's *Essay on Man*. The correct wording is:

> Vice is a monster of so frightful mien,
> As, to be hated, needs but to be seen.

(Epistle II, ll.217–8)

42 Dayes, *Works*, I, p. 224.
43 [Landseer], *Review of the Publications of Art*, no. 2 (1808), p. 188.
44 *Le Beau Monde, and Monthly Register*, n.s. I (July 1809), pp. 341–2. The philosopher in question may be Edmund Burke.
45 Heaphy's *Fish Market* of 1809, now in a private collection, is reproduced in Smith, *Emergence of the Professional Watercolourist*, pl. XII.
46 Although we have no way of knowing if the two works were hung as a pair, they are both the same size, and would have made sense as a juxtaposition of various dichotomous elements: good/evil, sacred/profane, home/street, calm/violent, mother/maidservant, etc. Hibbert (1757–1837) was a wealthy West India merchant (and presumably a slave-owner) whose residence was in Clapham, and who bought 25 works from the SPWC exhibitions between 1808 and 1824. This collection, including the two Heaphys, was sold at Sotheby's on 22 March 2000. Here once again I must acknowledge Greg Smith's generous assistance.
47 *Morning Herald*, 23 April 1810. Due to an error made by Whitley (*Thomas Heaphy*, p. 36), and perpetuated by subsequent scholars, the Newcastle picture has hitherto been called *A Fisherman's Cottage*, and has not been identified with *Domestic Happiness* (SPWC 1810, cat. no. 166), which is clearly the original title.
48 Heaphy enjoyed his greatest financial success between 1808 and 1810; at the SPWC of 1811, where he returned in a minority of exhibits to the 'vulgar' subjects that had previously been so popular with rich collectors, his major works remained unsold. In 1812 he abandoned the Society in favour of showing at the Royal Academy, where he was represented by a mix of genre scenes and portraits, and thereafter he concentrated almost exclusively on portraiture. For a discussion of some of the other factors that may have been responsible for the downturn in Heaphy's fortunes, see Smith, *Emergence of the Professional Watercolourist*, p. 145.
49 *Le Beau Monde, and Monthly Register*, n.s. I (July 1809), p. 340n.
50 Apart from this comment and the watercolours themselves, the only other evidence for Heaphy's religiosity comes from a note of *c*.1868 by John Jenkins in

the archive of the Royal Watercolour Society (folio J46), apparently based on information provided by the artist's son, Thomas, Jr. Here the latter is reported as recalling how, in the early years of the Society of British Artists (founded 1824, with Heaphy Sr. as its first President), his father had taken offence when the Royal Family visited the Society's annual exhibition on a Sunday, and threatened to resign should this ever happen again. Presumably as President he had been principally responsible for the decree passed in 1824, 'That the rooms of the Society shall not be used on the Sabbath Day for any pretence whatsoever'. See Whitley, *Thomas Heaphy*, p. 24.

51   Donna T. Andrew, *Philanthropy and Police: London Charity in the Eighteenth Century* (Princeton, NJ: Princeton University Press, 1989), p. 165.

52   *Reports of the Society for Bettering the Condition and Increasing the Comforts of the Poor*, Sir Thomas Bernard, ed. (London 1798–1808), 5 vols, II, pp. 35–6.

53   Hannah More, 'Tawny Rachel; or, the Fortune Teller: with some Account of Dreams, Omens, and Conjurers', in *Works*, V, p. 448.

54   More, 'Parley the Porter. An Allegory. Shewing how Robbers without can never get into an House, unless there are Traitors within', in *Works*, IV, pp. 455–6.

55   More, 'The Shepherd of Salisbury Plain', in *Works*, V, p. 44.

56   *Ibid.*, pp. 36–8.

57   George Crabbe, too, was a master of allegorizing physical detail; but his moral vision was more in line with the Anglican mainstream than with the Evangelical insistence on the fallen nature of Creation that we find in Hannah More and Thomas Heaphy.

58   *The Exhibition of the Society of Painters in Water Colours. The Fourth* (London, 1808), p. 8, no. 100.

59   [W.H. Pyne], *Repository of Arts*, I (June 1809), p. 492.

60   *Le Beau Monde, and Monthly Register* n.s. I (July 1809), p. 338.

61   David Wilkie, diary for 24 May 1810, q. Allan Cunningham, *The Life of Sir David Wilkie, with his journals, tours, and critical remarks on art; and a selection from his correspondence* (London: John Murray, 1843), 3 vols, I, p. 298.

62   Catherine Hall and Leonore Davidoff, *Family Fortunes: Men and Women of the English Middle Class 1780–1850* (London: Routledge, 1997), p. 111.

63   Barrell, *Dark Side*, pp. 86–7.

64   *The Exhibition of the Society of Painters in Water Colours. The Third* (London, 1807), p. 14, no. 273.

# 4

# Chardin at the Edge of Belief: Overlooked Issues of Religion and Dissent in Eighteenth-Century French Painting

*Thomas Crow*

John Barrell taught a generation to think about British art of the eighteenth century within the interplay of deep assumptions about civic virtue, its carriers and its responsibilities. *The Political Theory of Painting* told a complex story and one that was new to most of its readers, even those well-versed in the intellectual, political and art history of the period.[1] It also represented a challenge to art historians, in that the ideological staging ground that Barrell situated in the century's early decades preceded its realization in paint on canvas. Ritual protestations about the primacy of 'the object' proved no defense against the implicit demands of history that scholarship first meet the standard of textual interpretation that Barrell had established as necessary for an adequate grasp of eighteenth-century British art.

To a specialist in French art of the same period, the parallels with Britain were tantalizing. Certainly there was the pronounced impact of English and Scottish liberal thinking on key Enlightenment thinkers like Voltaire. By mid-century, the semi-annual public exhibitions by the French Academy of Painting and Sculpture – the *Salons* – provided a dissident cadre of writers with both an object lesson and an audience in their efforts to promulgate a civic ideal with strong roots across the Channel. And like the British writers responsible for the new aesthetic of civic duty, the first *salonniers* were likewise forced to make their arguments in the absence of any truly persuasive exemplification for their ideas in actual works of art.[2] Their efforts aimed to create legitimacy in vulnerable corners of prevailing public ideologies for an art that did not yet exist – not until the arrival of a like-minded arts administration at the accession of Louis XVI and a generation of artists, dominated by Jacques-Louis David, prepared to realize a reformist programme.

That represents one time-tested story, the Enlightenment narrative whereby a patrician notion of the monarch's accountability to the nation eventually marshalled for its purposes the Italianate artistic ideals of unified *historiae* and compulsory elevation in style and subject matter – and the painters, after a long delay, followed suit. Not every form of dissent, however, could afford to announce itself in this way; if it were to find form in art, it would instead be forced to code its protests in silent material form.

The immediate object of this hypothesis hangs today in the Art Institute of Chicago: a modest canvas by Jean-Siméon Chardin that has come to be called *The White Tablecloth* (Illustration 4.1). An early still life, probably painted in 1732, its aspect is unassuming and without distinctive marks of originality.[3] Comparison to any number of Netherlandish prototypes of the seventeenth century reveals a large measure of convention in Chardin's choice and arrangement of his objects. But this was the motif of Chardin's early career, as dramatized in the well-known story of Chardin's admission to membership in the Academy of Painting and Sculpture just four years earlier. The story goes that he set up *The Ray* (Illustration 4.2) alongside its companion, *The Buffet*, in the Academy's vestibule rather than the examination room, successfully garnering the unguarded praise of the senior members as they entered.[4] They had taken the work to be by an accomplished Flemish

*Illustration 4.1*  Jean-Siméon Chardin, *The White Tablecloth*, c. 1732, oil on canvas, 96×24 cm. (Copyright the Art Institute of Chicago)

*Illustration 4.2* Jean-Siméon Chardin, *The Skate/The Ray*, 1726, oil on canvas, 144 × 146 cm (Paris, Louvre)

master of the still-life genre. Asking to see Chardin's entry, they were told they had already seen it and already made their judgment.[5]

It makes for a great punch line, no matter how much of the tale is actually true.[6] As was customary in the period, Chardin's early biographers threaded their accounts through a few loaded anecdotes, rather than offering anything resembling a continuous life-narrative, and these nodal points need to be unpacked like little parables. Among other things, this one underscores how much Chardin built his reputation on conventional Netherlandish foundations. *The White Tablecloth*, though much less celebrated, silently tells a similar story, but its debts to the North are of a more limited and superficial character than those of his brilliant culinary virtuosity displayed in *The Ray* and *The Buffet*. In that slightly later work, all sparkle and suavity are gone (well- beyond the evident effects of abrasion on the surface as one sees it today). More than a third of the total area of the white table cloth features nothing but an expanse of white cotton cloth. A virtual surrogate for the canvas support beneath, its modest disorder lacks picturesque accident, and its texture is unrefined, with visible marks of mending. Shapely vessels find themselves tucked out of view on the floor in a rough brown cylinder. A tangle of circular strokes serves to notate the edge of the torn loaf. In its convoluted energy and indifference to pleasing the eye, compounded by the awkward way that it laps over the edge of the platter, this passage enacts a kind of violence toward customary decorum. The adjoining shape of the remaining loaf, by contrast, settles for flat two-dimensionality divorced from the drama of the torn interior.

The two wine glasses, one carelessly overturned, compound this same play of associations. Nor has much trouble been taken to give them particularly convincingly volume. *The White Tablecloth* transforms Chardin's inviting goblet in *The Buffet* into an opaque, flattened trapezoid of crimson. The knife, just used to cut the sausage, picks up the red note, but the effect is curious, in that the reflection of the wine – the only thing it could be – appears to slide off the blade, clinging only to the handle, which further invites a grip by the left hand.

One astute modern-day authority has written: 'it is a somewhat awkward and perhaps hastily executed work, lacking the careful arrangement and exquisite handling of Chardin's cabinet pictures'.[7] And so it is, certainly by the technical standards of *The Ray* or any number of his preternaturally assured later works, the ones that have awakened all those non-cognitive exclamations of magic and mystery in Chardin's supernatural touch. Diderot could write of *The Ray*: 'The object is revolting, but this is the very flesh of the fish. This is its skin. This is its blood.... Oh Chardin! It is not white, red, or black pigment that you spread onto your palette; it is the very substance of your objects.'[8] But not everyone among the painter's contemporaries agreed. While the perceived shortcomings of *The White Tablecloth* may seem an anomaly in the body of work conjured up by Diderot's encomia, one equally seasoned commentator, Pierre-Jean Mariette, wrote that the painter's style 'smacked too much of effort and labor. His touch is heavy and never varied. There is no ease in his brushstrokes; everything is expressed in the same manner and with a certain indecision – all of which makes his work seem cold.'[9]

Could it be that Diderot and Mariette were not so much in disagreement as they were attending to different strands in Chardin's work, the latter addressing something like the technique on view in *The White Tablecloth*, the failings of which may have been sufficient to colour his view of the artist's work as a whole – it is difficult otherwise to credit his verdict at all. And Chardin further distinguished that work from the rest of his output by subjecting it to a sub-artistic function. The current rectangular format of the picture has been modified from its earlier shape, with a scalloped upper border, which was fitted to serve as a fireplace screen in the summer months.[10] That is to say, he inserted it in a common, low place in the domestic household. It would never have been a splendid material possession in the manner of its traditional Dutch cognate nor could it have circulated in the marketplace in the same way.

Despite this relegation to the zone of the low and soiled, however, the painting attracted an anecdote fully as realized as the one attached to *The Ray*. Chardin' friend, the portraitist Joseph Aved, had just turned down a commission because he judged the offered price unworthy of his talents. Chardin tartly observed that the offer seemed plenty for just a portrait, particularly as Aved was only beginning to acquire a reputation. His friend shot back that Chardin was under the misapprehension that painting a human being was no more difficult than painting a sausage – precisely what Chardin happened to be doing at that moment. Stung by this disparagement of his lowly genre, he is said to have painted his first picture incorporating the human figure (either *The Young Man Blowing Bubbles* or *The Serving Maid at the Copper Cistern*, depending on the account) thereby leaving still-life behind and launching himself into a more ambitious and rewarding two decades painting the pastimes of children, the routines of domestic servants and the everyday exchanges, almost below the level of conscious reflection, between mothers and their offspring.[11]

*The White Tablecloth* was certainly the object of Aved's disparaging retort, and the chronology of Chardin's paintings suggest that it indeed stands close to this watershed in his career – though so far-reaching a transition will surely have had a longer and more complex preparation. Granting its symbolic status, however, it may nonetheless be the case that he turned away from the genre of inanimate objects with a defiant demonstration of its capacity to represent a form of truth unknown to Aved's pricey portraiture. His friend's irritated comment joined the lowly sausage to a human presence. Chardin presents it divided into segments for distribution. Highlights of white in the cut surfaces may be meant as globules of fat, but their similarly cursive rendering echoes the torn bread above, drawing a non-mimetic link between the two foodstuffs. The platter presents this cheap meat, while the wildly rendered tearing of the bread intrudes on its surface. The red wine stains the hand like blood. The curious disposition of the white cloth itself, so honoured in the picture's traditional title, disguises the wooden support underneath and makes the whole arrangement undergo a kind of levitation. In this alternative scenario, Chardin refuses to abandon his exclusive devotion to the still-life genre without first defiantly raising its subject matter to the plane of the Eucharist[12].

There is little else in the painting to distract one's thoughts from these analogies, certainly not the unrelieved murk of its shadowed background. At the same time, everything about its design and manufacture serves to subtract splendour and mysterious allure from the central mystery of Christian faith. Chardin enumerates the elements of Catholic communion, yet withholds the painterly effects – along with the honorific mode of display – that might have lent the customary aura of sanctity and splendour to the ceremony. He abandons his expected virtuosity with the brush in favour of a harsh and abrupt manner, going so far as to equate the body of Christ with an everyday item of *charcuterie*. In its function, the painting was intended to be hidden away, yet it appears to have served as some kind of demonstration piece, even if it remained concealed from most eyes.

There is, in fact, a contemporaneous context of ideas and beliefs centred on the Eucharist, in light of which virtually all of these apparent discrepancies and contradictions snap into a significant degree of coherence. Beginning in the 1640s, the French followers of the Belgian theologian Jansensius threw into doubt all comfortable assumptions concerning confession and absolution. Against the Jesuit reliance on good works and intermediate institutions of this world, the Jansenists (as they came to be known) opposed a fundamentally tragic vision of the condition of humanity. The fall from innocence, the utter catastrophe of Adam's disobedient pride, was for them, in their strict Augustinianism, total and final. The only mitigation for this condition lay in the unbidden and unpredictable manifestations of divine grace.

In strictest practice, its adherents were enjoined to renounce worldly honours and temptations. Blaise Pascal, to take the most famous case, abandoned his previously meteoric career in mathematics and science in favour of theological meditation. His anonymously published *Provincial Letters* of 1656 were the second great popular success among published defences of Jansenist beliefs, and he launched them on behalf of the imprisoned author of the first, a tract entitled *On Frequent Communion* by Antoine Arnauld, published in 1643. Arnauld had, of course, recommended the opposite, judging even fear of damnation to be an insufficient motive for absolution if not accompanied by an inner contrition so thorough that its achievement might take years for even the most sincere and pious penitent. Subsequent generations of Jansenists came to regard frequent communion by the unprepared as simply presumptuous, manifesting a prideful confidence in individual initiative and the instruments of the Church as paths to absolution.

The issue remained a source of deep contention – social and political as well as theological – for more than a century afterward. Louis XIV and his ministers chose to make a capital issue out of Jansenist independence and, one surmises, their refusal to credit the world's 'intermediate' institutions with any element of the divine. By 1711, the might of the state had seen to the complete demolition of the convent Port-Royal des Champs, around which key male figures like Arnauld and Pascal had gathered over the years. 1713 brought the papal bull *Unigenitus*, fulminated at the behest of the French government, which forbade the faithful to teach, read, discuss or even think about the key tenets ascribed to Jansenism. But resistance – through clandestine journalism, covert legal maneuver and overt popular demonstrations – continued to smoulder and flare well into the mid-century.[13] After a century of conflict, a prominent Jesuit preacher was still inveighing against a 'voluntary and considered profanation' of the Eucharist: 'it was reserved to our century', he lamented, 'to accredit, to authorize, to consecrate, as it were, a voluntary withdrawal from the sacraments...under a hypocritical respect for the most holy mysteries, a sorrow for the decline of discipline, a nostalgia for the severity of ancient canons'.[14]

Within the particular realm of the visual arts, the research of Christian Michel has unearthed a network of Jansenist sympathizers inside the Academy of Painting and Sculpture.[15] Jean Restout the elder, a contemporary of Chardin, was one painter who overtly identified himself with Jansenist belief.[16] His son, also a painter, followed in the same path, and the list can be considerably expanded. The history painter Pierre-Jacques Cazes was allied with Restout, as well as with the equally Jansenist extended family that included successive academic generations of Cochins, Tardieus and Belles. The mother of the younger Cochin, Charles-Nicolas, was one of three sisters who were all zealous Jansenists and wives of academic artists.[17] Cochin rose to the post of permanent secretary of the Academy, but that ascent did not prevent him from providing frontispieces for the proscribed, clandestine Jansenist periodical *Les Nouvelles eccésiastiques* (at some earlier point, he drew and engraved a small image of the crucified Christ that certain inspired Jansenist militants credited with the miraculous power to exude blood from the five wounds).[18] Chardin was first a student of Cazes and then continually supported by Cochin's friendship and institutional advocacy.[19] In short, Jansenism was all around him in both his earliest formation and his subsequent career. Its commonplaces would have been his.[20]

The elder Restout brought the issue of the sacrament and grace together in his version of *The Supper at Emmaus* of 1735 (Illustration 4.3), the theme encompassing both the revelation of the risen Christ to his disciples and a typological recapitulation of the Last Supper.[21] As related in Luke (24: 15–45):

> Jesus himself drew near and went with them. But their eyes were holden that they should not know them ... as he sat at meat with them, he took bread with them and blessed it, and brake and gave it to them. And their eyes were opened, and they knew him; and he vanished out of their sight. And they said to one another, Did not our heart burn within us ... while he opened to us the scriptures.[22]

In that Christ comes and goes, leaving mortals alternatively inspired and dismayed, this final reiteration of the Last Supper figures the fugitive nature of grace. And the sentence about scripture, seized upon by Pascal, fed the preoccupation among all underground Jansenist networks with 'Figurist' readings of the bible among the laity, whereby their contemporary travails and witnessing of truth could be read, when properly decoded, as prefigured in holy writ.[23] Restout evokes an ideal communion effected in the breaking of the loaf, here transfigured by grace but, too often, in the fallen world before Christ's return, travestied in empty magic by those who expect mere ceremony to substitute for true contrition, charity and unforced love of God.

Figurist doctrines sustained the militancy of a self-conscious elect that alone could decipher the secret, divine meaning behind familiar appearances. In the analysis of historian Catherine Maire, their appeal lay at the

*Illustration 4.3*   Jean Restout, *Le Souper à Emmaüs* (Lille, Musée des Beaux-Arts)

heart of the revival of Jansenism in the eighteenth century: its transformation from, at the turn of the century, an isolated sect mourning the defeat of Port-Royal to the major cultural force it became by the later 1720s.[24] Restout's *Supper at Emmaus* adapts the conventional idiom of religious painting to signal the unbidden, unpredictable nature of divine visitation, abundantly manifested for the emboldened Jansenists in a profusion of perceived miracles in the streets of Paris during the first half of the 1730s.[25] At the start of the decade, the King's chief minister, cardinal Fleury, had finally overcome the Jansenists' last legal defenses against *Unigenitus* becoming the law of the land in France; Chardin painted his fire-screen after two years of renewed public battles over the attempt by the established church to deny the sacraments to all those suspected of resistance to the strictures of the papal bull. As William Doyle comments: 'Although it was basic Jansenist spiritual strategy not to profane the sacraments by seeking them too often with insufficient preparation, this was the corollary of a veneration that made their total loss unbearable.'[26] The subtlety of this understanding of the Eucharist required its negation alongside its realization: What would be its value if God did not choose at that moment to inhabit the host? And what mortal could guarantee that event? Thus, would not any viewer sympathetic to the Jansenist cause, his or her Figurist sensitivities attuned to a scriptural image of communion, have been just as ready to discern the signs of its worldly failure in Chardin's canvas. The barren ritual table provides the necessary complement to the miracle celebrated by Restout, its mystery cancelled by official travesty and a tragic absence of grace. Or did it go beyond Restout's accomplished but literal effort to find form for both Figurist doctrine and the complicated ambivalence of Jansenist attitudes towards the sacrament? The fact that the image was husbanded within a household suggests that it possessed some consoling meaning. And might that meaning have been some truly radical sense of the immanence of the divine in the least prepossessing vessels imaginable? The slightest trace of worldly aspiration manifested in the material trappings of Holy Communion would thus represent the true travesty of the sacrament and the greatest obstacle to genuine contrition and absolution. Somewhere within these coordinates, the *White Tablecloth* locates its iconography.

To make of one's very instrument of success a humble domestic implement, withdrawn from the world and exposed only to an elect viewership, personifies the painting itself as solitary and penitent. It has been too easy to assimilate all advanced eighteenth-century painting in France under a broadly Enlightenment programme of social improvement and optimism. Within this framework, Chardin's still-life subjects are seen to have shed the last vestige of an older Dutch preoccupation with moralizing allegories, substituting new values of formal composition and the capture of vision itself. But there are many ways of mapping a religious sensibility in art, and not all of them entail overt iconography. At the heart of Jansenist Figurism lay the assumption that it was the destiny of the true church to undergo in historical time the suffering originally visited upon the body of Christ. In the times of episcopal apostasy and despotism, the persecuted minority – very much including the lay faithful – could take heart from the meanings inscribed in their own day-to-day experiences: Divine importance could attach itself to any secular event or condition.

In that light, Chardin's eloquent recorded account of his own vocation takes on a potentially deeper significance. In remarks famously recorded by Diderot in 1765, his vision of the artist's life under the aegis of the state is one of penitential suffering in the face of the world's cold indifference. He challenges all critics, his friend Diderot included, to take on board 'the perils' faced by any aspiring artist and the near-unattainability of excellence:

> Find the worst painting in the Salon and bear in mind that two thousand wretches have broken brushes between their teeth in despair at ever producing anything as good... The chalk-holder is placed in our hands at the age of seven or eight years. We begin to draw eyes, mouths, noses, and ears after patterns, then feet and hands. After having crouched over our portfolios for an eternity, we're placed in front of the *Hercules* or the *Torso*, and you've never seen such tears...

> Then, after having spent entire days and even nights by lamplight in front of immobile, inanimate nature, we're presented with living nature, and suddenly the work of all the preceding years seems reduced to nothing... Those who've never felt art's difficulty will never produce anything of value; those, like my own son, who feel it too early, produce nothing at all. Rest assured that most of the high positions in our society would remain empty if one gained access to them only after trials as severe as those to which we artists must submit.[27]

Those who fail the test of this martyrdom, he laments, are destined to find themselves stranded in a hostile society, without preparation for any other honest career and likely to drift into one or another inherently sinful occupation.

   Lest this be read as the rueful recriminations of an old man and disappointed father, one can discover the very personification of this passage in one of Chardin's earliest figure paintings, the first of numerous versions completed within a few years of *The White Tablecloth* and his 'conversion' from still-life to human subject matter. The *Young Student Drawing* (Illustration 4.4) is a tiny but intensely worked picture, evidently complex in conception.[28] Its subject, head bowed and back slumped, submits to his duty, the thankless routines excoriated by Chardin in his commentary to Diderot ('crouched over our portfolios for an eternity'). His face is hidden, but his back is marked with the most distinctive single incident in the painting: the hole in his thick, roughly-woven coat. The coat itself signals a frugal shortage of coal; the unmended hole poverty's indifference to appearance. Ostensibly, the gap simply reveals a glimpse of the lining underneath, but the choice of colour and the fact that it is rendered with a single stroke of red visibly on top of its neighbours make it the unmissable surrogate for a wound – which burns in a way that the unseen stove does not. The dark brown touches adjacent to it lend the opening the depth of an incision. The large and lethal-looking knife dropped on the floor nearby (to sharpen the chalk? to

*Illustration 4.4* Jean-Siméon Chardin, *The Draughtsman/Young Student Drawing*, c. 1733–34, oil on canvas,19.5 × 17.5 cm (National Museum, Stockholm)

cut the paper?) might be the instrument of a butcher or an assassin. A further, dragged touch of red paint draws a livid note along the handle.

As the wounded body of Christ prefigures the persecuted body of his true, primitive church, so the body of this ragged pupil stands in for the condition of art stretched on the rack of its worldly institutions. Is it going then too far to see the raw wood of the cross in the background, juxtaposed to the livid wound? David would do nothing less for Marat. The thought lends weight to René Démoris's observations about *The Ray*, to go back before *The White Tablecloth* to the very onset of Chardin's mature career. 'Discreetly active in *The Ray*', he states, 'is a disposition familiar in scenes of martyrdom: the bodies of the victims are not only subjected to various outrages and mutilations; they are also arranged in unnatural postures to be put on public exhibition. This display of the body can stand as the visual essence of torture, in particular for the many types of crucifixion (of Christ but also of Saints Peter and Andrew).' As nearly every viewer can attest, the ventral orifice lends *The Ray* itself the uncanny appearance of bearing a human face above a mutilated chest and splayed arms. While there are plenty of precedents in northern still-life for the motif of a suspended fish, Démoris finds no prototype for 'this conjunction of suspension and wounding' of the gutted animal. He asks, 'if in some involuntary manner, the flesh and blood evoked by Diderot is not the way in which the evangelical text – this is my body, this is my blood – comes in some way to "transpire" throughout the canvas. It happens that the martyr-fish is also destined to be eaten'.[29]

In his contribution to the catalogue of the latest retrospective, Démoris raises the stakes by asking, 'does not Chardin's painting take over the task of *unveiling* to which the art of his day no longer paid any attention, having lost its religious vocation'.[30] Given that the history painters of the day continued to paint religious subjects in considerable numbers, the form of the question assumes some kind of Jansenist answer.[31] The Academy's highest genre is blocked from any persuasive manifestation of Christianity's fundamental truth, in that the history painter improves and elevates the things of this world towards an ideal; like the monarchy and the established church, it seeks a middle zone between the human and divine. To a Jansenist temperament, this manifests nothing but vain aspiration to effect some intermediate approach to God by means of individual will and hierarchical privilege. When embodied in an academic *machine*, such presumption required a profusion of preparatory studies and an elaborately artificial architecture of lines and contours before a final clothing of color could be applied. In Chardin's way with paint, by contrast, there is refusal of any model or preconceived idea; the objects before one's eyes were enacted in the moment, in the matter of the world to which paint belongs, without abstract lines or contours.[32]

Could there be in this a filtered effect of the Port-Royal abhorrence of pedantry and of Pascal's idea of intuition, that is, sensitivity to nuances of experience so fine – the famous *je ne sais quoi* – as to defy clear categorical contours?[33] Chardin carried that same technique into his treatment of human figures, which legend tells us followed directly from the experiment with *The White Tablecloth*. And in this may lie the truer moral significance of Chardin's evident rejection of the moralizing motifs common in the

Netherlandish prototypes for such scenes. The prosperous households conjured up in these paintings – with their upright mistresses, attentive children, and (mostly) industrious servants – seem to spring from a milieu of moderate social advancement; but worldly, male-dominated pursuits are always far away from his domestic interiors. The giving and receiving of lessons, the principal occupation of his characters, remains a modest and unchanging affair away from the public eye. Any form of ostentatious virtue paraded for worldly gain contradicted the humility most prized in Jansenist thought.[34]

Did then the arrival on the Salon scene of Greuze, who synthesized Chardin's bourgeois subject matter with the morally exemplary narrative of academic painting, change the rules of the game in such a way that Chardin had no effective reply? His own established popular success had handed Greuze an instrument that the younger artist initially applied to the theme of lay reading of the Bible in 1755, and then shifted to a complete secularization of the marriage sacrament in *The Village Betrothal* of 1762[35] (Illustration 4.5). In a second act of renunciation, Chardin abandoned his own scenes of everyday life by the mid-1750s. Despite the clamour of demand from princely collectors across Europe, he never returned to the genre and once more devoted himself to still-life for the considerable remainder of his career, an act for which there has never been any persuasive explanation.[36]

*Illustration 4.5* Jean-Baptiste Greuze, *The Village Betrothal*, 1761. Photo: J.G. Berizzi, Copyright © Réunion des Musées Nationaux/Art Resource

This essay has been studded with rhetorical questions, a mark of the elusiveness of the connections it has attempted to draw. But the same is true of any attempt to connect the inwardness of the self with its outward manifestations. That difficulty is always intensified when those manifestations carry the expressive promise of a work of art. The case of eighteenth-century Jansenism, which was both clandestine and given to the occult practices of Figurism, would seem to compound the difficulty. But perhaps the opposite is true. Jansenist practices provide an empirically historical cognate for the privacy of the self and its unveiling. Their charge was to reveal the hidden and unpredictable workings of grace, the occult signs of the divine. The last rhetorical question will be to ask whether Chardin was a Jansenist who happened to paint or was a painter who required sectarian encouragement that his brush could be a means of revelation.

## Notes

1  John Barrell, *The Political Theory Of Painting From Reynolds To Hazlitt: 'The Body of the Public'* (New Haven and London: Yale University Press, 1995).

2  On this point, see the author's *Painters and Public Life in Eighteenth-Century Paris* (New Haven and London: Yale University Press, 1985), pp. 129–33.

3  See entry on the painting by Susan Wise, 'Jean-Siméon Chardin: *The White Table-cloth*', in Larry J. Feinberg and Martha Wolff eds, *French and British Paintings from 1600 to 1800 in the Art Institute of Chicago: A Catalogue of the Collection* (Princeton, NJ: Princeton University Press, 1996), pp. 24–8.

4  On the two paintings, see most recently Pierre Rosenberg, ed., *Chardin*, exhibition catalogue (London and New York: Royal Academy of Arts and Metropolitan Museum of Art, 1999), no. 2, pp. 118–19, no. 12, pp. 138–9.

5  See Haillet de Couronne, 'Eloge de M. Chardin sur les mémoires fournis par M. Cochin', (1780), reproduced in Georges Wildenstein, *Chardin* (Les Beaux-Arts: Paris, 1933), p. 42.

6  Charles-Nicolas Cochin, 'Essai sur la vie de Chardin' (1780), reprinted in Wildenstein, *Chardin*, p. 37, relates that the encounter with Largillierre, the academician who pronounced them 'de quelque bon peintre flamand', took place 'chez lui', though in other respects the description of the scene parallels that of Haillet de Couronne.

7  Philip Conisbee, *Chardin* (Oxford: Phaidon, 1985), p. 94.

8  Denis Diderot, 'Salon de 1763', in Jean Seznec and Jean Adhémar, eds, *Diderot, Salons* (Oxford: Oxford University Press, 1975), I., p. 223 (author's translation).

9  Pierre-Jean Mariette, *Abécédario*, 1749, reprinted in Wildenstein, *Chardin*, p. 31 (author's translation). The view persists, in defiance of the contrary visual evidence. See Rosenberg, 'Chardin: the Unknowing Subversive', p. 32: 'All his life, doggedly and tirelessly, Chardin battled to overcome his lack of natural talent.' The confusion here seems to be one between talent and facility.

10  Mariette is the contemporary source for identifying this particular canvas, 'un tableau de devant de cheminée', as he terms it, with the Aved anecdote and the sausage motif, *ibid.*, p. 30; Marianne Roland-Michel, *Chardin* (New York: Thames & Hudson, 1996), p. 156, observes that the perspective of the painting implies a viewing position from above. For a discussion and photograph of the original scalloped upper border, see Wise, 'Chardin: *The White Tablecloth*', pp. 26–7.

11  See the biographical notices by Mariette and Cochin in Wildenstein, *Chardin*, pp. 30–1; *Woman Sealing a Letter*, Berlin, Schloss Charlottenburg is now generally taken to be the first of Chardin's figure paintings of the 1730s: see Rosenberg, *Chardin* (1999), no. 33, p. 190.

12  *Pace* Rosenberg, 'Chardin: the Unknowing Subversive', in Rosenberg, *Chardin* (1999), p. 33: 'defying iconographic analysis, his paintings obstinately challenge any attempt at interpretation'.

13  There has been a flowering of new scholarship on Jansenism, emphasizing particularly the continuities between its first, seventeenth-century phases and its strong afterlife in the eighteenth century. See Dale Van Kley, *The Jansenists and the Expulsion of the Jesuits from France, 1757–1765* (New Haven and London: Yale University Press, 1975) and *The Religious Origins of the French Revolution* (New Haven and London: Yale University Press, 1996); Catherine-Laurence Maire, *Les Convulsionnaires de Saint-Médard. Miracles, convulsions et prophéties au XVIIIe siècle* (Paris: Collection Archives, 1981) and *De la cause de Dieu à la cause de la nation. Les Jansénistes au XVIIIe siècle* (Paris: Gallimard, 1998); B. Robert Kreiser, *Miracles, Convusions and Ecclesiastical Politics in Eighteenth-Century Paris* (Princeton: Princeton University Press, 1978); and Peter R. Campbell, *Power and Politics in Old-Regime France, 1720–1745* (London: Routledge, 1994).

14  See Van Kley, *The Religious Origins of the French Revolution*, p. 168, quoting Henri Griffet, *Sermons pour l'Avent, le carême, et les principaux fêtes de l'année, prêchés par M. père H. Griffet, prédicateur ordinaire de Sa Majesté Très-Catholique* (Liège, 1773), III: pp. 116–17.

15  See Christian Michel, *Charles-Nicolas Cochin et l'art des lumières* (Rome: Ecole française de Rome, 1993), pp. 27–35.

16  See Christine Gouzi, *Jean Restout, 1692–1768: peintre d'histoire à Paris* (Paris: Athena, 2000), pp. 39–40; also John Goodman, 'Jansenism, parlementaire politics and dissidence in the art world of eighteenth-century Paris', *Oxford Art Journal*, XVIII (1995), pp. 74–95.

17  See Michel, *Cochin* (1993), p. 29; also the account written in the 1760s by Cochin's student Simon-Charles Miger, quoted in Bellier de la Chavignerie, *Biographie et Catalogue de l'oeuvre du graveur Miger* (Paris: Dumoulin, 1856), p. 20, who describes not only Cochin's 80-year-old mother, but his sister and a younger cousin as being 'trois femmes très dévotes et jansénistes par-dessus le marché'.

18  The annual collections of *Les Nouvelles ecclésiastiques* concerned extended from 1737 to 1742. See Charles-Antoine Jombert, *Catalogue de l'oeuvre de Ch. Nic. Cochin fils* (Paris, 1770), p. 16. On the crucifix, see Jombert, *Catalogue*, p. 36: 'Le petit Crucifix étant tombé entre les mains de quelques convulsionnaires, ils l'ont trouvé digne de faire des miracles, & l'on assure qu'ils avoient le talent de faire paroître du sang à ses cinq playes.' See also Michel, *Charles-Nicolas Cochin et le livre illustré au XVIIIe siècle* (Geneva: Droz, 1987), nos 3 and 180bis, pp. 173–4, 365–6; Michel, *Cochin* (1993), p. 30, writes 'Le clan janséniste de l'Académie formera, semble-t-il, un véritable groupe de pression dans les années 40.'

19  See documents reprinted in Wildenstein, *Chardin*, pp. 334–40; also Michel, *Cochin* (1993), pp. 9–10: '…il est impossible de savoir si l'amitié a conduit Cochin à construire un système esthétique qui permît de réévaluer l'art de Chardin par rapport à la doctrine traditionelle et à la hiérarchie des genres, ou si au contraire il a cultivé l'amitié d'un homme qui lui paraissait un des plus grands artistes vivants. Il peut être aussi tentant de considérer qu'un graveur, qui professionnellement privilégie la technique et le sentiment et néglige l'invention poétique, a cherché, en se liant avec Chardin… à constituer un clan académique capable de contrebalancer les peintres d'histoire, en

chargeant en même temps d'élaborer une doctrine qui mette sur le même pied la peinture de genre et la peinture d'histoire.'

20 Rosenberg, *Chardin: New Thoughts* (Lawrence, Kansas: Spencer Museum of Art, 1983), p. 16, broached the topic of a link between Chardin and Jansenism, but in an inconclusive way, based on the purchase by the artist and his brother of the prints and books of the son of Jean Racine. René Démoris, 'Chardin and the Far Side of Illusion', in Rosenberg, *Chardin* (1999), p. 100, has extended the idea in a number of suggestive ways.

21 See Gouzi, *Restout*, p. 234.

22 Authorized (King James) Version.

23 Blaise Pascal *Pensées* XIX: 253, in *Oeuvres Complètes*, ed. Louis Lafuma (Paris: Editions du Seuil, 1963), p. 532: 'J.-C. leur ouvrit l'esprit pour entendre les Ecritures'. On early eighteenth-century Figurism, Kreiser, *Miracles*, pp. 246–9, 263–6, offers a succinct, well-documented synopsis; see also Van Kley, *Religious Origins*, pp. 92–3; Campbell, *Power and Politics*, pp. 204–5; and most importantly Maire, *De la cause de Dieu*, pp. 163ff.

24 See Maire, *De la cause de Dieu*, pp. 163–4.

25 The catalyst for these events was the modest grave of a local cleric who had died proclaiming his Jansenist beliefs and opposition to *Unigenitus*. In 1732, the government closed down the cemetery of the church of Saint Médard, where for the previous five years the tomb had drawn growing crowds of so-called 'convulsionaries' claiming miraculous cures and ecstatic transports they attributed to possession by the holy spirit. See Maire, *Convulsionnaires, passim*; also Kreiser, *Miracles, passim*.

26 William Doyle, *Jansenism: Catholic Resistance to Authority from the Reformation to the Revolution* (Basingstoke: Palgrave Macmillan, 2000), p. 60.

27 Diderot, *Salons*, II, pp. 58–9; trans. (slightly modified) John Goodman, *Diderot on Art* (New Haven and London: Yale University Press, 1995), pp. 4–5.

28 See the discussion by Michael Baxandall, *Shadows of Enlightenment* (New Haven and London: Yale University Press, 1995) pp. 139–43.

29 Démoris, *Chardin, le chair et l'objet* (Paris: Olbia, 1999), p. 33. (author's translation)

30 Démoris, 'Chardin and the Far Side of Illusion', p. 99.

31 Démoris, *ibid.*, p. 100, offers a guarded one.

32 See the apposite comments of Démoris, *ibid.*, p. 104, on Chardin's art in general: 'It is a *lowly* zone, an *anterior* zone; the time of sensation and presence in the world. And that can be disturbing.'

33 See Jacqueline Lichtenstein, *The Eloquence of Color: Rhetoric and Painting in the French Classical Age*, trans. E. McVarish (Berkeley and Los Angeles: University of California Press, 1993), pp. 15–29.

34 The leading voice for a renewed 'aesthetic of grandeur' and public demonstration of virtue was the elusive Etienne La Font de Saint-Yenne. On what is known of his life, see Etienne Jollet, *La Font de Saint-Yenne, Oeuvre critique* (Paris: Ecole Nationale Supérieure des Beaux-Arts, 2001), pp. 7–25. While one witness reported La Font's presence at 'une réunion de convulsionnaires', his long service to the deeply pious and orthodox Maria Lezczynska as 'gentilhomme servant de la reine' (1729–37) places him in the orbit of the court *parti dévot*. Resurgent during the 1740s, this group renewed the practice of refusing sacraments to those who would not publicly embrace the terms of *Unigenitus* – precipitating the crisis that led to the expulsion of the Jesuits in 1762 and the brief high-water mark of Jansenist political power (see Van Kley, *Jansenists, passim*). That outcome, however, depended

upon a minority Jansenist core within the *parlements* successfully mobilizing a much larger constituency by painting their grievances as those of threatened Gallican 'liberties' and the prerogatives of the nation as a whole in the face of ministerial 'despotism'. La Font's devotion to reviving the magnificence of the state, as well as his celebration of the magistrates of the *parlements*, advanced the cause of this nascent *parti patriote*. But this evolution of patriotic dissent elevated the nation as an object of veneration that old-style Jansenists could only have regarded as idolatrous. Those Salon writers who echoed La Font's general critique also proved unable to register Chardin's art in any but trivializing terms, if they paid attention to him at all (see Crow, *Painters*, p. 130).

35  Démoris, 'Chardin and the Far Side of Illusion', p. 104: '. . .in *Reading the Bible* [by Greuze], the spectator is invited to recognize the accomplishment of the family's social ritual, and the values attached to it'.

36  The best efforts by the established authorities are reflected in this unsatisfying pronouncement by Rosenberg, 'Chardin: the Unknowing Subversive', p. 35: 'That "the work cost him infinite pains" seems to be the best answer. He no longer had the strength to persevere.' There is no actual supporting evidence for this verdict. Démoris, 'Chardin and the Far Side of Illusion', p. 106, comes closer to the view advanced here: 'Competition and some of the critics may have played a part in this, but more influential, it seems to me, was the intensive and inescapable verbalisation that went with the Salons. . . . Perhaps Chardin's renunciation of the Salons was necessary so that the human element could make a new entrance – in stunning fashion – into what I have elsewhere referred to as a "theatre of objects".'

# 5

# The Sabine Women and Lévi-Strauss

*T.J. Clark*

> The total relationship of exchange which constitutes marriage is not established between a man and a woman, where each owes and receives something, but between two groups of men, and the woman figures only as one of the objects in the exchange, not as one of the partners between whom the exchange takes place. This remains true even when the young woman's feelings are taken into consideration, as, moreover, is usually the case.
>
> (C. Lévi-Strauss, *The Elementary Structures of Kinship*)[1]

> Women are not primarily a sign of social value, but a natural stimulant; and the stimulant of the only instinct the satisfaction of which can be deferred, and consequently the only one for which, in the act of exchange, and through the awareness of reciprocity, the transformation from stimulant to sign can take place, and, defining by this fundamental process the transformation from nature to culture, assume the character of an institution.
>
> (*Ibid.*)[2]

In a letter Poussin wrote to his patron Paul Fréart de Chantelou in April 1639, instructing him how best to come to terms with the new painting Poussin had sent him – patron and painter were at the start of their long relationship, so basic advice was in order – the following phrase occurs. 'Lisés l'istoire et le tableau, afin de cognoistre si chasque chose est appropriée au subiect.'[3] (Read the story and the picture, so as to know if each thing is appropriate to the subject.) I think of this as a John Barrell-type instruction. Therefore it is not surprising that the phrase itself, for all its apparent straightforwardness, is open to interpretation. I for one doubt that Poussin intended Chantelou to look at the painting – it is the *Israelites Gathering Manna* now in the Louvre – Bible in hand, checking off visual incident against precise textual instigation. This is what a certain kind of

114

scholarship wants the letter to mean. I think Poussin assumed that he and Chantelou had the gist of the episode from Exodus, and even some of its more dramatic details, as common ground. When he says 'lisés l'istoire et le tableau', I believe we should understand *l'istoire* to mean something close to Alberti's *historia*, and unpack the implied contrast with *le tableau* in the light of another phrase occurring earlier in the same sentence: 'et que tout ensemble vous considériés le tableau'. In other words (and again I should say that I feel Poussin is offering, tactfully, very basic advice), one should look at pictures paying attention to the story they tell, but also as entities that exist *tout ensemble*, as visual wholes, with much in them exceeding – qualifying, amplifying, even diverging from – their narrative instance.

My interpretation of Poussin's letter is tentative. How textual a painter Poussin was, and how textbound a 'reader' he expected his viewer to be, are questions that will never be crisply resolved. At the very least, however, Poussin's instruction can serve to take us back to a world of art in which texts – classical and Biblical – mattered intensely. I am proposing that in Poussin's case (and in David's) we should consider them as themes for variation rather than scripts for point-by-point visual exegesis. But perhaps this meant they mattered all the more. I think we should try to reenter a world in which the making of a painting involved a painter pondering – in David's case, working on *The Intervention of the Sabine Women* (Illustration 5.1), pondering for years on end – a small range of textual materials relevant to the task, and dreaming how best, how deeply and completely, to visualize them. Not just to make one see their story, but to find form for what the story was about – what made it take the shape of a narrative in the first place, and above all what made it go on being spellbinding as the narrative was warped and embroidered in retellings through the years.

This is a side of painting we now tend to shy away from. I can see why. We are still modernists, after a fashion; still suspicious of the narrative or illustrative in art; and that prejudice is abetted by a further impatience with the kinds of text that David and Poussin dreamt over, and the absoluteness of their belief in the worth of what they were doing. Not Plutarch, Livy and Ovid again! Do not many of us have the feeling that if we too enter, imaginatively, into the same reverie we shall end up reproducing – and in one way or another validating – the over-intensity of this past culture's hermeneutics? Therefore we shy away from a painting's textual connotations – its openness to its written source, its mobilization of the source's uncertainties – and move instinctively towards its historical, contextual, circumstantial ones. I am not against this. In the case of David's *Sabines*, thinking of it as a painting of 1799 – as a picture set up in a specially designed room in the Louvre one had to pay 1fr80 to get into, a picture whose message of Revolutionary reconciliation could hardly have been more lightly coded, a painting hung eventually

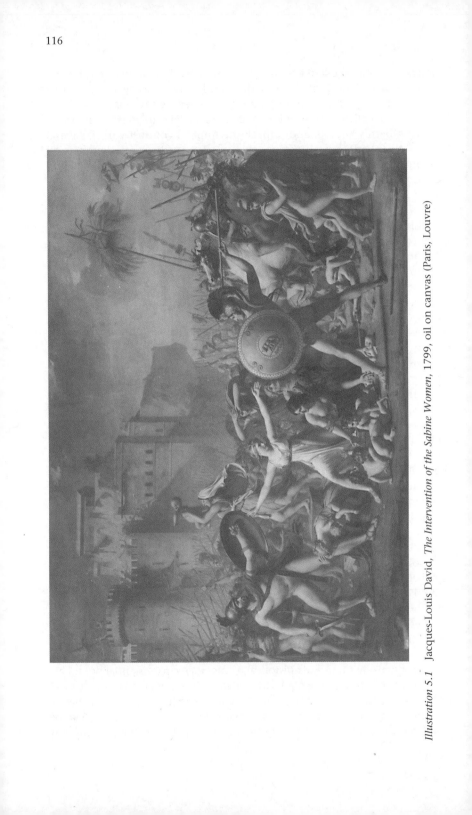

*Illustration 5.1*  Jacques-Louis David, *The Intervention of the Sabine Women*, 1799, oil on canvas (Paris, Louvre)

between two (two!) images of the young Bonaparte crossing the Alps – has been of late deeply productive.[4] All I want to offer as supplement to these approaches is a view of the *Sabines* capable of seeing, somewhere at the heart of its achievement, the ways in which it deeply did *not* belong to 1799 and the Directory. It belonged to the distant past. It went back to the scandalous birth pangs of the state.

Of course in doing so it could hardly have been more eighteenth-century. The wish to imagine the moment of inauguration of human society, in all its terror and power and urge to orderliness, had been central to the project of Enlightenment. The David I am proposing is a reader – an ordinary reader – of Rousseau and Bougainville just as much as the *Vies des hommes illustres*. Of course. The two tastes reinforced one another. Eighteenth-century readers went to their Livy and *Life of Romulus* for many reasons, but certainly in part because they were interested in humanity's first steps, fatal or otherwise – especially the moment of state-formation. We know that many such readers processed the old stories with bland condescension or triumphalism, but equally we know that the century they lived in was dogged by the suspicion – grandly voiced, ruthlessly acted upon – that the first steps had been some kind of Fall, or, at best, an entry into a world of arrangements, bindings, guilts, reparations, against which the body of Nature would always protest. Perhaps this was the story Livy and Plutarch were almost telling, and that David would help make manifest. I should like to reconstitute a David, in other words, who not only 'read the story' in Livy and Plutarch, but returned and returned to what both his authors had to say about causes and consequences, in and around the central atrocity – about what the rape had been for, and how it lived on in the state's unconscious – the strange pattern of seemingly inconsequential, weirdly vivid, momentarily philological or ethnographic material that surfaces in both texts, and which points, I believe, to things in the story of state formation that can only rarely be stated out loud.

Again, I believe that to do so is to follow in John Barrell's footsteps. I remember long ago a would-be historical reviewer of Barrell's *The Political Theory of Painting* headlining his piece 'The Political Theory of Painting without the Politics'. The jibe depended (typically) on just the sort of simple-mindedness about the meaning of 'politics' in the eighteenth century – in just what register of distance and reverie politics was consti-tuted then, so often with deadly results – against which the present essay is aimed.

Of the paintings David went back to over the years employed in putting the *Sabines* together – and I am not suggesting that he spent more time with *Ab urbe condita* than with Raphael engravings and the sketchbooks he had brought from Rome – the most important seems to me Guercino's (Illustration 5.2).[5] It had been confiscated from its aristocratic owners

*Illustration 5.2*   Guercino, *The Intervention of the Sabine Women*, 1799, oil on canvas
(Paris, Louvre)

in 1794, and taken from the Hôtel de Penthièvre to the Louvre. In any case its
place in the great sequence of pictures done originally for La Vrillière had long
been celebrated. I doubt David got his first sight of it when he came out of gaol
in December. There are, I think, aspects of the Guercino that lived on specifically
in David's visual memory through Years V, VI, and VII: the counterpoint of feet
on the smooth gray floor of the floodplain (Plutarch makes much of this feature
of the terrain), the shape of Tatius's shield and the inside view we get of his
hold on it, the shield's intersection with the body of a woman in a loose-flowing
gown, the idea of Tatius in particular being held onto gently by a Sabine at
his side (in the David that happens likewise to Tatius, and seemingly to no
other man in the crush), even the invention of the distant battle done in
grisaille, glimpsed through the front screen of limbs. But of course the true
importance of the Guercino was that it was strong enough to put David in mind
of what he wanted to do instead, almost in despite, of the precedent. I think he

admired the Guercino's naïve intimacy, and its easy erotic decorum; but he thought that the earlier painter had turned the great moment into too much of a finite theatrical episode, with its main actors front-stage. For all the obvious differences, Guercino's *Intervention* was essentially similar, in its view of history, to David's own *Horatii* and *Brutus*. History, or paintable history, happened indoors – or in a proximity set off from the scene of mass struggle by what looks to be, unmistakably, a stage flat rolled on at one side. David's *Sabines* was to be unlike his great paintings of the 1780s, unlike the *Marat* and even the *Tennis Court Oath*, above all in its having history happen fully in public, with its heroes and heroines locked into the matrix of the crowd (or the phalanx). The Guercino was vital because it gave such touching form to just the separation – of great men and women from the society their deeds summon into being – that David wanted to imagine not yet in place.

'Their deeds summon into being.' Eighteenth-century readers, as I have said, warmed to the story of Romulus because they were interested in how societies were founded. They knew, of course, that the narratives offered by Livy and Plutarch were poetic, mythological – the writers themselves admitted as much. 'L'origine de l'empire romain', reads the first sentence of David's *explication de texte* for his picture in Year VIII, 'est enveloppé d'obscurité'.[6] 'Whether in tracing the history of the Roman people from the very foundation of the city (*a primordio urbis*) I shall do something worth the trouble, I am neither very certain, nor, if I were, would I dare say so out loud.'[7] But the fact that most people recognized Livy and Plutarch were telling the tales of the tribe, in the way of Ossian as much as Vico, made what they had to say more interesting, not less. Readers wanted to know what *Rome* thought was involved in her beginnings. For Rome still had the primordial in sight. Confusedly, no doubt; episodically and irresponsibly; but in ways that still resonated (this was the eighteenth-century wager) with the first facts of life.

Rome thought one of those facts was rape. (Or, to be technical, what the anthropologists now call 'bride theft' – often a collective activity, and not necessarily followed by forced sexual intercourse.[8]) The bare bones of the story of the Sabine women are, I am assuming, sufficiently well-known. Romulus's city lacked females, and attempts to persuade neighbouring, better established communities to grant Rome rights of intermarriage broke down. So Romulus invited his neighbours to a festival of the corn god Consus, and at a pre-arranged signal the Romans carried off 30 of the women guests – unmarried women, all but one of them – and put their fathers and brothers to flight. Three years passed. The women were bribed and blandished into matrimony. 'Romulus himself went among them and explained that the pride of their parents had caused this deed, when they had refused their neighbors the right to intermarry' (L, 36–7). Children were born. Some of the lesser cities whose daughters had been abducted tried for vengeance on the battlefield, without success; but the richest and most powerful of the neighbours, the tribe of Sabines ruled by Tatius, held back. Finally the Sabines marched on

Rome. Battle was joined in the valley between the Palatine and Capitoline; the Sabines took the Roman's citadel, the armies gained and lost local advantage, and eventually it seemed as if Romulus's men were poised for the final offensive; maybe the two chiefs, Romulus and Tatius, were moving into position for single combat; when suddenly the Sabine women themselves, sons and daughters held high, came careering onto the battlefield pleading for a stop to death. What has happened, they said, has already enmeshed us all in a web of kinship. Look on your grandsons and decide if you will make them orphans. Look on your enemies and recognize them as brothers-in-law. 'Movet res cum multitudinem tum duces; silentium et repentina fit quies; inde ad foedus faciendum duces prodeunt; nec pacem modo, sed civitatem unam ex duabus faciunt' (L, 48–9: The thing touches the multitude as well as the leaders; a stillness falls on them, and a sudden hush; at this the leaders come forward to make a truce; and not only do they agree on peace, but make one city out of two).

These are the bare bones of the story. Nothing I go on to say is meant to detract from David's clumsy, irresistible determination to make these bare bones live. The story was paramount for him. The picture would recapitulate it, massively and comprehensively, so as to make it believable again, with every movement solid and persuasive. But David, I am proposing, was an eighteenth-century reader. Stories mattered to him, but also structures. He was dreamer and mythographer as much as stage technician. He was out to paint a moment, but also an eternity – the moment when a great silence and stillness falls, as much on the mass of men as their leaders, because the whole body of humanity is suddenly in the presence of the one great thing – *civitas, regnum, imperium* – that will now give the body form. That is the silence the *Sabines* intends to recreate.

What, then, in Plutarch and Livy, would have set David dreaming most deeply? Two threads, I think. First, the stress these writers (and also Ovid in the *Fasti*, which no doubt David looked at as well) put on Rome's utter *inferiority* as a society before the rape took place – its improvised and ragtag social structure, its lack of grounding in a place and population with local roots, its merely martial character, its dependence on a recruiting policy for citizens that drew to it aliens, criminals and slaves; and therefore the deep contempt in which it was held by the communities surrounding it.

Some of this, obviously, would have appealed to the defeated Jacobin. 'Next, lest the size of his city should be all in vain [Romulus's first act as chieftain had been to build walls and push out the city limits], he resorted to a plan for increasing the population which had long been a favorite strategy for the founders of cities, who gather about them an obscure and lowly multitude and pretend that these are offspring born of the very earth' (L, 32–3). The essence of the plan was to provide sanctuary for those in need – between two groves on the slopes of the Capitoline. 'Thither fled, from the surrounding peoples, a miscellaneous rabble, without distinction between freemen and slaves, all of them eager for change' (L, 32–3). Plutarch, naturally, allows himself a little more aristocratic disdain on the subject. 'A mixed rabble of the needy and obscure', is how he describes the city before the rape.[9] David in his pamphlet sums this material up in full *Journal des hommes libres* vein: 'Il n'oublia rien pour attirer à lui les bergers des contrées voisines, les esclaves fugitifs, et tous les étrangers propres à des grandes entreprises. Tels furent les foibles commencements d'un empire qui, par la suite, subjugua l'univers'[10] (There was nothing he left undone to attract to his side the shepherds of the surrounding countryside, fugitive slaves, and all foreigners fit for great undertakings. Such were the feeble beginnings of an empire which ended by subjugating the universe). I fancy him peopling the Palatine with Giotto, Spartacus and Tom Paine.

Even David, you will notice, sees the problem. A city of immigrants and desperadoes is still barely worthy of the name. It lacks cohesion, and above all it lacks status. When Romulus first tried to solve the problem by sending envoys to the neighbouring peoples, pleading for alliance and rights of intermarriage, the answers reported in Livy and Ovid have the flavour of studied insult. 'Wealthy neighbors scorned to take poor men for their sons-in-law... It counted against the Romans that they dwelt in cattle-stalls, and fed sheep, and owned a few acres of waste land (*in stabulis habitasse et oves pavisse nocebat/iugeraque inculti pauca tenere soli*).'[11] 'The envoys were frequently asked, on being dismissed, whether they had opened a sanctuary for women as well as men, for only in that way would they obtain suitable wives' (L, 34–5).

The rape, so the ancient writers argue, was a way out of this impasse. It was designed to produce alliance – *koinonia* is the word in Plutarch, meaning 'partnership', but also, more strongly, specific and enduring marriage arrangements – and therefore to enforce acknowledgement of Rome as a city, not an armed camp of peasants and runaways.[12] I think these accounts of causes were important to David: they were what excused the subject, we might say, and gave it political dignity. It mattered greatly to him that this was a picture of a rabble becoming a people – of course the word *peuple* is the one David prefers at the key moment in his pamphlet, as opposed to Livy's *civitas* or Plutarch's inevitable *polis* – and of humans still living in the shadow of a truly primordial past. One sign of that is a feature of the painting that David seems to have introduced very late – there is no hint of it in any of the preparatory studies – the bale of fresh-mown hay filling the sky to the right, held aloft on a massive ceremonial spear by a young warrior wearing a Phrygian cap. (The agrarian insignia carried at the head of each company in Romulus's army are again a detail borrowed from Plutarch.[13]) The hay sways in counterpoint to the teetering she-wolf next door, and the trophy armour (could it still be Acron's, paraded as reminder to the enemy?), the standards (one with what looks like an abstract sign for 'citadel' at the top), the pikes and axes. It is a world of totems. 'If you ask what my son's palace was [this is Mars speaking in the *Fasti*, referring to Romulus], behold yon house of reeds and straw' (O, 132–3).

Another sign is simply the effort David put into making the mass of his armies both a unity – the control of tone and the wonderful spidery density of the sea of pikes are the key to this – and a gathering of the clans. Chaussard, in the essay-cum-advertisement he wrote for the exhibition in Year VIII, seizes on just this aspect. His paragraph will serve to sum up the argument so far, and to suggest how much it mattered to some of David's viewers (maybe almost as much as Adèle de Bellegarde's hairdo):

> Tout est contraste dans ce tableau... Vous suivez ce contraste dans les groupes; vous le saisissez dans les accessoires. La troupe de Romulus, com-posée d'aventuriers audacieux rassemblés de toutes parts, présente une foule de physionomies et de costumes divers, des Gaulois, des Phrygiens, des Daces, des Germains, mêlés dans les rangs de la jeunesse belliqueuse des différents états de l'Italie... tout ce qui caractérise des brigands, le mélange d'une pauvreté primitive et d'une richesse acquise par la force; ici des bottes de foin portées en étendard; là des armures brillantes, cette parure de l'audace guerrière.[14] (All is contrast in this picture... You follow the contrast in the groups; you notice it in the details. Romulus's army, made up of daring adventurers drawn from all parts of the earth, presents a crowd of diverse physiognomies and costumes, Gauls, Phrygians, Dacians, Germans, mixed among the ranks of warlike youths from the different Italian states... everything characteristic of brigands, the mixture of a primitive poverty with riches acquired by force; here, bales of hay carried as standards; there, shining armor, that finery of the warlike and the bold.)

The second strand was sexual. Again, I am less concerned at this point with how the classical sources staged the first level of the drama – the brutality, the blandishments, the pathos of the women's plea for peace – than with what they seemed to think resulted from the rape and intervention. What kind of social ordering, that is – what sort of transition from one pattern of human dealings to another. From here onward we begin to make our way toward Lévi-Strauss's abominable sentences.

Two things should be pointed to. First, that though there is certainly wildness and desperation to the Sabine women's rushing onto the field (even Livy has them letting their hair down and rending their garments, like maenads in the woods of Cithaeron), what the writers finally give them to say is strangely formal, strangely instructional. They are expounders of a new (an inaugural) kinship system. Perhaps this is to overstate the case slightly. Certainly Plutarch has them first launch into a series of reproaches to their Sabine relatives for having delayed the war for years on end, so that they have learnt to love their ravishers; and Livy depicts them calling for their own death, in preference to widowhood or orphanage. Ovid brings on the babies to pipe 'Grandfather!' like bit players in a novel by Mrs Oliphant. But the crux of the women's argument is positional, almost grammatical. 'Even if there were other grounds for conflict, you would do best to cease for our sakes, now that you have become fathers-in-law and grandfathers, and have ties of affiliation with your enemies. If, however, the war is fought on our behalf, carry us off with your sons-in-law and their children, and so give us back our fathers and kinsfolk, but do not rob us of children and husbands' (P, 148–51). 'Hinc patres hinc viros orantes ne se sanguine nefando soceri generique respergent, ne parricidio macularent partus suos, nepotum illi, hi liberium progenium' (L, 48–9: Pleading with their fathers on the one hand, and with their husbands on the other, that fathers-in-law and sons-in-law should not contaminate themselves with impious blood, nor pollute their children with parricide, being grandsons to one party and sons to the other). Of course the various 'in-laws' smuggled in by the English language here betray the true force of what is being said. Law is in the making. Its bedrock is exogamy – the discovery (the elucidation) of an overlapping, formalizable system of human bonds and oppositions, which only the crispness of parts of speech (the *soceri generisque*, the *nepotum illi, hi liberum progeniem*) can bring to the surface of consciousness. The silence that greets the women's exposition, we could say, is the silence of grammar itself – the sound of its *unanswerability*.

Second, and more deeply embedded as the texts' unconscious, is the question of how relations between the sexes were to be regulated after the women had done their work. How was the rape to be atoned for? Could the first act of force ever be integrated into the new world of rules? What happened to maleness – to warlikeness, to the claims of *virtus*, to the fabulous rabble of strangers and escapees Romulus had made into an army – when Tatius put down his shield?

Answers here are fragmentary, like the bits of a dream that even the dreamer thinks are beside the point. Livy and Plutarch both say that in the division of the new city into three tribes and 30 phratries – a mathematical sorting of kinship groups that looks to have followed on the heels of exogamy with true Lévi-Straussian promptness – the phratries, or some of them, were named after the original women victims. Maybe a dubious compliment. It is Plutarch who seems to feel there is something more – something strange but essential – to add. He tells us twice that Roman wives were henceforth released from all tasks inside the household except those connected with spinning. And then adds the following sentence:

> However, they made many other concessions to the women, to do them honor, some of which are as follow: to yield right of way to them when walking in the street; not to utter any indecent word in their presence; that no man should appear naked before them, or else be liable to prosecution before the judges of homicide; and that their children should wear a sort

of necklace, the 'bulla', so called from its shape (which was that of a bubble), and a robe bordered with purple. (P, 152–3)

Translators struggle with this passage, not surprisingly. There is a strong feeling, especially with the French, that readers from early on wanted to rationalize what Plutarch was telling them. Jacques Amyot, whose great version of Plutarch David could hardly have avoided – we cannot be sure exactly which translation the painter mainly depended on, as what seems to be a direct quotation in his pamphlet from the *Life of Romulus* turns out to be clever paraphrase – flinches in particular at the thought of male nakedness as now a capital crime.[15] So does the preferred eighteenth-century translation by André Dacier. It is such an un-Winckelmannian suggestion. But whatever the exact form of words David was faced with in the text at his disposal, he had more than enough to go on. The sentence told the story of the transition from one regime of sexuality – let us call it the realm of permanent warfare and homosociality, and with it an acted, flaunted, *public* male dominance, a parading of the phallus – to another, more covert and reparative, more decent and family-centred. To that extent the insight of David's great paintings of the 1780s still stood: the state was a binding together of households, not streets and squares. Politics was a private matter, founded essentially (interminably) on a suppression of bodies – male bodies – mouthing obscenities and displaying their proletarian credentials.

I am pointing, then, to two moments in Livy's and Plutarch's story that direct any reader to something beyond the glamour and horror of first level events: what exactly the women say on the battlefield, and how the new social order tries to make amends to them for its first crime. I believe David was interested in this 'something beyond'. Thinking of him musing over it may help us, I think, to get into focus two great aspects of the painting that have always divided interpreters: his treatment of the extraordinary central spokeswoman in the drama, clad in white with arms flung wide, and the contrast between her energy and fluency and 'la nudité de mes héros'.

The woman in white is named Hersilia. Plutarch is specific that at the key moment she acted as the Sabine women's main speaker. Livy does not single her out in the same way, but he is categorical that she was Romulus's wife – and David in his pamphlet introduces her as such, and gives her the crucial speech. The other main fact that the ancient sources want us to know about her is that she alone of the stolen women was already married when she was carried off. It was a mistake, Plutarch says; but in the end a fortunate – I would say a structurally necessary – one. Hersilia in the painting is deeply tied into a whirling circle of wives and children immediately surrounding her. Six women, sharply differentiated in costume, age, affect and vigour; and six children, all but one of them naked, and each reacting to the mayhem in a recognizable, more or less fetching, way. I say Hersilia is 'deeply tied in', but this does not do justice to what is special in David's handling of his heroine – that she is made part of the matrix of female assertion and emotion attending her, and yet kept utterly distinct from it, standing in a kind of vortex at its centre, white and bright against its reds and greens. It is almost as if she were lit from within.

Commentators lately have been in agreement that Hersilia steals the show in David's picture, or solders its overweight action together. She does so by her vitality and elegance, they agree, and by her balance – her foursquare standing on the ground. (Of course we do not see the actual contact of her left foot with the earth of the Forum, and sometimes one comes to believe she may be partly resting a knee against a low plinth or altar stone. But nothing can shake the illusion of her centered, poised stability. She makes Romulus look like a statue and Tatius like a model hanging on to studio ropes.) I would want to add to this only that the ultimate clue to her power over the image is her apartness from it. It is as if David intended Hersilia to take her stand, aesthetically and conceptually, in a space just slightly – but irrevocably – detached from the world of bodies she is out to save. In this he responds profoundly, I think, to what he encountered her saying – and how he encountered her saying it – in the two ancient texts.

Hersilia is Romulus's wife. Writers tell us nothing about her original ties to her native city, but I am not alone in having sometimes imagined that the story would be perfect if she had been Tatius's daughter. Too perfect, in fact. That would make what she is saying to the symmetrical chieftains too particular and personal, and anyway have her be a kind of abstract transformation-operation straight from the pages of *Mythologiques*. The clue to her abstractness – or her unique mixture of the abstract and embodied – lies elsewhere. It is enough that Hersilia, alone among the Sabine women, has been married twice. She has *repeated* the passage from nature to culture, as if to get it by heart. She is the full (pedagogical) embodiment of Lévi-Strauss's 'transformation from stimulant to sign'. Therefore she is the perfect speaker for marriage. She can expound the true artificiality, the endless ramifications, of the institution, launching her words from deep within its world of rules – on the other side of desire and biology. She is the virgin mother, I dare say: her whiteness and brightness stand, as they so often do, partly for that imagining away of the dangers of childbirth. But more: she is the figure of marriage *as opposed to* maternity – marriage with maternity as mere provider of morphemes to be swallowed and regurgitated by endless generative grammar. She is the figure of conjunction, of crossing, multiplication and loss. She is – she does not merely take the shape of, she *is* – the letter 'x', copula and placeholder. (Stevens's 'vital, arrogant, fatal, dominant X'.)

She is pure discursiveness, to put it another way: the body that truly and finally stands for the power of the letter. What diction we imagine coming from her lips! What lapidary phrases! What hardwired well-formedness! *Nepotum illi, ni liberum progeniem.* No wonder viewers have always been puzzled by the force of the gesture belonging to the woman who is most obviously her shadow – the one in red right next to her, with two arms shading an anguished face, seemingly pressing away some hideous insight. I think she is Hersilia's best listener. What she fends off (for a moment) is knowledge of the place allotted her in the state's new grammar.

Hersilia – let me adopt Lévi-Strauss's perspective explicitly for a moment – is the voice of full entry into, and acceptance of, the multiple alienations of kinship.[16] As a twice-married woman, she has left the realm of the nuclear family irreversibly behind – said goodbye to it on two occasions, as if to acknowledge but also subdue its dreadful, intimate, bodily attractions. The taboo against incest has finally *worked*. (This is why it would have been wrong to have Hersilia be Tatius's daughter. She has to face him finally as the Figure of the Father, not any father she once knew and desired.) Therefore she can mediate between Tatius and Romulus, in a way that no other mother and daughter could. Tatius, as the picture works hard to make explicit, is simply a second sovereign in her scheme of things, an alternative husband as opposed to a father substitute. He is essentially her own age. This is what gives her her freedom. She is free because she has entered the realm of exogamy. She lives in a world where women accept their place – and their power – in the space of exchange, as makers of sons, sons-in-law, grandfathers, fathers-in-law, *soceri generique*. She has left home, and set up house.

Of course what is wonderful about David's picture is the fact that it manages to show us the power of Hersilia's vision of humanity and at the same time everything that Hersilia's diction is struggling (again, interminably) to sublimate. There will never be a more seductive figure of *mere* maternity than the woman on the ground below the anguished listener, black-haired, bare-breasted, from whom naked boy children tumble as from Gaea herself. And this extraordinary consciousness in the picture of what the state is made out of – made against – brings me back to Plutarch's glimpses of men minding their language, passing on the left side, and girding their loins going home from the gym.

Again we could take a Lévi-Straussian view. Kinship systems are the quintessential human creation. They enact – they give form to, ultimately they *are* – the passage from the realm of biology to that of introjected cultural constraint. The systems are inescapable and constitutive, but that does not mean they are ever fully acceptable to the human animal, or the animal in the human. They fly in the face of the great facts of reproduction, and the pull of the first, incestuously bonded triad. This will never go away, this pull. The sacred horror surrounding the incest taboo testifies to the magic still needed to keep the unspeakable tendency in check. And there is another permanent opponent, continually reproduced within the systems by the fact of the systems being predicated on patriarchy. Putting an end to incest is bound up, as Plutarch and Livy seem aware, with putting an end to the other 'primordial' sexual economy – that of male prowess, military bonding and sparring, homosociality informed (often flagrantly) by outright homoeroticism, with power over women deployed as a sign language between competing, desiring, infatuated men – men wanting women as messengers or metaphors of their love for others more like themselves. There will never be an end to this dream of the human, either. The incest taboo and the taboo on homosexuality are two sides of the same coin of Law, Civilization, Non-Identity.

David's picture is full of this.[17] Stage centre stand Romulus and Tatius, hearing the message of heterosexuality and already frozen by it, immobilized, encumbered, their phallic attributes sheathed for good. (Romulus's spear echoed by its twin on the ground with buckled point; Tatius's sword as much a dead weight in his hand as the one still grasped automatically by the corpse.) But this can never be the last word. The little boys on the mud floor are still rough housing, and look somewhat disappointed that their elders have thought the better of physical force. And off to the right and left of the canvas are perfect, unrepentant figures of the world Romulus is about to leave behind. To the left an exquisite ephebe in profile, his curls and buttocks salaciously modelled, holding the bridle of Tatius's charger, as much apart from the eddy of battle as Hersilia herself, profoundly and proudly self-absorbed; and to the right, yet more astonishing, a wild naked boy in the cap of liberty, nuzzling the muzzle of a frisky chestnut, turning it, calming it, revelling in its animal high spirits. No covering up and walking on the left side for him!

There may be one more level to David's dreaming here. I offer it tentatively, and in a sense reluctantly, because it points to an episode in the picture that I am sure is charged – overdetermined – but which it seems almost cruel to push at too hard. It is the juxtaposition – what seems to be the direct confrontation – between Romulus and the elderly woman in green, to his left. She is old enough for her withered neck to be unavoidable, and what hair she has is unstylishly covered by a matron's loose cap. She seems to be pulling down her green dress, and looking up directly at Romulus as she does so. It could be she is inviting him to strike – 'Here! Strike here if you dare!' – but the fact of her being so closely aligned with the overflowing mother on the ground makes it irresistible to read her as about to repeat that woman's baring of her breasts. Or maybe threatening to, as if thinking it her last weapon. What is notable about her, of course, is preeminently her age, which does not in the least fit into Livy's and Plutarch's story. None of the Sabine women were old enough to be Romulus's mother. But that is what she is – fantastically, symbolically, within the dream logic of David's central group. No more nor less fantastically than the wolf-mother next door to her on Romulus's shield. Romulus is hemmed in by totems and taboos.

I believe this texture of juxtapositions is truly the key to what makes Romulus an image of himself – an alienated *figure* of masculinity, as schematic as the emblem on his shield. But I do not intend to turn the key in the lock. We have no business seeing what Romulus recoils from. Suffice it to say that maleness, for him, seems precisely to be wedged – sandwiched – in a space between two projections of what first gave him sustenance. On the shield – already mythical, that is, already flattened into the status of a sign – the wonderful, terrible, naked, available animal called 'Mother'. And on the ground in front of him, the Mother whose very being for him is *not to be seen* – not to be seen naked, and, in the long moment to follow, not to see him naked in return. He is face to face with everything exogamy represses.

David's painting is of its time. But in the way David is always of his time – that is, deeply absorbed in dreaming an other to the present. Making paintings for him was a matter of setting up, irresistibly, the space of a distant past, into which, through the looking glass, we were invited to enter; but enter as suitors, misfits, overdressed suppliants – invited back to the inaugural moment, yes, but at the same time chastened by it, by the comparison of our standing to theirs. 'Can we attain to the business of state-formation again?' is the *Sabines'* question. 'So this is what is involved in the process! This is what brought on the hush! Are we up to it? Can we find ourselves in it? Is there room for us too under the bale of hay?'

Much has been said in the past 20 years of commentary about the *Sabines'* extraordinary investment in illusionism, and in devices – conditions of viewing – which seemed designed to break the last barrier between the spectator and the scene on the wall.[18] There was, notoriously now, a body length mirror set up towards the back of the room in the Louvre, and in it viewers were supposed to lose hold of the paintedness of the *Sabines* altogether, and see themselves as actors by Hersilia's side. I believe that what drove illusionism to this kind of hypertrophy in David's case was a wish, in the *Sabines* specifically, to make the brute fact of the body almost irresistible, the better to have the essential counter-movement in the Sabines story – the stilling and regulating of its energies – register as the human miracle it is. (*How on earth*, the spectator is meant to ask, does the being-in-the-body of the baby sucking its thumb on the mud ever turn into the pantomime hero standing over him?) The crowding and layering of the picture, close to the point of illegibility, which surely was one of the things that caused David most trouble over the years, was necessary because the picture was nothing, for him, if it did not actually demonstrate an almost uncontrollable heterogeneity becoming a single sentence. The state had to be visibly a near rabble; the ground hardly dry from the flood; nudity had to be ludicrous, delectable and dangerous at the same time; kinsfolk and phratries still at daggers drawn. The painting was to be as dense and intricate and algorithmic as the diagrams in 'The Chao Mu Order' or 'Harmonic and Disharmonic Regimes'[19] – in order to show in the end, to persuade us conclusively, that even *this* much of desire and aggression could be stopped dead in its tracks. For the time being, at any rate. Don't bank on the boy babies resting long from their squabbles. Or do I mean embraces?

# Notes

1 Claude Lévi-Strauss, *The Elementary Structures of Kinship*, translated by James Harle Bell, John Richard von Sturmer and Rodney Needham (Boston, MA: Beacon Press, 1967), p. 115. Warmest thanks to Jessica Buskirk for her help with the research toward this article, to Darcy Grimaldo Grigsby and Anne Wagner for their advice, and to Christopher Hallett for his generous and pointed comments on the text. Some of the ideas developed here emerged first in a seminar I gave on 'Description in Art History' at Berkeley in 1998, and I am grateful to participants for their enthusiasm and generosity at that stage.

2 *Ibid.*, pp. 62–3.

3 Charles Jouanny, *Correspondance de Nicolas Poussin* (Paris: F. de Nobele, reimpression, 1968), p. 21.

4 See especially the discoveries and arguments of Ewa Lajer-Burcharth, put forward most sharply in her 'David's *Sabine Women*: Body, Gender and Republican Culture under the Directory', *Art History*, vol. 14, no. 3, September 1991, pp. 397–430, and expanded and summed up in Ewa Lajer-Burcharth, *Necklines: The Art of Jacques-Louis David after the Terror* (New Haven and London: Yale University Press, 1999), chapter 3; and of Darcy Grimaldo Grigsby, 'Nudity *à la grecque* in 1799', *Art Bulletin*, LXXX, no. 2, June 1998, pp. 311–35. Both Grigsby's and Lajer-Burcharth's approaches are intense and suggestive, and much of what follows is in dialogue with their findings. Compare Stefan Germer and Hubertus Kohle, 'From the Theatrical to the Aesthetic Hero: On the Privatization of the Idea of Virtue in David's *Brutus* and *Sabines*', *Art History*, vol. 9, no. 2, June 1986, pp. 168–84. I end up disagreeing with Germer and Kohle's verdict on the *Sabines*, but their thinking about the public–private distinction in David's paintings of the 1780s remains fundamental.

5 See especially Denis Mahon, *Guercino: Master Painter of the Baroque* (Washington, DC: National Gallery of Art, 1992), pp. 262–4; Stéphane Loire, *Le Guerchin en France* (Paris: Réunion des musées nationaux, 1990), pp. 54–6; and Stéphane Loire, *Musée du Louvre: École italienne, XVIIe siècle: 1. Bologne* (Paris: Réunion des musées nationaux, 1996), pp. 253–7. For discussion of the *Sabines*' sources, see Robert Rosenblum, 'A New Source for David's "Sabines"', *Burlington Magazine*, April 1962, pp. 158–62. Rosenblum was the first to suggest that a painting by François-André Vincent of the *Intervention*, shown in the Salon of 1781 and undoubtedly seen at that time by David, might also be relevant. Perhaps so – the bodies struggling on the ground in the 1781 painting may have become part of David's image bank – but ultimately I see Vincent's episodic, centrifugal, deliberately overwrought treatment of the subject as too remote from David's view of things to have counted for much two decades later.

6 *Le tableau des Sabines, exposé publiquement au palais national des sciences et des arts* (Paris: P. Didot, An VIII), p. 9; cited in Daniel Wildenstein, *Documents complémentaires au catalogue de l'oeuvre de Louis David* (Paris: Fondation Wildenstein, 1973), p. 149.

7 Livy, *History of Rome*, with English translation by B.O. Foster (Cambridge, MA: Harvard University Press [Loeb Classical Library], 14 vols, 1982–98), vol. 1, pp. 1–2. Hereafter cited in text as L, 1–2, etc., with translations sometimes modified. Christopher Hallett believes that a case could be made for the Romans' own excavation of their deep past being powered, in ways analogous to David's, by a feeling of crisis in the state they inhabited. The key sources date from the era of proscriptions, the assassination of Caesar, the 'Roman Revolution'. Augustus at one point considered taking the name Romulus, but opted for a title that invoked the founder more indirectly.

8 See the material summarized in Gary Miles, *Livy: Reconstructing Early Rome* (Ithaca and London: Cornell University Press, 1995), pp. 186–7.

9   *Plutarch's Lives,* with English trans. by Bernadotte Perrin (Cambridge, MA: Harvard University Press [Loeb Classical Library], 11 vols, reprinted 1948), vol. 1, pp. 126–9. Hereafter cited in text as P, 126–9, etc., with translations sometimes modified.

10  *Le tableau des Sabines,* pp. 10–11; Wildenstein *Documents,* p. 149.

11  *Ovid in Six Volumes,* with English translation by James George Frazer (Cambridge, MA and London: Harvard University Press and William Heinemann [Loeb Classical Library], revised edition, 1931–9), vol. 5, pp. 134–5. Hereafter cited in text as O, 134–5, etc.

12  See Miles, *Livy: Reconstructing Early Rome,* p. 184. Miles's whole discussion of the Sabines story (pp. 179–219) is helpful, as is T. Peter Wiseman, 'The Wife and Children of Romulus', *Classical Quarterly* vol. 33, no. 2, 1983, pp. 445–52, and Jacques Boulogne, 'L'utilisation du mythe de l'enlèvement des Sabines chez Plutarque', *Bulletin de l'Association Guillaume Budé,* 4, December 2000, pp. 353–63.

13  My thanks to Christopher Hallett for pointing this out. The Phrygian cap is (among other things) again an antiquarian reference to the Romans' part-Trojan origins.

14  Pierre Chaussard, *Sur le tableau des Sabines, par David* (Paris: Charles Pougens, An VIII), pp. 20–1.

15  Amyot translates the key phrase: 'de ne se dépouiller point à nu devant elles, ni pouvoir être appelées en justice devant les juges criminels connaissant des homicides'. See Jacques Amyot, *Les Vies des hommes illustres* (Paris: P. Dupont, new edition, 1826), p. 108. Dacier corrects this to: 'qu'on ne paroîtroit point nu devant elles; qu'elles ne pourroient être obligées de comparoître devant les juges établis pour juger des meutres'. See André Dacier, *Les Vies des hommes illustres de Plutarque* (Paris: Duprat-Duverger, new edition, 1811), p. 145. (Amyot's famous translation, a staple of private libraries, was given a new edition in the 1780s; Dacier's Plutarch, first published in 1721, had three new editions before 1800.) Clearly the Greek is difficult here. From Dryden to Loeb, English translators opt for the idea of nudity as a capital crime, or, at least, one now to be judged in the courts set up to deal with such life and death matters. The milder French tradition persists, though I notice one recent translation adopting the English reading.

16  What follows is dependent on all of the first ten dazzling chapters of Claude Lévi-Strauss, *The Elementary Structures of Kinship,* but perhaps particularly Chapter IV, 'Endogamy and Exogamy', Chapter V, 'The Principle of Reciprocity', and Chapter VIII, 'Alliance and Descent'.

17  On the question of homosociality and/or homoeroticism in David's studio, which may or may not be relevant here, see, among much recent literature – often at loggerheads – Thomas Crow, *Emulation: Making Artists for Revolutionary France* (New Haven and London: Yale University Press, 1995), and Whitney Davis, 'The Renunciation of Reaction in Girodet's *Sleep of Endymion*', in Norman Bryson *et al.,* eds, *Visual Culture: Images and Interpretations* (Hanover, NH: Wesleyan University Press, 1994), pp. 168–201.

18  In addition to Lajer-Burcharth and Grigsby, see Frédérique Desbuissons, 'A Ruin: Jacques-Louis David's *Sabine Women*', *Art History,* vol. 20, no. 3, September 1997, pp. 432–48. Note that Chaussard seems to see the mirror more as a test of David's illusionism than an enhancement of it: 'Une glace, disposée à l'extrémité de la salle, répète et réfléchit la scène et l'illusion. C'est là qu'on voit combien le peintre a été vrai: le ton des figures s'y confond avec celui des spectateurs'. Chaussard, *Sur le tableau des Sabines,* p. 18.

19  Lévi-Strauss, *Elementary Structures,* Chapters XX and XIII.

# 6
## 'Love and Madness': Sentimental Narratives and the Spectacle of Suffering in Late-Eighteenth-Century Romance

*John Brewer*

On 7 April 1779, a 27-year-old clergyman, James Hackman, shot Martha Ray through the head in front of a large crowd of horrified onlookers, as she stepped into her carriage outside the Covent Garden Theatre. 'With another pistol he then attempted to shoot himself, but the ball grazing his brow, he tried to dash out his own brains with the pistol, and is more wounded by those blows than by the ball.'[1] Martha Ray, the mistress of John Montagu fourth Earl of Sandwich died instantly, leaving Hackman on the ground 'beating himself about the head...crying, "o! kill me!...for God's sake kill me!" '[2]

In those few moments, a tortured private affair was transformed into an event of exceptional public notoriety which would preoccupy Grub Street writers, novelists, lawyers, poets and doctors for years to come. The passion (if such it was) between Ray and Hackman and its violent end prompted a fierce debate about madness, love and suicide, and about the diseased imagination and the sentimental literature which many believed to lie behind the *crime passionelle* committed that evening.

The stories of Ray and Hackman were, for reasons that will become apparent, difficult to disentangle, but most accounts agree on the broad outlines. Hackman, a 'Person of Abilities...descended from a very reputable family, distinguished for Taste and Delicacy of Sentiment', as the papers put it[3] – it's important to nearly all accounts that apart from his crime Hackman was a person of blameless character – had been besotted with his victim, whom he had first met some years earlier at Hinchingbrooke, Lord Sandwich's country seat. At that time Hackman was a protégé of the earl, a 19-year-old army officer, who as a house guest played cards and rode the countryside with Ray.

Martha Ray had become the mistress of the Earl of Sandwich in the early 1760s, when she was 17 and he was 44. She was the daughter of a staymaker and a milliner's apprentice, he was an aristocratic politician, roué, patron of the arts and government administrator (most famously as First Lord of the Admiralty) separated from his wife, who in 1767 had been formally found insane and made a ward of the court of Chancery.[4] Sandwich saw that Martha Ray was taught the accomplishments of any polite lady of leisure. As one admirer wrote, 'She was a mistress of the Modern Languages, a fine singer, and an excellent performer on the harpsichord.' 'Of the women in her rank of life', he added – and its not clear what rank he was alluding to – 'few have deserved to be so well spoken of, and scarce any have borne a fairer character.'[5]

Sandwich, one of the most important patrons of late eighteenth-century music – a founder member of the Concerts of Ancient Music and one of the three original organizers of the Handel Centenary Concerts which began in 1784 – supported Ray's singing.[6] She had lessons from the Italian mezzo-soprano Catherina Galli, who had come to London to work with Handel in 1743, and from Joah Bates, who led Sandwich's private orchestra and who was to lead the Handel centenary concerts. Everyone agreed that she had great talent: 'her voice was powerful and pleasing', wrote one of Sandwich's friends,[7] and she sang most of the female solos in the private oratorios staged at Hinchingbrooke. But she was best known in Sandwich's circle for her role as Iphis, the daughter of Jephtha in Handel's final oratorio. Joseph Cradock wrote, 'she has never been excelled in that fine air of Jephtha, "Brighter scenes I seek above"';[8] and when she was painted by Nathaniel Dance two years before her death, she was portrayed with her right hand resting on a copy of the oratorio.[9]

This detail is important. Iphis is the daughter whom Jephtha, because of a vow, must sacrifice in return for his victory over the Ammonites. Ray sings an air in which she accepts that she must be destroyed for the good of others – 'The call of heav'n with humble resignation I obey' – and dutifully agrees to abandon the world for 'Brighter scenes . . . in the realms of peace and love'.[10] It was a moment which combined female suffering with passive acceptance – the woman as virtuous victim – which in the aesthetics of sensibility was regarded as exceptionally erotic and appealing. The Abbé Du Bos in his *Reflexions critiques sur la poesie et sur la peinture* (1719), one of the most influential works on taste and arts in eighteenth-century Europe, singled out the representation of the sacrifice of Jephtha's daughter in his discussion of why such moving representations ('representations pathetiques') are seen both as so affecting and so beautiful.[11] One admirer of Martha Ray wrote of her performance, 'I look on her as a second Cleopatra – a woman of thousands and capable of producing those effects on the heart which the poets talk so much of and which we are apt to think chimerical'.[12] Even before her murder, she played the role of sentimental victim.

Hackman was promptly arrested and tried on 16 April, a little more than a week after the murder. His lawyers entered a defence of temporary insanity. In an important and early example of such a defence they argued that though Hackman was not mad he had been temporarily insane and had yielded to a sudden and 'irresistible impulse', prompted by a fit of jealousy at seeing Ray on the arm of another man. This was Hackman's own account in the speech he made to the court: 'I protest, with that regard for truth which becomes my situation, that the will to destroy her who was ever dearer to me than life, was never mine, until a momentary phrenzy overcame me, and induced me to commit the deed I deplore'.[13] But the bench – Sir William Blackstone and the Deputy-Recorder of London Frances Maseres – was not persuaded of the defence's case. Even though evidence was offered at the trial that Hackman had attempted to kill himself twice the same evening, but had been prevented from doing so by the crowd milling round the theatre, Blackstone argued that the presence of two pistols showed felonious intent and premeditation. The trial attracted a great deal of attention. There were full reports in almost all the newspapers – the *London Evening Post*, the *London Chronicle*, the *General Evening Post*, *St James's Chronicle*, the *General Advertiser*, and the *Gazetteer*[14] – and James Boswell, who sat with Hackman's Counsel at the trial and wrote an account for the newspapers, preened himself at a meeting later that night at Johnson's club – 'I was a man of consequence, as I could talk of it'.[15] Eighteenth-century justice was swift. Hackman was executed a few days after the trial, 'turned off' at Tyburn before a vast crowd of onlookers. Again there were numerous and extensive reports in the press, all of which commented on his lack of fear in the face of death, his contrition and repentance.

Several features of the press coverage of the murder, trial and execution stand out. The accounts of Ray and Hackman and the gradual obsession of the murderer with his victim were plotted to portray the two as leading characters in a sentimental story. From the outset it was emphasized that Hackman was a fine, upright and handsome young man, and that Martha Ray, despite her status as aristocratic mistress was a women of virtue and talent. Thus the *St James's Chronicle* of 10 April 1779: 'It appears that Miss Ray ... hath herself been irreproachable in her Conduct, any otherwise than what perhaps was not well in her Power to prevent, that she was unprotected by the legal Marriage Ceremony: It appears likewise that Mr. Hackman, so far from being an abandoned and insensible Profligate, was rather distinguished for Taste and Delicacy of Sentiment'. These characters, rounded out in the repeated telling, became the protagonists in a tragic romantic story.

In fact, the earliest accounts of Hackman's murder of Ray used sentimental narrative to portray all three protagonists as victims. Hackman was a victim of youthful love and passion, Ray a fallen woman whose acquired respectability did not prevent her destruction, and Sandwich a reformed rake whose domestic felicity with his mistress and their five children had been ended by Hackman's bullet. The story was one without agency – no-one was responsible, all suffered. But it was a story cooked up after Ray's murder by Sandwich and his lawyers and Hackman and his friends, and fed to the press in an effort to close down debate about the case. It was an exercise in damage limitation. It deliberately overlooked the sexual economy that underpinned Ray's liaison with Sandwich, it suppressed Sandwich's notorious libertinage, and it evaded the question of Hackman's madness. Everyone was reduced to a passive figure in a spectacle of suffering.

But with Ray dead and Sandwich moving out of the public eye, it was Hackman who hogged the limelight. The newspapers were preoccupied with Hackman's bearing and conduct, with what I think we can legitimately call his performance in court and on the scaffold. Nearly all the papers characterized Hackman's conduct in the same way. As one of several press reports remarked, 'he repeated that affecting acknowledgment of his guilt .. and seemed in a state of composure, unruffled with the idea of punishment... His whole behavior was manly, but not bold; his mind seemed to be quite calm, from a firm belief in the mercies of his Saviour.'[16] Nearly all commentators spoke of Hackman's manliness. The rhetoric was one in which Hackman in committing the murder had lost his masculine identity, but had recovered it through his stoical conduct during the trial and execution. The murderer was now himself cast as a victim, constantly referred to as 'the unfortunate' Mr Hackman.

Interestingly, press coverage was as much concerned with the responses that Hackman evoked from the many people who attended his trial and execution as with the crime itself. The *London Evening Post* reported: 'His behaviour was decent, and he seemed quite resigned to his fate; yet the agitations of his mind were strongly visible; insomuch that all present were deeply affected; and however we may detest the *crime, a tear of pity will fall from every humane eye upon the fate of the unhappy (my emphasis)* criminal'.[17] As another report put it, 'his manifest agitation, contrition and poignant grief, too sensibly affected all present to wish to add affliction to such heart-felt misery...the whole court were in tears'.[18]

Hackman's comportment, the legibility of his feelings as they manifested themselves in his conduct, fashioned bonds of sympathy, despite the crime he had perpetrated. As Boswell was to write in an essay on executions in *The Hypochondriack*, a few years after Hackman's execution, 'the curiosity which impels people to be present at such affecting scenes, is certainly a proof of sensibility not of callousness'.[19]

The entrepreneurs of Grub Street quickly moved in. James Boswell was disgruntled to learn that his attempt to publish an account of Hackman's trial was preempted by a newspaper hack.[20] Between April and June a succession of pamphlets were published purporting to tell the true stories of Hackman and Ray; a number of periodicals like the *London Magazine* also published their version of events; two engravings of Hackman from drawings by Robert Dighton were published, while Valentine Green succeeded in borrowing the portrait of Ray by Dance, which he sold as an engraving in late May.[21]

Though such a rash of publications would probably have been produced at almost any point in the eighteenth and early nineteenth centuries, the materials on Hackman and Ray grew out of a particular literary and publishing milieu. One, to which I will return, was not particularly a product of the 1760s and 1770s, but an old genre that went back into the late seventeenth century, namely, the confession or life of a notorious murderer or criminal.[22] But three other genres, generally of more recent pedigree, shaped the accounts of the murder. The first is that of political journalism, particularly associated with the followers of John Wilkes, which sought to link private immorality in high places with the corrupt state of national politics. In the pages of the *Middlesex Journal*, pamphlets like the series *Critical Memoirs of the Times* which appeared in 1769, satirical prints on high life, and in scandal sheets which revealed the sexual peccadilloes of the likes of the Prime Minister Duke of Grafton, critics of the government not only attacked the morality of particular individuals, but made the case that corrupt aristocratic rule was also marked by personal depravity.[23] This overtly political muck raking was paralleled by the emergence in the 1760s of a number of magazines – the most famous was *The Town and Country Magazine* – which were scandal sheets *tout court*, offering their readers titillating accounts of the affairs between actresses and peers, courtesans and Dukes. And thirdly, of course, the story of Hackman and Ray was both published in the form and told in terms which would have been familiar to the many readers of the extraordinarily popular sentimental novels that were published in the 1760s and 1770s by the circulating library proprietors, John and Francis Noble.[24]

The most important of the new publications about the crime was *The Case and Memoirs of James Hackman*, a pamphlet written by Manasseh Dawes, a reforming lawyer who had taken up Hackman's case. It went through nine editions in a few months and was published by an old political enemy of Sandwich, George Kearsley, who had once been the publisher of John Wilkes's *North Briton*.

*The Case and Memoirs of Hackman* looks at first sight like the usual memoir of a notorious murder, but is a far cry from such sensational works. It assumes the conventional format of such literature with a biography, an account of the crime and trial, and reflections on the character of the accused, but *The Case* is framed as the story of a young man of 'great tenderness and humanity... particularly bashful in his behavior',[25] who is misled by his lover, Martha Ray, who promises him marriage but reneges on her vow, and by the perfidious Italian, Galli, who either at her own instigation, or at the prompting of Sandwich or Ray, lies to Hackman when she tells him that the earl's mistress no longer wishes to see him and that she has found a new admirer. The victim of perfidy and intrigue in high life, Hackman falls into a decline 'becoming melancholy, pensive and grave'.[26] His last desperate effort is a plea to Ray to end his 'pleasing pain' and 'sufferings' by marrying him, bringing her youngest child with her to live a life of rural felicity as a cleric's wife. 'I know you are not fond of the follies and vanities of the town. How tranquil and agreeably, and with what uninterrupted felicity, unlike to anything we have yet enjoyed, shall we then wear our time away together on my living'.[27]

In *The Case* the murderer is lost in the lover:

> he was a lover...He was a slave to its influence, and sought a cure in death, when a supposed contempt from her, on whose account he had long been miserable, robbed him of his reasons, and in his phrenzy compelled him to execute that deed, which, peculiar as it was, will be remembered with compassion, not remorse; with pity, not abhorrence; with charity, not indifference; and whenever we think of the man we shall exclaim – Alas! Poor Hackman![28]

Hackman's case was one of 'imprudence, impolicy and folly...powerful ingredients in love' opposed to 'the colder considerations of lucre, rank, and fortune'.[29] This was a sentimental tale, but one, like Thomas Day's later *The History of Sanford and Merton*, with a political twist. Hackman emerges as a sincere, ordinary man caught up in the intrigues and moral depravity of a vicious aristocratic milieu of which he has little understanding. His innocence explains his guilt.

Though Hackman was the chief object of fascination, and his defenders far more numerous than his detractors, the spectacle of this murderous 'man of feeling' clearly made many commentators uneasy. They were almost all profoundly relieved that he reverted to a masculine type at his trial and execution, that, although he remained the object of sentiment, he ceased to be either palpably mad or visibly sentimental. As Horace Walpole remarked of Hackman's conduct at his trial, 'He behaved very unlike a madman'.[30] Male stoicism triumphed. Libertine friends of Boswell privately expressed the view that Hackman's action, while wrong, was justified,[31] while the defense of 'irresistible impulse', which all of Hackman's apologists, both legal and literary, chose to emphasize, separated his single action from his general mental state. He was not mad, he had just acted madly. He was not wicked but misled. His character, in contrast to that of other killers as depicted in their biographical histories, had not undergone a progressive deterioration; on the contrary, he had always, it was stressed, been a man of virtue and feeling. Paradoxically, therefore, the sentimental account of Hackman helped legitimize a brutal act of the sort normally associated with the villains in sentimental stories – rakes, libertines and roués – or with the lives of the most brutal murderers. The libertine crime, of course, was more usually abduction and rape – offenses which were usually premeditated and planned in ways that demonstrated the power and control of their perpetrator; romantic murder, on the other hand, was impulsive. To a very large degree, then, the notion of irresistible impulse was contingent upon a particular idea of sentimental love. The legal category and the literary narrative were inseparable. But, at the same time, we must add a caveat, for its my strong impression that 'irresistible impulse' was overwhelmingly used in cases involving male rather than female murderers. And I suspect that female crimes of passion involved questions of premeditation and madness rather than premeditation and 'irresistible impulse'.

The views expressed about Hackman's case embodied a number of unresolved tensions. If the murder was not evidence of madness, what about Hackman's intention to commit suicide? Hackman's apologists had to admit his (publicly acknowledged) determination to kill himself, but they treated it less as a symptom of Hackman's illness than a sign of the perfidy of others. It could therefore be construed as further evidence that Hackman's momentary irresistible impulse was justified.[32]

The unease shown at Hackman's representation as an object of distress is partly explained by the difficulty of placing him in the conventional context of sentimental narratives. Gentlemen of feeling were onlookers, provoked into sentimental response by their role as observers; they were not conventionally the objects of pity, a role that was normally left to women. In sentimental novels and poems the conventional plot was one in which women suffered because of men – notably the arbitrary father, the predatory rake, or the cruel husband.[33] Such women excited sentimental feeling either by bearing their misfortunes with a dignity derived from their acceptance of their role in society (the position of Iphis in Jephtha) or they were driven to madness by their suffering (as in the case of Maria in Sterne's *Sentimental Journey*).[34] In both cases, the woman in distress is fetishized as the male object of desire.

The problem for Martha Ray, of course, was that, though she might act the sentimental victim in Jephtha, her story could not be easily accommodated to either of these narratives. She did not meekly accept her place in society; she showed no signs of love's madness. Her life seems to be more in accord with a modern feminist narrative than with an eighteenth-century sentimental story: the narrative of a woman who, though exploited and commodified through the structures of patriarchy, nevertheless carved out a life for herself, using her talents and force of character to the advantage of herself and her children. (A somewhat similar story, also with a tragic ending, is now being told in recent revisionist accounts of the life and career of Emma Hart, Lady Hamilton.) Ray's story resists and resisted sentimental interpretation. Despite her terrible and brutal death, it was hard (though as we shall see it was not impossible) to represent her as a sentimental victim.

Between the summer of 1779 and the spring of 1780, the Hackman–Ray case went cold, but revived with the publication, again by George Kearsley, of a book, entitled *Love and Madness. A Story too True*.[35] *Love and Madness* supposedly consisted of letters between Ray and Hackman, which Kearsley claimed had been given to him by Frederick Booth, Hackman's brother-in-law.

Their 'discovery' was something of a sensation; now the true story would be revealed in the words of its most important participants.

In fact the book was compiled, written or edited by a clerical hack, Herbert Croft, who was, like Hackman, shabby genteel, and who had written advice manuals and religious tracts for young girls, a life of Edward Young, the graveyard poet whose *Night Thoughts* was one of the era's most popular poems, and who had also launched proposals for an English Dictionary to rival Dr Johnson's.[36] He was, in short, a typical product of Grub Street.

Croft's epistolary text is an extraordinary mish-mash, a book which combines the conventional correspondence of a love-affair with Grub Street gossip and literary reflection. Cashing in on the notoriety of the Hackman–Ray affair was undoubtedly one of Croft's purposes. Most notably, in order to promote his own work on English poets, Croft inserted into Hackman's letters a number of documents that he had procured by dubious means from the sister of the young Bristol poet, Thomas Chatterton, who had committed suicide in 1770 after failing to achieve literary success with a series of forgeries of mediaeval chivalric verse. These documents caused almost as much of a stir as the purported letters of Hackman and Ray.[37] Croft's book was an instant bestseller and quickly went through nine editions; it was still in print in the 1820s.[38]

From the outset the status of the book was in question. It was widely denounced as a fiction – not a collection of 'real' letters, but an epistolary novel. Others claimed that only the insertion of the Chatterton letters was a falsehood – how could Hackman have had such correspondence – and that the other letters were true. Some believed the Chatterton material authentic, but the rest not.[39] This was the position of critics like Dr Johnson, to whom the ninth edition was dedicated, who condemned it for what he took to be its deliberate mixture of fact and fiction.[40]

One of the most skillful aspects of *Love and Madness* is the way that it repeatedly plays on the reader's anxiety about the status of the text. The challenge is issued in the very title – '*Love and Madness. A Story Too True*'. On the one hand the reader is titillated with the prospect of an intimate view into the true feelings of the protagonists as expressed in a passionate private correspondence. 'These papers', Croft quotes of Hackman, 'which will be delivered to you after my death, my dear friend, are not letters. Nor know I what to call them. They will exhibit, however, the picture of a heart'.[41] On the other, long discussions of literary controversies about which it is scarcely credible that Hackman could have known, stretch the reader's credulity to the limit.[42] Are these letters, or are they not a window into the soul of their creator (s)? And who is their creator? At one point, as the text cheekily remarks, 'We cannot bear to see the author only peeping over the top of every page, to observe how we like him.'[43]

*Love and Madness* fitted into a recognizable genre of works whose appeal lay in their effective negotiation of the boundary between history and fiction. Novels had long used the term history in their titles; indeed in the 1760s, the Scottish critic Hugh Blair designated novels and romances as 'fictitious histories'. And novelists frequently used the techniques of authentication employed by historians – the quotation of documents and records, the recording of the testimony of eyewitnesses, an account of how and where they had obtained their source materials. Daniel Defoe, of course, was the master of this genre – his *Memoirs of a Cavalier* (1720) and *A Journal of the Plague Year* (1722) are both presented as historical documents and reflect on the way in which we determine what is 'authentic'. It was important to many writers of fiction that their work be treated as if it were history – hence Samuel Richardson's protestations when Warburton proposed that he preface *Clarissa* with a declaration that the work was entirely fiction. Richardson wanted 'to avoid hurting that kind of Historical Faith which Fiction itself is generally read with, tho' we know it to be Fiction'.[44] Such faith was important to those who wanted to legitimate fiction by claiming that, like history, it embodied an instructive truth, even if it were not a story of what actually happened. The moral effectiveness of the fiction depended upon its plausibility.

It was but a short move from fiction being written and read as if it were history to fictions that were based on contemporary historical characters and circumstances. The growth of the newspaper press – the vehicle by which the world were first acquainted with Hackman's murder of Ray – and spread of biography made this possible. In the 1770s a succession of widely reported, high-profile aristocratic scandals spawned a number of novels whose success depended on readers' recognition of the figures on which they were based. Works like *The Unhappy Wife* (1770) based on Lady Sarah Bunbury's break-up with her horse-loving but emotionally tepid husband, *Harriet, or the Innocent Adulteress* (1771) which used materials from the scandal of the Duke of Cumberland's affair with Lady Grosvenor, and *The Correspondents* (1775), which purported to be letters between Lord Lyttelton and his mistress, Mrs Peach, all used fiction to elaborate on fact. The pleasure in reading them lay in the possibility that they might be true, a prospect that could only be contemplated if they were known to be works of fiction. (If they were works of history they had to be true.) At the same time they could play with the idea that, even if all the facts were not correct, they nevertheless contained a moral truth about the story they told. The genre affirmed the boundary between history and fiction by asking the reader to move back and forth across it.

But Croft does more than contribute to this genre. *Love and Madness*, itself a work of fiction masquerading as fact, argues that true creative genius is the ability to convince readers that the fiction they are reading is true. 'Most readily I admit', concludes Croft, 'that, if Chatterton be an impostor (i.e. the wonderful human being I firmly believe him), he imposed on every soul who knew him. This with me, is the trait of greatness.'[45]

The test of a great work is not its adherence to factual accuracy but its ability to move the reader, to convince and persuade them because of its aesthetic and moral power. Elsewhere *Love and Madness* makes the same point when discussing the other great forgery of the period, James Macpherson's 'reconstruction' and translation of the ancient Gaelic poems of Ossian. When Hackman discusses the verses with Ray, he subordinates the issue of their authenticity and authorship to the quality of their effects: 'They who do not refuse their admiration of the compositions, still think themselves justified to abuse Macpherson, for pretending *not* to be the author of what they still admire. Is not this strange?'[46]

Croft, who constructs a story from a few fragments, just as Macpherson and Chatterton created their forgeries, wants to be seen in the best company, along with authors whose fictional powers have led readers to take as fact what was the work of their creator's fertile imagination.

Yet if *Love and Madness* encourages a certain skepticism and achieves a degree of playful distance from the genre it purports to adopt, it is nevertheless a credible account of the Hackman–Ray affair, one sufficiently plausible to lead some of its readers to accept the letters' authenticity. The plausibility of *Love and Madness* is sustained not only by its scrupulous adherence to the known facts of the Hackman–Ray affair but by virtue of the fact that it is telling a story which is already well-known. Croft's work confirms and elaborates the link that the earlier *Case and Memoirs* published by Kearsley had established between the story of Hackman and Ray and sentimental narrative. The story of Hackman and Ray becomes an epistolary novel.

There are nevertheless some important differences between *Love and Madness* and the *Case and Memoirs of James Hackman*. Croft's text is more literary than political, its point of reference less the social forces that produce a sentimental tragedy than a reflection (made all the more powerfully because of the material on Chatterton) on the delicate sensibility that accompanies and is a sign of literary skill or even genius.

Croft's account makes Hackman an author, a literary figure who both creates and comments upon texts. The full panoply of sentimental cliché is displayed to plot the progressive desperation of Hackman as he fails to persuade Ray that love should triumph over duty, and youth over old age. His letters are filled with palpitations of the heart, that key organ of sensibility, and of tears and weeping;[47] and, true to genre, is also replete with literary reference and allusion to Rousseau, Sterne, Mackenzie and minor sentimental versifiers.[48] In speaking of his response to Martha's musical talents Hackman writes:

> Observe, when I write to you I never pretend to write sense. I have no head; you have made me all heart from top to bottom. Sense why, I am out of my senses, and have been these six weeks. Were it possible my scrawls to you could ever be read by any one but you I should be called

a madman. I certainly am either curst or blest (I know not which) with passions wild as the torrent's roar. Notwithstanding I take this simile from water, the element out of which I am formed is fire... I have a burning coal of fire; your hand can light it up to rapture, rage, or madness. Men, real men, have never been wild enough for my admiration; it has wandered into ideal world of fancy. Othello (but he should have put *himself* to death in his wife's sight, *not* his wife), Zanga, are *my* heroes. Milkandwater passions are like sentimental comedy. Give me (you see how, like your friend Montaigne, I strip myself of my skin, and show you all my veins and arteries, even the playing of my heart), give *me*, I say, tragedy, affecting tragedy, in the world, as well as in the theatre. I would massacre all mankind sooner than lose you... Inconsistent being! While I am ranting thus about tragedy and blood and murder, behold, I am as weak as a woman. My tears flow at the idea of losing you; yes, they do not drop only, they pour. I sob like a child.[49]

Not only is much of the structure of the narrative derived from Goethe's *The Sorrows of Young Werther*, which had been translated into English in 1779, but the novel in its 1776 French translation features prominently in the letters. Hackman urges Ray to get him the book. 'Nonsense, to say it will make me unhappy, or that I shall not be able to read it! Must I pistol myself, because a thickblooded German has been fool enough to set the example, or because a German novelist had feigned such a story?'[50] But she is terrified by his request: 'The book you mentioned is just the only book you should never read. On my knees I beg that you will never, never read it! Perhaps you *have* read it. Perhaps! I am distracted.'[51]

While the language attributed to Hackman is all of the heart, palpitations and passion, the letters purportedly written by Ray (and there are many fewer of them) are cautious and caring. Though she is portrayed as loving Hackman almost to the last, she consistently chooses prudence over passion. But we get little sense of Ray as a subject; she is the object of Hackman's desire, and her own subjectivity an obstacle to its fulfillment. What *Love and Madness* elaborates is a theory of male romantic desire and possession. What Hackman seeks is another form of possession. Certainly what is at stake here is not physical or bodily possession, the object of the rake or libertine rather than the true lover. In *Love and Madness* Ray and Hackman enjoy a sexual relationship, but it is largely irrelevant to the main plot. Rather what Hackman wants is a union of the spirit, the dissolution of the distinction between the lover and the loved one, the achievement of a degree of interpersonal transparency that dissolves the self in the other, or, perhaps, to put it more accurately in the case of Hackman, of the other in the self. As he says 'I wish you happy, *most* happy; but I cannot bear the thoughts of your receiving happiness from any hands (man, woman, or child) but mine'.[52] (When he is awaiting execution in prison, he claims to be plagued by the idea that Ray is possessed by another in heaven, and his dying wish was that he should be buried at her side.[53]) The pleasure and desire here are linked to the pain of their unattainability, to their constant delay, the impossibility of their fulfillment except in fleeting moments and through the imagination.

The letters reach a climax with the murder, which has come to be seen as inevitable, almost unavoidable, but once the deed is done a curious peace remains. In the novel Hackman displays the same sense of tranquillity as in the press reports of the trial. In one of the final fragments that fill the end of Croft's text Hackman is given the words, 'Without her I do not think I can exist. Yet I will be, you shall see, a *man*, as well as a lover.'[54] This is the moral at the end of the novel, which is reminiscent of Goethe's remark in the revised edition of *Werther*: 'Be a man and do not follow me.'

Like the earlier *Case and Memoirs of James Hackman*, *Love and Madness*, despite its charting of the progressive derangement of Hackman, takes the view that he is the victim of a special kind of love: 'the torture of my situation is this, that not a word can be said in my favour, unless you will say that I am mad. But God knows, I possess all my senses and feelings much too exquisitely'.[55] And, once again, *Love and Madness* argues the case of 'irresistible impulse'. In both texts there is a repeated desire both to acknowledge and to reject the notion that male romantic love is a form of madness, a contradiction that the legal notion of 'irresistible impulse' so neatly elided.

One of the most important effects of *Love and Madness* was to sketch Hackman as a proto-Romantic hero whose memory would survive into the nineteenth century, and to highlight the issue of Hackman's madness which many of the earlier accounts had downplayed or tried to evade. *Love and Madness* recast a story which had previously had many actors and inter-twined plots into a single, inexorable story line with only one protagonist, the progressively maddened James Hackman. It made the case into an exploration of individual pathology rather than a complex social drama.

Largely because of the commercial success of Croft's book, Hackman's case passed into the medical literature on insanity, being cited by Erasmus Darwin's *Zoonomia: or the Laws of Organic Life* (1794–97) as the example of the third stage of 'erotomania, or sentimental love', and by Joseph Mason Cox in his influential *Practical Observations on Insanity* (1806).[56] Darwin wrote:

> When the pain of love is so great, as not to be relieved by the exertions of reverie, as above described; as when it is misplaced on an object, of which the lover cannot possess himself; it may still be counteracted or conquered by the stoic philosophy, which strips all things of their ornaments... Of which lessons may be found in the meditations of Marcus Antoninus... the third stage of the disease I suppose is irremediable; when a lover has previously been much encouraged, and at length meets with neglect or disdain; the maniacal idea is so painful as not to be for a moment relievable by the exertions of reverie, but is instantly followed

by furious or melancholy insanity; and suicide, or revenge, have frequently been the consequence, as was lately exemplified in Mr. Hackman, who shot Miss Ray in the lobby of the playhouse.[57]

The idea of love madness was not, of course, new, dating back to Plato's *Phaedrus* and receiving its most eloquent expression in English in Robert Burton's *Anatomy of Melancholy* (1621). But Darwin, and he was not alone in this, saw love madness as a modern condition, a consequence of the leisure, refinement and taste which were made possible by modern society. Apparent in Darwin's analysis – as in non-medical works which were concerned to examine modern man and his place in society – was a theory of the mind and body which is at once a physiological view derived from Enlightenment associationalist psychology (a theory of the human nervous system and the place of the human heart in the physiology) and a social theory, most brilliantly expounded by the Scottish political economists, about the contemporary condition – about European modernity – and its effect on people's feelings. The medical and social argument was that modern living had made man more and more nervous, more and more refined in his feelings, a condition attributable to luxury, commerce and excess. This was at once desirable and pathological. Greater refinement, greater sensibility was associated with persons of nervous, even hysterical disposition.[58]

And, though this theory was originally a view about man, it quickly became gendered, and came to be associated with women. As David Hume put it in his essay on 'Delicacy of Taste and Passion': 'How far delicacy of taste, and that of passion, are connected together in the original frame of mind, it is hard to determine. To me there always appears very considerable connection between them. For we may observe that women, who have more delicate passions than men, have also a more delicate taste of the ornaments of life . . . and the ordinary decencies of behaviour.'[59] The civilizing process was at once pathological or had pathological consequences, and was associated with women.

So, although Hackman appears in such works as Darwin's as a test-case of love's madness, there are ways in which he is also viewed as an anomaly: a case of male erotomania at a time when such sickness, both in imaginative and medical literature, was increasingly linked with women. (Female patients in mental hospitals confined because of love's madness considerably outnumbered men in this period.[60]) This anomaly is revealed in Darwin's examples which follow his mention of Hackman, whom he compares to Dido, who killed herself when left by her lover, and Medea who murdered her rival lover and her own children to avenge the loss of Jason's love. Darwin concludes his remarks with a quote from Dryden:[61]

> Earth has no rage like love to hatred turn'd,
> Nor hell a fury like a woman scorn'd.

Darwin is aware that there is a male as well as female clinical pathology, but seems driven to consider it a purely feminine or female sensibility. But then again, perhaps Hackman is a good example for Darwin to choose, for his famous case demonstrates that men may be temporarily unhinged rather than carrying any innate disposition or propensity to love madness.

The association of women and love's madness was explored by William Wordsworth in one of the *Lyrical Ballads*, 'The Thorn', composed in 1798. In March of that year Wordsworth borrowed a copy of Erasmus Darwin's *Zoonomia* from a circulating library,[62] and in the same month and while the son of his close friend Basil Montagu, Basil Caroline Montagu, Martha Ray's grandchild, was living with and being tutored by Dorothy Wordsworth and by William himself, he began what was eventually to be one of the *Lyrical Ballads*, 'The Thorn'.[63] The poem, partly based on popular ballad variants of 'The Cruel Mother', tells of a woman who repeatedly returns to a small mound on a hilltop by a thorn tree.[64] She had been deserted and left pregnant by her lover. I quote from the poem:[65]

> She was with child and she was mad. . .
> More know I not, I wish I did,
> And it should all be told to you;
> For what became of this poor child
> No mortal ever knew;
> Nay – if a child to her was born
> No earthly tongue could ever tell;
> And if twas born alive or dead,
> Far less could this with proof be said;
> But some remember well,
> That Martha Ray about this time
> Would up the mountain often climb. . .
> I did not speak – I saw her face;
> Her face! – it was enough for me;
> I turned about and heard her cry,
> Oh misery! Oh misery!

Wordsworth's radical recontextualization of Martha Ray – her transformation from victim of a mad lover to her portrayal as a woman driven mad by the desertion of her lover and condemned, in the voice Wordsworth adopts, if not by the poet himself, as the perpetrator of infanticide – has long troubled critics. But Wordsworth's verse is a self-avowed investigation, through the voice of the old sea captain who narrates the poem, 'of the general laws by which superstition acts upon the mind'.[66] The memory of the historical Martha Ray, far more alive in the 1790s especially in the Wordsworth circle whose members knew Basil Montagu's story of his mother's death, serves to make his point about superstition more poignant.

Over the course of twenty years, a period when *Love and Madness* was always in print, the case of Hackman and Ray was stripped of its historical context and its characters removed into the realms of medical pathology and poetry. James Hackman and Martha Ray became two different archetypes of love's madness, one apparently based on fact and posing awkward problems for medical science; the other a strange fiction, but one much more in accord both with clinical analysis and a prevailing literary sensibility.

## Notes

1   Horace Walpole to Lady Ossory, 9 April 1779, *Horace Walpole's Correspondence*, ed. W.S. Lewis, 48 volumes (New Haven and Oxford: Yale and Oxford University Presses, 1937–83), vol. 33 p. 100. This account closely follows the report in *London Evening Post*, 10 April 1779.
2   *London Evening Post*, 10 April 1779.
3   The wording is almost identical in *St James's Chronicle*, 8 April 1779 and *London Chronicle*, 8 April 1779. Compare *General Advertiser* 16 April 1779.
4   On Sandwich's life and his relations with Martha Ray, see N.A.M. Rodger, *The Insatiable Earl. A Life of John Montagu, fourth earl of Sandwich 1718–1792* (London: HarperCollins, 1993), especially pp. 122–5; George Martinelli, *Jemmy Twitcher. A Life of the Fourth Earl of Sandwich* (London: Cape, 1962), especially pp. 165–77.
5   *Westminster Magazine* (April 1779), p. 173
6   On Sandwich as a musical patron see Rodger, *Insatiable Earl*, pp. 116–21, 310–14, 329–30; Martinelli, *Jemmy Twitcher*, pp. 84–6; William Weber, *The Rise of the Musical Classics in Eighteenth-century England: A Study in Canon, Ritual and Ideology* (Oxford: Clarendon, 1992), pp. 147–55.
7   *Literary Memoirs of Cradock*, vol. 1, p. 118.
8   *Westminster Magazine* (April 1779), p. 173.
9   The portrait is in the possession of the current Earl of Sandwich.
10  In fact in Handel's version of the story Jephtha is not sacrificed but made to go into a nunnery, a change in the plot that exposed him to criticism.
11  Abbe Du Bos, *Reflexions critiques sur la poesie et sur peinture* (Ecole Nationale Superieure des Beaux-Arts, Paris, 1993), Premiere Partie, section 1. For a general discussion of this text see David Marshall, *The Surprising Effects of Sympathy. Marivaux, Diderot, Rousseau and Mary Shelley* (Chicago and London: University of Chicago, 1988), pp. 1–49.
12  Richard Cumberland to George Cumberland [April 1779], *The Cumberland Letters, being the correspondence of Richard Dennison Cumberland and George Cumberland, between the years 1771 and 1784*, ed. Clementina Black (London: Martin Secker, 1912), p. 228.
13  Hackman's speech was reported in all the trial accounts, for which see note 14.
14  *London Evening Post*, 15–17 April 1779; *Gazetteer*, 17 April, 1779; *St James's Chronicle*, 15–17 April 1779; *London Chronicle*, 15–17 April 1779; *General Advertiser*, 17 April 1779; *General Evening Post*, 17 April 1779.
15  *Boswell, Laird of Auchinleck 1778–1782. The Private Papers of James Boswell*, ed. Joseph W. Reed and Frederick A. Pottle (Edinburgh: Edinburgh University Press, 1993), p. 85.
16  *General Evening Post*, 17 April 1779.
17  *London Evening Post*, 15–17 April 1779.
18  *St James's Chronicle*, 15–17 April 1779. Cf. *London Chronicle*, 15–17 April 1779.

19   *The Hypochondriack. Being the Seventy Essays of the celebrated Biographer, JAMES BOSWELL, appearing in the LONDON MAGAZINE, from November 1778 to August 1783, and here first reprinted*, ed. Margery Bailey, 2 vols (Stanford, CA: Stanford University Press, 1928), vol. 2 p. 282.

20   *Boswell Laird of Auchinleck*, p. 85.

21   *The Case and Memoirs of Hackman*, passim; *The Case and Memoirs of Miss Martha Ray* (London, 1779); *The London Magazine* vol. XLVIII (1779), pp. 188–9; *Universal Magazine*, April 1779, pp. 202–3.

22   For which see Lincoln B. Faller, *Turned to Account: the forms and functions of criminal biography in late seventeenth and early eighteenth-century England* (Cambridge: Cambridge University Press, 1987).

23   John Brewer, 'The Wilkites and the law', *An Ungovernable People. The English and their law in the seventeenth and eighteenth centuries*, ed. John Brewer and John Styles (London: Hutchinson, 1980), pp. 142–3, 145, 147–9. Cf. the French cases discussed in Sarah Maza, *Private Lives and Public Affairs. The Causes Celebres of Pre-Revolutionary France* (Berkeley and Los Angeles: California University Press, 1993).

24   James Raven, *British fiction 1750–1770. A Chronological check-list of prose fiction printed in Britain and Ireland* (University of Delaware, 1987), pp. 36–7.

25   *The Case and Memoirs of the late Rev. Mr. James Hackman* (London: G. Kearsley, 1779), pp. 17, 32.

26   *Case and Memoirs of Hackman*, p. 4.

27   *Ibid.*, pp. 29–31.

28   *Ibid.*, no pagination, should be p. 18.

29   *Ibid.*, p. 32.

30   Horace Walpole to Horace Mann, 17 April 1779, *Horace Walpole's Correspondence*, vol. 24, p. 459.

31   *Boswell Laird of Auchinleck*, p. 92.

32   This was the position of *The Case and Memoirs of Hackman*, pp. 6–7.

33   On this genre see Janet Todd, *Sensibility: An Introduction* (London: Methuen, 1986) *passim* and R.F. Brissenden, *Virtue in Distress: Studies in the Novel of Sentiment from Richardson to Sade* (New York: Harper & Row, 1974).

34   Laurence Sterne, *A Sentimental Journey Through France and Italy by Mr. Yorick*, ed. Gardner D. Stout (Berkeley and Los Angeles: University of California, 1967), pp. 13–17, 268–76.

35   *Love and Madness. A Story too True. in a series of letters between parties, whose names would perhaps be mentioned, were they less known, or less lamented* (London: G. Kearsley, 1780).

36   See *Dictionary of National Biography* entry: Herbert Croft.

37   On Croft and Chatterton see Michael Macdonald and Terence R. Murphy, *Sleepless Souls. Suicide in early modern England* (Oxford: Clarendon, 1990), pp. 191–3; *Love and Madness*, pp. 51–7, 112, 125–244, 253–4.

38   For a recent attempt to rehabilitate Croft's text see Max Novak, 'The Sensibility of Sir Herbert Croft in *Love and Madness* and the "Life of Edward Young" ', *The Age of Johnson*, 8 (1997), 187–207.

39   Typical responses are to be found in *Gentleman's Magazine*, vol. L (June 1780), pp. 287–8; *Town and Country Magazine*, vol. XII (April 1780), p. 211; *Monthly Review*, 62 (April 1780), p. 326.

40   *Boswell's Life of Johnson*, Vol. 4, p. 187.

41   *Love and Madness*, p. 280

42  *Ibid.*, pp. 103–07, 292.
43  *Ibid.*, p. 31.
44  Cited in A.D. McKillop, *The Early Masters of English Fiction* (Lawrence, KA: University of Kansas Press,1956), p. 42.
45  *Love and Madness*, p. 140.
46  *Ibid.*, p. 27.
47  *Ibid.*, pp. 26–7, 47, 49, 51, 53–4, 56, 87, 100, 246, 282, 289–90.
48  *Ibid.*, pp. 6, 33, 43, 88, 90, 267–8.
49  *Ibid.*, pp. 23–7.
50  *Ibid.*, pp. 73–4, cf. 283–6.
51  *Ibid.*, p. 75.
52  *Ibid.*, p. 73.
53  *General Evening Post*, 17 April 1779; *Case and Memoirs of Hackman*, p. 10; *Love and Madness*, p. 282.
54  *Love and Madness*, p. 263.
55  *Ibid.*, p. 296.
56  Roy Porter, 'Love, Sex and Madness in Eighteenth-Century England', *Social Research*, vol. 53, no. 2 (summer 1986), pp. 215–17.
57  Erasmus Darwin, *Zoonomia; or the Laws of Organic Life* 2 vols (London: Joseph Johnson, 1794–96), Vol. 2, p. 365.
58  See Porter, 'Love, Sex and Madness', *Social Research*, pp. 211–19; G.J. Barker-Benfield, *The Culture of Sensibility: sex and society in eighteenth-century Britain* (Chicago and London: University of Chicago, 1992), and for a later period Helen Small, *Love's Madness* (Oxford: Oxford University Press, 1996).
59  David Hume, 'Of the Delicacy of Taste and Passion', in *Essays, Moral, Political and Literary*, ed. Eugene F Miller (Indianapolis, IN: Liberty Found 1987), p. 603.
60  Porter, 'Love, Sex and Madness', *Social Research* (1986), pp. 217–19; Small, *Love's Madness*, p. 33.
61  Darwin, *Zoonomia*, Vol. 2, p. 363.
62  Duncan Wu, *Wordsworth's Reading 1770–1799* (Cambridge: Cambridge University Press, 1993), p. 45.
63  On the relations between the Wordsworths, young Basil and his father Basil senior see Mark L. Reed, *Wordsworth. The Chronology of the early years 1770–1799* (Cambridge, MA: Harvard University Press, 1967), esp. pp. 163, 172, 180, 182, 190, 194, 196, 204, 210, 221, 227, 282.
64  *Lyrical Ballads, and other Poems, 1797–1800 by William Wordsworth*, ed. James Butler and Karen Green (Ithaca and London: Cornell University Press, 1992), pp. 77–85
65  I quote lines 155–65; 199–202.
66  *Lyrical Ballads*, p. 351

# 7

## 'A Submission, Sir!' Who has the Right to Person in Eighteenth-Century Britain?

*Peter de Bolla*

On 19 February 1747 the actor-manager Thomas Sheridan was tried in the court of Oyer and Terminer for assault and acquitted. Immediately following this case the court heard a suit that Sheridan himself brought against one Edward Kelly, a young man from Galway, and also for assault, and found for Sheridan. Kelly was sent down, fined £500 and imprisoned. Although these two interconnecting cases do not have the same reputation in the history of theatre as Charles Macklin's later suit brought against some members of the audience who had attempted to have Macklin barred from acting on account of his refusal to be whipped, 'Sheridan's Case', as I will refer to it, should be thought of as a landmark case.[1] And its significance is not confined to the cultural history of the theatre, or the social and political inflections of acting; 'Sheridan's Case' is caught up in the deep structures of practice, precedent, behaviour and aspiration which underpin the conceptual formation of person. As will become clear such structures, in so far as they may be understood to be located in the individual, become visible once we begin to see the practices of subjectivity as fully cultural and political forms; that is, once we begin to read the formation of the category 'person' historically. And, when seen in this light, what may initially seem to be a minor skirmish in the development of Irish theatre will become part of the larger – perhaps the largest – story about subjectivity in which the category 'person' is constantly under pressure and in need of containment or precise definition because who 'one' is, what person is, strikes to the core of our beliefs in and conceptions of society, culture, nation and state. 'Sheridan's Case', then, is one of the bricks in the edifice that is our legal, social, political and cultural home (and perhaps prison): subjectivity or personhood.

Thomas Sheridan is primarily known to most literary scholars as a contributor to mid-to late eighteenth-century debates on education and elocution, and of course as the father of Richard Brinsley.[2] But before he made a living giving lectures on elocution all over the country he had been an actor on the Dublin stage. To theatre historians he is known primarily for his intervention into the customs and practice of eighteenth-century theatre which resulted in a change that was to prove to be decisive in respect of the audience's physical relationship to the stage, namely their being barred access behind the scenes and on the stage and removed or confined solely to the auditorium.[3] As is relatively well-known, early to mid-eighteenth-century theatregoers were far from constrained in their habits and practices of attendance at performances: they talked pretty much throughout the play, often shouted abuse at the actors, threw rotten fruit and other materials at the stage and each other, sat on the stage and wandered about on it during performances.[4] Indeed the sense one has, reading accounts of theatre performances from the Restoration up to the mid-century, is that the play, players or performance in general was pretty much the last thing the audience was interested in or attended to. Sheridan himself gave a vivid description of the playhouse in the years immediately preceding his becoming the manager of the Theatre Royal in Dublin. He writes:

> One Part of the House was Bear-Garden, the other a Brothel. If the Numberers Accounts in those Days could be produced, they would make an extraordinary Figure. It was no uncommon Thing to see about twenty persons in the Pit, not a Creature in the Boxes; one Row of the middle Gallery filled, and more than an hundred People on the Stage, who mixed with the Actors in such a Manner as scarce to be distinguished from them. The upper Gallery indeed, as every one could get Admission into it for two Pence, was generally crowded, and the Time constantly passed in Squabbles, and Battles between the Footmen and the Mob.[5]

Even if the audience restrained itself from these diversions it nevertheless found entertainment in itself before and beyond any interest in the performance. It is useful to recall here that theatres were public spaces in which patrons were displayed both to and for each other; along with other such spaces – the pleasure garden, exhibition room, auction room and so on – they provided a site or location for the display of person. Thus play-houses both in London and as we shall see in Dublin afforded the opportunity for the audience to see and be seen by one another – it was a common observation that, at the theatre last night, a particular person, usually a young beau, had climed up on to the railing above the pit and decorously displayed himself for the benefit of the audience. As for the gentry, who sat in the boxes, they are often described sitting facing towards the audience with their backs to the stage. Restoration theatre acknowledged this aspect of performance to such a degree that many plays can be said to *be about* the practices of theatregoing. Lansdowne's *The She Gallants*, for example, comments from within the play on the audience:

They spread themselves in parties all over the house; some in the pit, some in the boxes, others in the galleries, but principally on the stage; they cough, sneeze, talk loud, and break silly jests; sometimes laughing, sometimes singing, sometimes whistling, till the house is in uproar; some laugh and clap; some hiss and are angry; swords are drawn, the actors interrupted, the sense broken off, and so the play's sent to the devil. (III. I)

'Sheridan's case' was certainly going to change the material conditions under which performance took place, and the actor, Sheridan, was not shy in promoting himself as the great reformer of the stage.[6] In the following section I shall describe the immediate theatrical context in which Sheridan claimed an assault to his person had occurred before turning to the wider social, political and cultural framings of the category 'person'. This will help in understanding the legal arguments which underpin the trial and form the basis for contemporary views about the rights of persons, the topic for the following section.[7]

## The Kelly riot

The 1746–47 season on the Dublin stage had been very volatile, partly on account of the lingering political fall out of the '45, and partly provoked by the increasing irritation of both actor/managers and some members of the audience, with the unruliness of theatre attendance. Precisely over its habits of interruption and inattention but also, as we will see, over the rights distinct persons had over the selection of the play, the disposition of the audience within the theatre, the manner of the production, the performance of the actors – in brief over the social, cultural and political space of theatre itself. Sheridan became the focus of this agitation since, it was widely known, he was in favour of removing the right of spectators to sit on the stage. The so-called Kelly riot at Smock Alley in January 1747 – the civil unrest that led to the trial I am going to return to in conclusion – has usually (in fact almost universally) been thought to have been provoked by Sheridan's notice in the 13–17 January issue of the *Dublin Journal* to the effect that: 'In the future no money will be taken nor no person admitted behind the Scenes except on benefit nights'. But in point of fact the immediate cause of the disturbance was not his announced intention to prevent audience members from occupying the stage – the advertisement for the performance of the play that evening makes it clear that tickets were offered for sale for 'box, stage, and lattices', and in any case that night was a benefit night, precisely one of those nights excluded by Sheridan in his announcement of this new measure in the *Dublin Journal*. It is true that Sheridan himself claimed later that the reason for the riot had been his attempt to exclude the audience from the stage, but the actual prompt to the riot tells a different, and even more interesting story. This is what happened.

On Monday 19 January 1747, Sheridan mounted the second performance of Vanbrugh's *Aesop*, a play that has a very patchy performance history (and which Sheridan was to revive later in his career, transforming it into a farce first performed at Drury Lane on 19 December 1778 with Henderson in the role of Aesop). Sheridan took the title role himself. We know from the avalanche of comment that followed the riot and lead up to the subsequent legal proceedings that the play was well under way when a young gentleman, the worse for wear, clambered out of the pit, over the spikes that were placed there precisely to prevent such action, and onto the stage. His action was accompanied by loud signals of approbation since many in the audience were fired up to protest Sheridan's proposed restriction of the audience to the auditorium. Once on the stage he proceeded, unaccosted – presumably because a large number of sitters were already present on the stage – to the greenroom. There he found one of the actresses, Mrs Dyer, who in her affidavit read out in the subsequent court hearing described what had happened in the following rather demure fashion. Her assailant had, she says, 'first designedly' trod on her foot and then put one of his knees between hers, she protesting all the while, so that he would 'spoil her cloaths'.[8] He then told her what he intended to do: 'he would do what her husband Mr Dyer, had done to her, using the obscene expression', and then continued further 'abusive obscene language'.[9]

At this point a second actress, George Anne Bellamy, appeared by chance in the greenroom and witnessed Mrs Dyer's discomfort – she interposed herself, momentarily distracting the young drunk thereby affording them both the opportunity to escape to a nearby dressing room where they locked themselves in. The drunk tried to force entry and was then struck by one of the dressers who was herself 'big with child'. The drunk continued to exclaim that he would have 'carnal knowledge' of one or other of the two actresses between the scenes.

Sheridan was on stage while all this fracas was ongoing and when word was conveyed to him he retired from the stage, leaving the play at an effective standstill, the players it is reported 'staring dumbly at one another'.[10] With great calm Sheridan ordered the young man to be taken into custody by the official guards who were stationed in the Theatre Royal at every performance.

When Sheridan next appeared on stage he was surprised to find that the young man had escaped his guards and was once more in the pit causing a commotion, and then, to give material weight as it were to his verbal abuse he threw an orange at Sheridan which struck him on the false nose he was wearing (made out of iron) and caused a severe dent to be made in his forehead. At this moment Sheridan removed the false nose, stepped out of character, walked to the front of the stage and addressed the audience. The record concerning what he actually said has more than one version of his speech but it is quite clear that the ensuing part of the story and the legal case that was to result both crucially turn on the words Sheridan uttered at this moment.

A friend and associate of Sheridan, Benjamin Victor, who was to become the manager of the Theatre Royal and to write a history of the London and Dublin stage, claims the following happened:

> the actor addressed the audience (which happened to be thin that night) for protection – as there were some gentlemen in the pit who knew the rioter, they silenced him, but it was with great difficulty, and not 'till he had let loose several abusive names, such as Scoundrel, &. Sheridan, who generally speaks with propriety, in return for scoundrel, said *he was as good a gentleman as he was*. – These words were the next day altered thus – *I am as good a gentleman as any in the house*.[11]

In order to understand why a court case might have hung on these words we need to bring into the picture both the general social and cultural freighting of the term 'gentleman' and the more specific legal and political context within which eighteenth-century actors worked.

## The gentleman

It is perhaps unsurprising that the history of the word 'gentleman' has most often been told from the perspective of status, since as Hippolyte Taine famously remarked the word contains 'the history of English Society'.[12] The social and political resonance of the word is plugged into its origins in the Latin *gentilis* which gets carried into Old French as *gentil*: to be *gentle* is to be highborn or noble. Throughout the Renaissance the terms 'nobility' and 'gentility' were to all intents and purposes interchangeable: they indicated a person who could demonstrate ancestry. On account of this the term 'gentleman' is often linked to conferral of arms through the Herald's College which confirmed those who had the right to display a coat of arms and sign themselves 'Gent'. But as has also frequently been pointed out, the basis of the word's usage in lineage was often muddied by the fact that coats of arms were purchased. Thus yeomen or merchants who became wealthy and lived as if they were gentlemen did, over time, become accepted as such and eventually purchased coats of arms. Even so, right up to the period that concerns my narrative of Sheridan's Case, a distinction continued to made between those who were elevated on account of fiat – a gift from someone empowered to confer status, say the monarch – and those who were born into their class. *Bailey's Dictionary* of 1707, for example, defines a gentleman as 'one who receives his nobility from his ancestors, and not from the gift of any prince or state', and Johnson confirms this in his 'man of ancestry'.

As we shall see when we turn to the law, this distinction causes an area of uncertainty with regard to the legal definition of a gentleman, which is only exacerbated by the difficulty of setting a minimum length of time for the qualification of 'ancestry'. The problem is well-illustrated by Defoe, who defines a gentleman as:

> A person Born (for there lies the essence of Quality) of some known or Ancient Family, whose Ancestors have at least for some time been rais'd above the class of Mechanics. If we examine for how long it must be that is a dangerous Inquiry, we dive too deep, and may indeed strike at the Root of both the Gentry and Nobility; for all must begin somewhere, and would be traced to some less Degree in their original than will suit the vanity of the Day. It is enough therefore that we can derive for a Line of two or three generations, or perhaps less.[13]

As this makes clear, while the term distinguishes rank and confers on the person so designated the authority of lineage, it nevertheless remains conceptually problematic since, as Defoe says: 'all must begin somewhere'. So how long is a length of ancestry? But the instability of the term's definition *vis-à-vis* rank was only a part of the difficulty for the period in question. Throughout the eighteenth century the stress or fautlines in the term were to enable a very particular account of both society and politics to emerge which was, crucially, centred in the malleability of the concept 'gentleman'. No one has done more that John Barrell to tease out how this came about, and how as he remarks in the final sentence of *English Literature in History 1730–80: An Equal, Wide Survey* the political culture of mid-eighteenth-century Britain was faced with a 'crisis of social knowledge'.[14]

Much of Barrell's argument in this book is concerned to elucidate the ways in which the category 'gentleman' was shaped, crafted or moulded to enable it to contain a particular kind of person who, through the virtue of disinterest, was able to survey the entire terrain of the social and political. It was, as Barrell is at pains to stress, only such 'gentlemen' who were able to 'grasp the unity of society' who by dint of their disinterestedness were 'qualified to observe' those who were 'qualified only to be the objects of others' observation'.[15] And in relation to this unique perspective on society it was, of course, of signal importance that the term 'gentleman' had such a protean character: in ways that will resonate significantly below, the unfixed or contestual aspect of the designator 'gentleman' will map onto the category 'actor' – perhaps the most dangerously protean category of subject for the period – to reveal what was at stake for Thomas Sheridan on his day in court on 19 February 1747.

In the long, central essay of *An Equal, Wide Survey* Barrell offers a penetrating account of the ways in which writers on language during the period conceived of the national tongue in terms of the law of the land. Indeed, according to Barrell, the constitution of Britain was understood as, in effect, an echo or analogy of the refinement of the language: both had their basis in custom rather than statute or decree. And, since this analogy was so forcefully perceived, the rule of the polite over the vulgar in terms of pronunciation, grammar or usage was as 'natural' as the law's dominion over its subjects. Sheridan has a role to play in the story Barrell tells since he was, of course, a significant figure in the elocution movement; precisely an enterprise focused on the transformation of one kind of person – say a rude mechanic – into another, a gentleman, through the reformation of his speech. This later incarnation of the Dublin actor takes on a particular sheen when seen in the light of 'Sheridan's Case' as will become clear below.

While Barrell's focus is on the constitutional and political inflections of this analogy – hence his interest in the gentleman's authority over the language – he nevertheless touches upon the more narrow legal usage of the term that I wish to bring to the foreground. For the 'gentleman' did not only participate in the arena of politics understood in its restricted sense; the category was also invoked in the contemporaneous efforts to describe, delimit and anatomize person. And this, of course, meant that the psychic, social and legal inflections of the term were activated and scrutinized. It is these senses that I wish to bring centre-stage in my attempt to demonstrate why 'Sheridan's Case' should be understood to be a landmark in the history of the formation of subjectivity.

Barrell helps us here through his forensic enquiry into the generality of the type 'gentleman'. As he points out, it was only such a general person, so refined or raised so far up above the particular who could occupy a viewpoint from which the design of society might be apprehended. Only the gentleman (so defined) can attain such a height since he, and only he, is without occupation and therefore impartial, uncontaminated 'by regional or occupational particularities'.[16] But how do such men, gentlemen, gain protection from the law, what are their rights *as persons*?

As I have already indicated the law was unclear as to a precise definition of the category 'gentleman' but there is one, essential, quality that seemed incontestable and which Barrell uses so effectively in his account. Here, in Blackstone's first volume of the *Commentaries on the Laws of England* devoted to the rights of persons, is the best the law can do:

> As for *gentlemen*, says sir Thomas Smith, they be made good cheap in this kingdom: for whosoever studieth the laws of the realm, who studieth in the universities, who professeth liberal sciences, and (to be short) who can live idly, and without manual labour, and will bear the port, charge, and countenance of a gentleman, he shall be called master, and shall be taken for a gentleman.[17]

This attempt at a definition occurs towards the end of a chapter concerned primarily with an account of the nobility. This itself is prompted by Blacktone's sketch of society at large: 'The civil state consists of the nobility and the commonalty.'[18] It is clear from the sequence of his discussion as much as from the logic of his dissection of the different categories of both nobility and the commonalty that the 'gentleman' ought to fall within the latter classification. But a problem arises since there is no precise legal definition of the term and, as Blackstone is at pains to admit, through use and custom the word has come to mean 'one *qui arma* gerit, who bears coat armour'.[19] Consequently the boundary between the nobility and gentlemen had become blurred or even permeable. This leads Blackstone to admit, almost apologetically, that 'Esquires and gentlemen are confounded together by Sir Edward Coke' (I, 393). There is only one way out of this confusion: a separation on categorial grounds of the term 'gentleman'. So Blackstone suggests that the word, although most commonly designating rank, may also be used in a slightly different way, as if it were a different kind of term that might designate a slightly different quality to person. Although the commonalty can be split into various categories, and even though the term 'gentleman' attaches to the commonalty rather than the nobility, it is nevertheless the case that like an overlay or superscription one might be either a gentleman and a lord, or a gentleman and part of the commonalty. It is as if the term refers to an additional quality, relating as much to modes of address, deportment or behaviour as to social rank. At its furthest or deepest remove it may refer to a mode of being perceived from within person, a kind of psychic self-image or self-reflection. This only compounds the problem, of course, since I might see in myself what is imperceptible to others. Blackstone could not go this far since, according to his schematic, the term gentleman always carries a residual index to rank; hence the gentleman could never be confused with 'the rest of the commonalty...*tradesmen, artificers*, and *labourers*'.[20] So can an actor, the most unstable and psychically divided type of person, be a gentleman?

## The actor

Here's (Illustration 7.1) a scene of a well-ordered and correctly functioning world, of domestic and social harmony: two characters – manifestly uncontaminated by occupational particularities and probably a man and wife – casually lean against the balustrade leading up to the entrance of a classical temple. In fact they are in animated conversation, he pointing with his cane towards the bank of the river that flows past, where, just behind the line of sight of the couple a man, not so well-dressed, seems to engaged in patrolling the perimeter of the property. He's there, for sure, in order to intensify the senses of propriety and property articulated by the image; included in order to ensure that we do not mistake this terrain for some public patch of land. It is, of course, the estate of a gentleman who has had himself depicted with his gentlemanly accoutrements: his property, wife and dogs.

*Illustration 7.1* Zoffany, 'David Garrick and his Wife by his Temple to Shakespeare, Hampton', c. 1762, oil on canvas, 102.2 × 134.6 cm. Yale Center for British Art, Paul Mellon Collection, New Haven, Connecticut

In the middle ground we see two boats on the river carrying others who are also most likely engaging in leisurely pursuits, and in the far background we see the Thames flowing away into the distant country. The light falls from the left, lighting up the low cloud and casting a shadow as it falls on the portico to the temple. Everything is marshalled in order to give the impression of cohesion and harmony: the central figure, the man we presume to be the husband, is at one in this setting. He is in his rightful place, a citizen of this world.

But he is also a master. What tells us this so forcefully is the immediate foreground of the image, occupied by an improbably large dog whose length within the relative perspective of the image is almost the height of his master. What are we to make of this? Why has the artist and/or whoever commissioned the painting (we assume the gentleman who is its subject) decided to direct the eye so pointedly towards this gargantuan pet? The answer, I think, lies in the history of the profession of acting.

I shall not rehearse in detail the long evolution of the craft of acting, from strolling player up to the actor-manager of Sheridan's day. For present purposes the immediate context of the late seventeenth century provides a good enough optic, since it is possible to discern from this time a clear alteration in the ways in which actors on the stage were perceived in British culture.[21] Instead of the anonymous individual whose name seldom, if ever, appeared on the playbill the actor was emerging as a personality, an object of public attention and curiosity. In the longer cultural history of acting this change must be weighed against the various ways in which actors had been distinguished from other types of person – their gender and sexuality, for example, has a long and curious history as a topic for suspicion and investigation.[22] But we do not need that longer perspective in order to note the intense scrutiny of the category 'person' which occurred on the restoration stage. Such scrutiny was, of course, most energized and exercised by male person. Indeed the restoration stage can be said to have provided a cultural space in which the topic of masculinity might be discussed, and the category of 'male person' inventoried, contested and in the most general way fabricated. Although it should be stressed that the playhouse was only one site in which such investigation and social and psychic construction took place, it provided, nevertheless, a particularly effective environment for the development of 'dissident' or non-standard accounts of sexuality and gender. The 'fop' for example, was a male type in the wider environs of culture at large, but he was also an obsessive character for dissection in the restoration playhouse.[23] Most importantly for my argument here the category fop provided a set of protocols for male behaviour that tied modes of masculine deportment – the gestural language of the body, public rituals of male–male kissing, extravagant dress – in society at large to the presentation of the male actor on stage.[24] Where before actors had been accorded marginal social status and suspected of being of uncertain sex – which allied them to other masculine marginals such as the libertine, rake or molly – they began to be seen in the same light as male types within the culture at large. Of course such a bond between men in society at large and actors on the stage was not universally perceived as a benefit or to be accepted without comment since the contested space of masculinity produced theoretically at least two (and in practice rather more) alternatives, divided by the standard bifurcation of gender, for masculine typing: the 'man's man', stereotypically masculine in habits and deportment, and the 'effeminate man' who took on the features of the fair sex. This contested cultural space includes the theatre but is not, of course, confined to it, but the social, cultural and most especially legal status of the actor has a leading part to play in this moment of the long history of the subject.

Something of the change in status of the actor around the first half of the eighteenth century can be gleaned from the bald fact that the first substantial autobiography of a stage actor, an *Apology for the Life of Mr Colley Cibber*, was not published until 1740. But even this engaging account of the profession of acting does not allay the fear that actors – since they are continually required to 'personate' others (in Cibber's terms) – are really a different species; they are not like us since, through the frequency with which they have to put on a habit not their own, they become, as it were, infected by the mobility of person, personation.[25] A good actor, in these terms, is someone who makes the audience believe he is someone else, and that must, at a deep psychic level, involve the actor himself believing it too. There is a continuing fear, then, that as Colley Cibber notes in his autobiography, actors in effect have no person.[26] In many ways the painting discussed above can be said to provide an alternative, even an antidote to this view about the personality of those who gain their living from the stage since it is of an actor, perhaps the most frequently depicted person in the entire eighteenth century: David Garrick and his wife.[27]

Now this psychic description must be weighed against the social and political dimension to the craft and profession of acting. And this is where Sheridan's case comes back in. The legal position of the actor was to a large extent dependent on the legislation governing the licensing of theatres. Plays were explicitly produced in a context in which the actors were designated on the title page of published texts as the monarch's 'servants' since the two royal theatres that were licensed to operate were bound by legislation that required each troupe to remain distinct and independent and formally cast the players as, precisely, the servants of the king. When unlicensed playhouses began to open up in the early decades of the eighteenth century the legal position of the actor became the topic for intense scrutiny. Some asserted that actors were bound by the law admitted to the statute book during the reign of Elizabeth. A pamphlet published in 1735 argues, for example, against what it takes to be the illegal proprietors of a playhouse that had begun to operate in Goodman's Fields in 1729. The author of the tract complains:

> But don't these Gentlemen know, as well as *Proprietor* as *Subscribers*, That, by the *Law of the Land* which they plead, all Persons of this *honest* and *lawful* Profession, need the exemption of a Royal Licence, from being rank'd among the most profligate of Mankind, and treated as Rogues, Vagabond, and Sturdy-Beggars?[28]

And our author is at pains to elucidate the precise legislation pertaining in regard to the category 'actor', making the point that even though revisions have occurred to the statute since Elizabeth's reign, such emendations nevertheless leave the status of actors unchanged:

> Tis true, the Act of the 39th of Queen Elizabeth, which makes a Licence, in express Words, requisite to intitle common Players to the above mentioned Exemption, is repealed by the Act of 12 Anne, Stat 2. Cap. 23. But by this very statute, S 1. 'All Fencers, Bear-words, *Common* Players of Interludes,

Minstrels, Jugglers & are included under the Denomination of Rogues and Vagabonds, and punishable accordingly.[29]

If the law exempted licensed players from the disenfranchised 'Vagabond', it remained the case that the common perception of the relationship between the actors and the audience was one of servitude. In effect, up through the mid-century actors in eighteenth-century Britain were the servants of the public who paid to see them act. The convention of the so-called 'benefit' was a performance commanded by a 'Lady or gentleman' who either paid for the seats in the house or guaranteed their sale, and in return selected the play to be performed. While these benefit performances had more than one role in the social and cultural practice of theatre-going – they can in part be understood as a means by which a citizen demonstrated his or her moral upstanding since they could also help raise funds for charities – they nevertheless perpetuated the uneasy situation in which actors and theatre managers were beholden to the socially superior patrons who comprised the audience. This is made explicit in Kelly's suit against Sheridan, reported by a 'Freeeman' to the citizens of Dublin, as is Kelly's enfranchisement in the category 'subject'. The 'Freeman' writes:

so to prove himself [Kelly] a good subject, he indicted the *Player* for hindering the *Gentleman* to ravish Actresses, abuse Actors, and for defending himself from the Outrages offered him.[30]

The relative social status of the different categories of person were embedded in the various practices – certainly to modern eyes unruly practices – engaged in by both actors and paying audience. The command that actors assume a kneeling position, sometimes with the backside exposed, in front of the audience as a symbolic gesture of their submissive status was frequent enough.[31] More disturbing still were the rights exercised by gentlemen in the audience to call for a cessation to the action in order to physically abuse the offending actor. It was precisely this that prompted the actor Charles Macklin to bring a case of assault in 1774. And actresses, of course, were deemed to be the right and lawful prey of any gentleman who took his fancy. Edward Kelly, in fact, was doing what any red-blooded gentleman assumed to be his right and privilege.

Such a position of servitude was clearly demeaning and sat very unhappily next to the burgeoning celebrity of actors during the first half of the century. Many actresses, of course, became known as society beauties while Garrick, the actor who rose through rank to become the equal of dukes and duchesses and intimate with philosophers, writers and politicians, was the prime example of the gentleman who happened to appear on stage. Garrick had, in fact, signalled his aspiration to such status on the very first occasion of his appearing on the London stage in Colley Cibber's version of *Richard III*, the playbill for which reads 'the part of King Richard III by a GENTLEMAN (*who never appear'd on any Stage*)'[32].

By the 1760s, when Zoffany painted Mr and Mrs Garrick in front of their Temple to Shakespeare at their home in Hampton on the river Thames, David Garrick had become renowned not only in his own country but throughout Europe.[33] He had no need to present his *bona fides* as a gentleman. Yet what does this image proclaim in tones as shrill as might be mustered if not that these people, and more importantly this man is certainly not a *mechanic, rogue* or *vagabond*. He is, if nothing else, the master of his comically enlarged pet, the English mastiff whom he named 'Dragon', and who sits obediently awaiting his master's command.[34] But even master and gentleman Garrick had to wait until 1762 before finally removing the audience from the stage at Drury Lane – a move that had been set in motion 15 years before by Sheridan in Dublin, the very actor who had staked his claim to the status of 'gentleman' in front of Lord Chief Justice Marlay in 1747. This is why I wish to claim that 'Sheridan's Case' is a landmark: it made explicit and legible within the enclosure of the legal process the uncertainty surrounding what might be called the 'subject status' of the actor – that is not only the political, social or economic status attaching to actors, but also the conceptual basis for actors claiming full rights as subjects or persons. Furthermore, it brought into the visible space of debate and discussion not only this, the subject status of actors, but also the very instability, permeability and transferability of the type of person characterized as 'gentleman'. This, it was genuinely feared, through dint of what in some circumstances was discerned as the very power and use of the term, precisely its plasticity and profligacy in reference, might lead to a confusion of the vulgar – say common players – with the polite. These fautlines in the term and the conceptual base for the category no less than such fears of miscegenation of rank were certainly evident to the participants in the pamphlet frenzy which broke out around the riot in Smock Alley in January 1747. In my concluding section I shall turn to that media furore and Sheridan's own defence.

## Sheridan's case

Immediately following the incidents in January, Sheridan closed the theatre in order to calm things down; he was unsuccessful in this aim since a barrage of comment in newspapers and occasional pamphlets continued to provide the talk of the town. Two and a half weeks elapsed before Sheridan decided to re-open with a performance of *Oroonoko*, without his own participation on stage. But at the last minute he substituted Cibber's adaptation of Richard III with himself in the title role. The theatre was packed on the evening of 9 Feb and at the end of the first scene a messenger appeared who announced – speaking away from the text – that if the audience wished it, Sheridan, in the role of Richard, was about to appear. At this moment cat-calls went up and on the appearance of Sheridan on stage a group of protesters exclaimed 'Submission, no Play, Acknowledgment, down upon your Knees, come, an Apology, we say.'[35] The story is now taken up by Benjamin Victor in his history of the theatre:

> It was in this Conjuncture that a CITIZEN, then well known for his struggles for Liberty in the City, rose up in the Pit, and asserted the rights of the Audience, and Freedom of the Stage. He expressed his Astonishment and Detestation of Men's bringing their *private* Quarrels with Managers or Players into the Theatre, and Such, he apprehended the present case to be.[36]

At this point the citizen asks the audience to decide the issue: should the play continue or should Sheridan be asked to make his submission? Before they can answer Sheridan addressed the audience in the following manner:

> As I am satisfied the Voice of the Publick can never be wrong, if it be their Opinion that I ought to make a Submission, I am ready to do it.[37]

So, submitting himself to the tribunal of the audience he readily acknowledged his position of subordination. As it turned out either by design or by luck the house was packed with his supporters:

> The whole House, except the Few, unanimously called out 'No Submission'. Notwithstanding which, the Gentlemen still persisted in giving Interruption, and making the same Demand; whereupon he [Sheridan] again addressed them in these Words: 'As I am a Servant of the Publick, I am under a Necessity of obeying their Directions' which was to make *no Submission*. The Play afterwards went on not only without Interruption, but with the greatest Stillness and Attention ever remembered in any Audience in this Kingdom.[38]

Although Sheridan and his supporters prevailed that night, the 'gentlemen', for this is how they were self-styled throughout the pamphlet war, were not yet done with their mischief. Two nights later on Wednesday 11 February the deferred benefit night for the Hospital for Incurables was presented – the play being Rowe's *The Fair Penitent*. As Sheridan entered the stage a group of armed men rose from the pit and ordered him off. The audience broke into a riot, hissing, clapping and shouting at which point Sheridan retired from the stage. Disputes then broke out between 'the gentlemen' and Sheridan's supporters and unrest spilt over to the next morning. The riot was serious enough to cause shopkeepers to close their shops along with the enforced closure, once again, of the theatres. Throughout the period from the first incident in January up to the court hearing on 19 February the local press was full of excited accounts, accusations and counter-accusations which construct a kind of palimpsest of what actually happened. But it is not the kaleidoscope of the history of the event that I want to draw attention to; in conclusion I wish to press the legal ramifications of Sheridan's case.

We can begin by recalling the precise context in which the initial disturbance took place. Sheridan was on stage on the evening of 19 January acting the lead role in Vanbrugh's *Aesop*, a play about a servant who is characterized throughout as the 'most deformed monster that copulation ever produced', precisely as anything but a gentleman. And the second part of this drama is quite explicitly about the relationships of power, of subordination and mastery, authority and licence that persisted in the theatre of the day. It begins:

> *Enter* Players
> Well, good People, who are all you?
> *Omnes.* Sir, we are Players
> *Aes.* Players? What Players?
> *Play.* Why, Sir, we are Stage-Players,
> That's our Calling:
> Tho' we play upon other things too; some of us play
> Upon the Fiddle; some play upon the Flute;
> We play upon one another, we play upon the Town,
> And we play upon the Patentees
> *Aes.* Patentees! Prithee, what are they?
> *Play.* Why, they are, Sir – Sir, they are – I Cod I don't know
> What they are – Fish or Flesh – Masters or Servants
> – Sometimes one – sometimes t'other, I think –
> Just as we are in the Mood
> *Aes.* Why, I thought they had a lawful Authority over you.
> *Play.* Lawful Authority, Sir – Sir, we are freeborn Englishmen,
> We care not for Law nor Authority neither,
> When we are out of Humour.[39]

We do not know if Mr Kelly made his lunge onto the stage at precisely this point in the performance, but in the documents surrounding the affair it is the presumption of the actor to the standard rights of any person that was the immediate cause of the disturbance. As Benjamin Victor wrote: 'I could not meet with a parallel to the case of *Sheridan*, which was no less than a violent dispute about the HONOUR of an *actor*.'[40] Sheridan himself couches his defence in the same terms:

> If the *Publick* is of Opinion, that *Mr Sheridan* ought to have submitted to such Treatment, and that by being on the Stage he is depriv'd of the *common Privileges of Man, they are Terms too hard for him to submit to, nor should any Consideration upon Earth prevail upon him to appear again on such Conditions.*[41]

And the reason for this is that, unlike the King's servants, Sheridan pleads a prior status, that of 'gentleman'.

Much ironic fun is made by Sheridan's supporters of the fact that Kelly's faction styled themselves the 'gentlemen' – as we have already seen the term was pliable enough to be used in both positive and negative ways. But it is also very clear that Sheridan himself wishes to be seen as, by birth, someone above the rank of the mere mechanic and certainly not a vagabond or slave. As his friend Victor states in a letter to *Faulkener's Journal* defending the actor:

> He is the son of the late reverend *Doctor Sheridan*, a gentleman that was well known in this kingdom. This, his son, was sent early in life, to Westminster School, and when fitted for university, was entered of this college, and class-fellow with most of the young nobility and gentry of Ireland, and took his degree there of bachelor of arts. Well then, he was born and has had the education of a *gentleman*.[42]

And Sheridan himself states that 'I am by Birth and Inclination a Gentleman'.[43] So it should come as little surprise that in court his line of defence is precisely over his status as a person.[44]

In *Kelly* v. *Sheridan*, the first case heard on 19 February 1747, the plaintiff attempted to indict Sheridan for 'hindering the Gentleman to ravish Actresses, abuse Actors, and for defending himself from the oranges offered him'.[45] And, in one of the pamphlets written by a 'Freeman', that alleged assault was 'a crime of which no fashionable Gentleman is ashamed'.[46] The case hung on whether the law in respect of the rights of persons reached into the environs of the theatre, and, as it were, once there if the actor, here the accused Sheridan, had rights in his person. Arguing against this Kelly's supporters claimed that : 'It is the incontestable Right of the bulk of an Audience to be entertained in what manner and by whom they please.'[47] The jury thought otherwise and found against the plaintiff before immediately hearing the subsequent case, *Sheridan* v. *Kelly*.

It began with Kelly's attorney sneeringly announcing to the court while looking in the plaintiff's direction: 'I have often seen a Gentleman Soldier, and a Gentleman tailor; but I have never seen a Gentleman Player'.[48] Sheridan, who had seen fit to dress for his day in court, immediately rose to his feet and replied: 'Sir, I hope you see one now'. But Sheridan's defence was not simply to claim that he was a person like any other. He did, of course, claim just this and he did so in terms which activate another set of arguments and beliefs, those upholding the notion of nation and the superiority of Britain. As he states in his *Full Vindication*:

> The only Privilege *Mr Sheridan* requires in his Publick Capacity is, provided that he offers no Insult to any Body, he should not be insulted. That is a

Right which, it is to be hoped, the meanest Subject of the King of *Great-Britain* enjoys.[49]

This immediately raises another set of issues, those that bear upon the political relations between Ireland and the English mainland. Dublin was, of course, under the rule of the monarch of Britain even if the Lord Chamberlain's office had no power of censorship over the Dublin stage. For Sheridan and his supporters British rule was something to be welcomed since it was held that the barbaric tribes of the native Irish were forced into more civilized behaviour. This is why so much is made of Sheridan's rights under the laws of Britain and why, according to his supporters, the supposed 'gentlemen' who had caused the riot were in danger of returning Ireland to its vulgar and uncivilized past. As the author of the *Letter from the Free Citizen* states:

> I must lay down the Proposition, which no *Freeman* or the *Protestant* can deny, To wit that *our State knows no Member who has any Power or Right to tyranize over or abuse the Person or Property of another, and that none, except Children or Apprentices, which are supposed under Age, are obliged to submit to Correction or Castigation, from any Man whatever.*[50]

So, having laid out the legal basis for the protection of person, the argument turns the screw of nationalism:

> If this be not true, our *Gentlemen* must confess themselves but a better kind of Slaves. For they must own some Superior to them, and these must allow others, and thus the Tyranny must somewhere Center in a Point. This is such Slavery as none but barefaced Enemies to our Establishment can assert. To oppose this and every other System of Tyranny, is the distinguishing Mark of *Britons*, and of none more than of us their Progeny.[51]

While Sheridan himself played the chauvinist card in his 1758 account of the reformation of the Irish theatre he claimed to have brought about it is the question of person that I wish to conclude with. In his later self-promotion he claims to have removed the theatre from 'the soil of Slavery':

> where for years it flourished. He had established the only FREE Stage ever remembered in these Kingdoms. Whilst it remained so; whilst the Actors were considered as on a common footing with the rest of the Subjects of the King of *Great-Britain*, he did not think himself dishonoured by his Station.[52]

But 11 years earlier he had not been quite so sure of his rights and in his defence in front of justice Marlay he tried another, more unusual tack.

Many of the quasi-legal commentaries in the publications surrounding the trial sought to ascertain whether or not Sheridan had 'degraded' his person, rescinded his rights as person when he turned actor.[53] And, having taken this step, whether it was possible to 'reassume the gentleman' as one of the pamphlets put it.[54] As I have indicated, the real kernel of the debate turned over the category 'gentleman' and whether or not an actor could be so considered.[55] Sheridan's statement to the court raised a far more interesting spectre *vis-à-vis* the constitution of the subject, namely the notion that person could, in some sense, be transferable and the subject divided.

It is not inconsequential in this regard that Sheridan referred to himself in the third person in all his published accounts of the incident from the *Full Vindication* on. And this strange locution helped break the continuity between selves, between the actor on stage and the person, subject of the King who appeared in the courtroom. There, speaking in the impersonal third person he stated that: Mr Sheridan was by birth and education a gentleman and that he has not degraded himself by any base behaviour or servile employment. He then goes on to clarify the fact that he is not a player since he had taken no salary to perform, always having been a director of the theatre and, therefore, had it as his option to perform or not. And then, in a marvellous turn he clinches his case by stating: 'tho' the Profession of an Actor, does not entitle a man to the Name of a Gentleman, yet neither can it take it from him if he had it before'.

So it turns out that the actor, that uncertain and dangerously promiscuous person, is in fact a precursor of the divided subject. Sheridan both is and is not a gentleman – as even his opponents admitted in their declaration that 'They bear no Enmity to Mr Sh—n, but to the Player.'[56] And of course there was no better theatre for the display of such an amalgam of persons as the courtroom. Perhaps nothing better could have prepared this Irish actor for his subsequent career as the reformer of British education and the elocutionary Svengali who enabled the rude and uncultivated to enter into the ranks of the polite through the expedient of their manner of speaking. Nation and state, culture and identity, law and society are all implicated in 'Sheridan's Case' which participated in the ongoing definition and containment of 'person'.

## Notes

1  See William W. Appleton, *Charles Macklin: An Actor's Life* (Cambridge, MA: Harvard University Press, 1960).
2  He was the author of, among other works, *British Education; or, The Source of the Disorders of Great Britain* (London, 1756); *A Course of Lectures on Elocution* (London, 1762); *Lectures on the Art of Reading*, 2 vols (London, 1775) and *A Complete Dictionary of the English Language* (London, 1789).
3  The exception here is Esther K. Sheldon, *Thomas Sheridan of Smock-Alley* (Princeton: Princeton University Press, 1967) to which the current essay is much indebted.
4  On eighteenth-century theatre see Allardyce Nicoll, *The Garrick Stage: Theatre and Audience in the Eighteenth Century* (Manchester: Manchester University Press, 1980);

H.W. Pedicord, *The Theatrical Public in the Time of Garrick* (New York: King's Crown Press, 1954); J.J. Lynds, *Box, Pit and Gallery* (Berkeley, CA: University of California Press, 1953); C.J.L Price, *Theatre in the Age of Garrick* (Oxford: Blackwell, 1973).

5   Thomas Sheridan, *An Humble Appeal to the Publick, together with some considerations on the present critical and dangerous State of the Stage in Ireland* (Dublin, 1758), p. 15.

6   See Thomas Sheridan, *An Humble Appeal to the Publick, together with some considerations on the present critical and dangerous State of the Stage in Ireland* (Dublin, 1758), pp. 33–4.

7   It is worth recalling that for the period in question the rights of person are quite explicitly framed or focused through the exemplary subject, the monarch. In effect rights are transferred from the sovereign to his or her subjects, or to put it another way, persons only have rights in so far as they are subjects of and for the sovereign. Within the period the clearest articulation of this legal doctrine is to be found in Blackstone's *Commentaries on the Laws of England*, 4 vols (London, 1765–69), the first volume of which is devoted to the rights of persons.

8   This affidavit appears in the *Dublin Journal*, 20–24 January 1747.

9   *Ibid.*

10  *An Humble Address to the Ladies of the City of Dublin. By a Plebeian.* (Dublin, 1747), p. 4.

11  Benjamin Victor, *Letters*, 3 vols (London, 1776), I, p. 127.

12  Hippolyte Taine, *Notes on England* (London: Thomson & Hudson, 1957), p. 144.

13  Daniel Befer, *The Complete English Gentleman*, ed. Karl Bulbring (London: David Nutt, 1890), p. 13.

14  John Barrell, *English Literature in History 1730–80: An Equal, Wide Survey* (London: Hutchinson, 1983), p. 209.

15  Barrell, *An Equal, Wide Survey*, pp. 34; 35.

16  *Ibid.*, p. 179.

17  Sir William Blackstone, *Commentaries on the Laws of England*, 4 vols (London, 1765–69), I, p. 394.

18  *Ibid.*, p. 384.

19  *Ibid.*, p. 393.

20  *Ibid.*, p. 394.

21  For a good account see the essays in Robert D. Hume, *The London Theatre World 1660–1800* (Carbondale, IL: University of Illinois Press, 1980).

22  There is now a significant bibliography on gender in the period. For a good survey see Michele Cohen, *Fashioning Masculinity: National Identity and Language in the Eighteenth Century* (London: Routledge, 1996). The question of gender and theatre in the period was opened up by Christina Straub, *Sexual Suspects: Eighteenth-Century Players and Sexual Ideology* (Princeton, NJ: Princeton University Press, 1992); see also Julia Epstein and Kristina Straub, eds, *Body Guards: The Cultural Politics of Gender Ambiguity* (London: Routledge, 1991). For an account of masculinity in relation to the visual arts see John Barrell, 'The Dangerous Goddess: Masculinity, Prestige and the Aesthetic in Early Eighteenth-Century Britain', in John Barrell, *The Birth of Pandora and the Division of Knowledge* (London: Macmillan, 1992); see also my *The Education of the Eye: Painting, Landscape and Architecture in Eighteenth-Century Britain* (Stanford, CA: Stanford University Press, 2003).

23  See Kristina Straub, *Sexual Suspects*, esp. ch. 3.

24  For a helpful guide through the complexities of this social type see Susan Staves, 'A Few Kind Words for the Fop', *Studies in English Literature*, 22 (1982) pp. 413–28.

25 A rather more strenuous description puts it in the following manner: 'Play-actors are the most profligate wretches, and the vilest vermine, that hell ever vomited out... they are the filth and garbage of the earth, the scum and stain of human nature, the excrements and refuse of all mankind, the pests and plagues of human society, the debauchers of mans minds and morals', *The Players Scourge* (London, 1757), p. 2. As Straub argues the basis for this suspicion is deeply connected to the sexual ambiguity of actors, a point she makes in respect of Cibber whose 'sexuality and gender neither exactly "fit" with nor oppose a masculinity defined as oppositional to the "femininity" of women and effeminate males', *Sexual Suspects*, p. 25.

26 See Colley Cibber, *An Apology for the Life of Colley Cibber*, ed. B.R.S. Fone (Ann Arbor, MI: University of Michigan Press, 1968), p. 6.

27 It would be difficult to ascertain the number of engravings in circulation of particular paintings, and it seems likely that if this form of the image was taken into account there would be other contenders – the royal family for example – for the most frequently depicted person. But it seems equally unlikely that any other individual was represented in a first state – painted in whatever media or sculpted – as often as Garrick. Among the artists who produced portraits, a large number of which were, of course, of the actor in character are: Batoni, Carmontelle, Dance, de Loutherbourg, Gainsborough, Hayman, Hogarth, Hone, Kaufman, Lemoine (a bust), Nollekens (a bust), Reynolds, Romney, West, Wilson and Zoffany. The last so many times it almost seems as if Garrick became that artist's muse.

28 *A Seasonable Examination of the Pleas and Pretension of the Proprietors of and Subscribers to PlayHouses erected in defiance of the Royal Licence* (London, 1735), p. 6.

29 *A Seasonable Examination*, p. 7.

30 *A Second Letter to the Free Citizens of Dublin* (Dublin, 1747), p. 6.

31 See Kristina Straub, *Sexual Suspects*, p. 72.

32 Playbill 19 October 1741.

33 The most thorough biography of the actor is Ian McIntyre, *Garrick* (London: Allen Lane, 1999).

34 The dog made occasional appearances at Drury Lane, which only intensifies the ennoblement of the Garricks in this image; see McIntyre, caption to plate 20.

35 *An Apology for Mr Sheridan*, newspaper cutting, n.d. The various reports are once again inconsistent on this point. Benjamin Victor has the mob shouting 'Submission, submission, off, off, off', *The History of the Theatres of London and Dublin*, 2 vols (London, 1761), I, p. 113.

36 Victor, *History of the Theatres*, I, pp. 113–4.

37 *A Full Vindication of the Conduct of the Manager of the Theatre Royal, written by Himself* (Dublin, 1747), p. 8.

38 *Ibid.*, pp. 8–9.

39 John Vanbrugh, *Aesop, part II*, in Bonamy Dobree and Geoffrey Webb, eds, *The Complete Works of Sir John Vanbrugh*, 4 vols (London, 1927), p. 67.

40 Benjamin Victor, *Letters*, 3 vols (London, 1776), I, p. 126.

41 *A Full Vindication of the Conduct of the Manager of the Theatre Royal, written by Himself* (Dublin, 1747), p. 6.

42 Victor, *Letters*, I, pp. 129–30.

43 *Mr Sh—n's Apology to the Town; with the Reasons which unfortunately induced him to his late Misconduct* (Dublin, 1754), p. 4.

44 Sheridan was, in fact, lucky to be admitted *in camera* – an actor in England, Arthur Murphy, was refused admission to the middle temple on the ground that

he was an actor. See Howard Hunter Dunbar, *The Dramatic Career of Arthur Murphy* (New York: Oxford University Press, 1946), p. 36.

45  *A Second Letter to the Free Citizens of Dublin* (Dublin, 1747), p. 6.

46  *Ibid.*

47  *An Humble Address to the Ladies of the City of Dublin. By a Plebeian* (Dublin, 1747), p. 12.

48  Benjamin Victor, *The History of the Theatres of London and Dublin*, 2 vols (London, 1761), I, p. 126.

49  *A Full Vindication of the conduct of the Manager of the Theatre Royal, written by Himself* (Dublin, 1747), p. 7.

50  *A Letter to the Free Citizens of Dublin*, 4th edn (Dublin, 1747), pp. 2–3.

51  *Ibid.*, p. 3. The trope of comparing actors to slaves seems to have been very commonly invoked through the 1740s; see on this Kristina Straub, *Sexual Suspects*, p. 164.

52  Thomas Sheridan, *An Humble Appeal to the Publick, together with some considerations on the present critical and dangerous State of the Stage in Ireland* (Dublin, 1758), p. 33.

53  John Barrell notes a similar anxiety over 'degrading' in relation to Smollet's Roderick Random. See *An Equal, Wide Survey*, p. 203.

54  *A Serious Enquiry into the Causes of the Present disorders in the City* (Dublin, 1747), p. 6.

55  See *An Apology for Mr Sheridan, by a Sch—r* (Dublin, 1746–47): '. . . this whole Affair turn'd and was manag'd [on] whether a Player can be a Gentleman', p. 1.

56  *An Humble Address to the Ladies of the City of Dublin, by a Plebeian* (Dublin, 1747), p. 12.

# 8

# Suspicious Minds: Spies and Surveillance in Charlotte Smith's Novels of the 1790s

*Harriet Guest**

In his influential essay of 1992 on 'Visualising the Division of Labour', John Barrell argued that the 'totalising discourse' of the division of labour articulates a 'subject which defines its own partiality even as it denies it'. The subject must claim for itself a viewpoint from which it can grasp the coherence of the social whole; a coherence invisible to all those pursuing their different occupations within society by virtue of the specialization their occupations demand. But the subject must also acknowledge its own view as partial, as the interested view made available by its peculiar occupation within the division of labour. It must therefore always admit the validity or authority of the competing discourses articulated from other subject positions, other occupational viewpoints. The discourse of the division of labour must define itself as both more than, and just one of, the 'hubbub of voices, which together produce the representation of a society irretrievably atomised and dispersed.'[1]

Since 1992, Barrell's work has centred on the 1790s. One strand of his work on the decade, developed in *Imagining the King's Death*, and elaborated most recently in his essay on 'Coffee-House Politicians', has explored the way changes in the nature of the categories of the 'public' and the 'private' which had evolved throughout the century were exposed and thrown into relief by political turmoil. In *Imagining* he showed how the introduction of the language of sentiment into political discourse 'necessarily had the effect

* This essay was first written for a conference on 'Spies and Surveillance' organized by Ian McCalman and John Barrell at the Humanities Research Centre, ANU, Canberra, and has benefited from the comments of audiences there and at the University of Chicago, as well as at the Centre for Eighteenth Century Studies at the University of York. I am particularly grateful to my colleague, James Watt, for his acute and helpful comments.

of blurring the distinction between public and private, and representing the ties which bound the nation and state as the affective ties which bound the family'. The language of sentiment, he concludes, effected 'the appropriation of the public by the private'.[2] In 'Coffee-House Politicians', Barrell returns to the theme of suspicious imaginings of plots and conspiracies on one hand, and spies and informers on the other, as the key note of the mid-1790s. The Loyalist Associations established in 1792–93 encouraged unofficial as well as paid spies to inform on what they took to be seditious conversations held in the privacy of the coffee house or the home. Liberal men, appalled by the curtailment of private freedom of speech, defended the right by advancing definitions of privacy in a range of competing discourses of place, class and gender difference. Barrell's persuasive account of differently construed privacies, defined through social exclusions and distinctions, brings into focus some of the cacophony of discourses involved in his earlier account of the representation of modern society as fragmented and dispersed.[3] In this essay, I use Charlotte Smith's novels of the 1790s to explore some of the themes raised by Barrell's work. Smith was undoubtedly one of the most politically alert novelists of the decade, and her novels are marked I suggest by their attention to the effects of a political culture of suspicion and surveillance on private life, which they represent as a symptom of the social atomization characteristic of modernity.

\*     \*     \*

Vicesimus Knox's analysis of the *Spirit of Despotism* pervading British society in the mid-1790s is based in the axiom that 'Public corruption must produce private'. He argues that the despotic spirit dominating 'the conduct of state affairs' will inevitably 'display itself in every part of domestic life ... from the palace of St. James's and the levee in Downing-street, to the rural mansion in the distant province – to the convivial table – to the fire-side – to the stable, and to the dog-kennel'. Alluding to the recent trials for treason and sedition, he argues that the use of spies and informers is an unmistakeable sign of public corruption, which destroys 'at once the confidential comforts, and the most valuable virtues of private life'. Urging the 'honest, independent, and thinking part of the community' to 'stem the torrent of corruption', he encourages them to shun 'as pestilences' not only paid agents of government, but '*every description of spies and informers, whether poor or rich, mercenary or volunteer*'. The manners of the 'friends of arbitrary power', Knox claims, are 'disgusting in private life', and 'are no less offensive to humanity, and injurious to all the sweet equality of social intercourse, than they are to public liberty'. Knox implies that men who favour despotic politics will extend their dominion into social and domestic life, and he points to a sexual politics interwoven with the exercise of arbitrary power in government. If unjust government infects every part of domestic life, it is, Knox insists, because it 'debases the morals, and injures the happiness, while it infringes on the civil rights of the people', driving the people to 'a mischievous activity in trifles' – to behaviour which is strongly reminiscent of what middle-class women are criticized for by Wollstonecraft, Hays and Charlotte Smith.[4]

Knox's energetic attack on despotism expresses the outrage of liberal opinion, and articulates clearly the perceived threat to areas of private life which are not understood to be directly involved in political controversy. He is not concerned to argue that private, domestic life should be fenced off and preserved from the contaminating influence of politics. He suggests, indeed, that the liberal education of the people to understand the principles of liberty and constitutional government is the most effective means of guaranteeing the political health of the nation. But he argues forcibly that corruption in high politics, of which the use of spies and informers is a clear sign, seeps irresistibly into the fabric of private life, rotting and perverting relations between men and women. Knox's account of the evils of despotism mediates between the opinions of those who see spies and informers as political agents, and those who represent surveillance as the independent activity of private individuals; views which seem broadly characteristic of the differences between the early and late 1790s, as well as between divergent political opinions.

William Godwin, for example, writes, in his Letters of Mucius to the *Morning Chronicle* in February 1793, in defence of the principles of 'civil and personal liberty' central to the British Constitution, which are now violated by the 'most crying evil of a despotic Government' – 'spies and informers'.[5] He focuses on the political role of spies and informers, citing the recent trials for sedition. For Knox, their definition is a little more uncertain and elastic – they may be unpaid, perhaps they may not even be knowingly acting as political agents, though they are the tools of despotism. In Godwin's *Caleb Williams* (1794), which Charlotte Smith much admired, spying and covert surveillance are of course pervasive, but their political significance is complex, most obviously because of the issue of class difference to which Barrell's recent article draws attention.[6] But by the late 1790s, spying and surveillance have become, in some accounts at least, an accepted if not necessarily welcome part of the social fabric, an important means of social regulation and control. In *Northanger Abbey* (which was probably written in 1798–99), to take a familiar example (the passage supplies the epigraph to Ian McEwen's *Atonement*, in which spying is the form of guilty conservative resistance to the destabilization of class differences in twentieth-century Britain), Henry Tilney disabuses Catherine Morland of her 'dreadful ... suspicions' about his father by asking her if 'such atrocities ... Could ... be perpetrated without being known, in a country like this, where social and literary intercourse is on such a footing; where every man is surrounded by a neighbourhood of voluntary spies, and where roads and newspapers lay every thing open?'[7] He also, of course, mocks the possibility that there might be a connection between gothic fantasy and any real political situation, insistently depoliticizing the novel even though the gothic genre in particular was so frequently the vehicle of political debate in the 1790s. For Austen's hero, spies are necessary to the constitution of modern British society as a kind of benevolent neighbourhood-watch scheme, policed not by any government or its agents but by a network of neighbours whose surveillance is reassuring and protective.

Charlotte Smith's major novels of the 1790s are riddled with suspicions (sometimes groundless) of spies and informers, covert observers and reporters on the actions of others. They reflect the national concern with espionage and surveillance that became prevalent after the onset of war with France, and which may have touched on Smith's personal life as a result of her political sympathies and personal connections. In November 1792, the British Club in Paris toasted Smith, Helen Maria Williams and Anna Barbauld as 'lady defenders of the Revolution';[8] Thomas Erskine, the great liberal advocate, befriended her and helped her with her legal difficulties; she was involved in the social circle of radical sympathisers that centred on Brighton, and seems to have provided Wordsworth with introductions to political leaders in Paris in late 1791.[9] But Smith's spies are by no means always political agents, tools of governments or of the law; they are also servants, gossips and scandal-mongers. Their prevalence is a sign of the extent to which notions of spying and surveillance are understood to have become a part of the fabric of a complex society in which actions are no longer transparent, in which suspicion and misrepresentation are perceived to be necessary to social interaction, or its evasion. They function as indices of the uncertainty with which society knows itself, or individuals see or understand the behaviour of one another; and the ubiquity of spies, or suspicions of spies, figures a degree of social fragmentation, disaffection and alienation, which only those perceived to be involved in intense domestic intimacies or secret and probably malevolent conspiracies seem able to counteract – though their conspiracies and intimacies reinforce the isolation of those they exclude. Smith's society of spies and gossips perhaps suggests an alternative account of public life, not founded in candour or the free exchange of ideas between privileged equals, but woven out of suspicious looks and stolen glances, out of the interconnections generated by increased mobility, and those fleeting peeps at the world through the loopholes of retreat that are afforded by newspapers and unreliable second-hand reports.

Surveillance, I suggest, is a characteristic of what is understood as a social organization burgeoning in complexity, which can no longer be imagined as capable of being grasped or perceived from a single identifiable viewpoint, or surveyed as a unified prospect – a characteristic, then, of those changes in the means of acquiring social information that can be clustered together in narratives on the incipient modernity of Britain in the second half of the eighteenth century. Spies, and suspicions of spies, in some general sense may be understood as a response to what T.J. Clark identifies as the fundamental 'blindness of modernity'. Alluding to Adam Smith, Clark explains that 'the great fact' of modernity 'is the hiddenness of the "hidden hand"; or rather the visibility of that hiddenness' – a visibility that spies and the need for surveillance underline.[10] For the perceived ubiquity of espionage suggests that those who wish to understand or control modern society can only gain necessary information about it indirectly, from secretive observers involved in its contingency. War with France, and the suspicion that British society is permeated with pestilential cells and networks of covert agents in the mid-1790s, provide a focus for fears of the pathological symptoms of modernity; give an edge and impetus to anxieties about the progressive destabilization of the social order that is peculiar to the decade, but has its roots in diverse responses to social or cultural change in the preceding half-century.

The role of spies and surveillance in Smith's novels can to some extent be mapped against the trajectory of rapidly heightened political awareness followed by progressive domestication marked by Godwin, Knox and Austen. In *Desmond* and *The Old Manor House* (published in 1792 and 1793 respectively), spying, or, to put it more neutrally, covert watching seems to have little political resonance. In *Desmond*, when the heroine, Geraldine, retreats with her children to the Wye valley, fleeing from her abusive husband, the hero secures lodgings which allow him to overlook her house, assuring his correspondent that 'this satisfaction, and that of witnessing her real situation (which I hoped to do without her knowing I was near her), were the only gratifications I proposed to myself: for many days I enjoyed it, and was content'.[11] He soon finds, however, 'that if I would really satisfy myself with the certain view of Geraldine, I must seek some spot, where, from its elevation, I could, by means of a small pocket telescope, have an uninterrupted view' (*D*, p. 231), and positions himself on a nearby hill, where 'the hand of time, rather than the art of man, has twisted [tree roots] into a sort of grotesque, rustic chair'(*D*, p. 222). As a result of this secretive manoeuvring, Desmond is able to spring to Geraldine's aid when her asylum is threatened with violation by the wicked French aristocrat to whom her husband has sold her. The detailed account of the elaborate means by which the hero achieves his scopic gratification suggests that there may be something twisted about it, but if he does emerge as a rather grotesque stalker, this is represented as the effect of the exigencies of his situation, and indeed of his delicacy in handling his passion for a married woman, which is rendered innocent and pastoral by the complicity of the landscape in offering him a comfortable natural seat, and by contrast with the intentions of the villainous aristocrat. As Nicola Watson points out, Geraldine 'is explicitly associated with the "Frenchness" of the Revolution', and her pathetic situation is compared with that of the Parisian mob.[12] The sexual politics of the novel are bound up with its analysis of the revolution. Perhaps Desmond's desirous but distanced surveillance is analogous to his restrained and largely indirect support for the revolution, but the potential for comparison is handled with delicacy, and in this incident the emphasis on the ingenuous idealism of his passion effectively conceals that possibility.[13]

In *The Old Manor House*, Vivien Jones has argued that 'we register [the heroine] Monimia's symbolic status through [the hero] Orlando's dominant point of view; she is constructed as the object of his (our) gaze'. Jones explains that 'the first half of the novel is obsessively concerned with the secret midnight visits which Orlando makes ... to Monimia's "turret"'', in the course of which Jones argues that Monimia's status as the object of the masculine gaze 'gives way ... to a fantasy of penetration'.[14] But if Orlando's gaze does, in Jones's terms, objectify the heroine, his secret and illicit access to her is nevertheless represented as innocent, polite even, in contrast to the dangers of less-exclusive visibility to which Monimia is exposed after Orlando's brother has caught sight of her. Smith writes that Orlando:

> foresaw that the beauty of Monimia, which had hitherto been quite unobserved, would now become the topic of common conversation ... Hitherto Monimia had seemed a beautiful and unique gem, of which none but himself had discovered the concealment, or knew the value. He had visited it with fonder idolatry, from alone possessing the knowledge where it was hid. But now half his happiness seemed to be destroyed, since his treasure was discovered.[15]

Orlando's gem seems to diminish in value, to lose its objectified definition and impregnability, when other eyes discover it. But the narrative constructs an elaborate set of circumstances to confirm the uniqueness and benevolence of his privileged gaze. During a secret meeting of the lovers in the darkened chapel of the house, Monimia is glimpsed by a smuggler, an 'unprincipled ruffian' who has been granted illicit access to the cellar by the greedy and lascivious butler, to whom he reports. But the butler mistakes the smuggler's account of the heroine for a description of the maidservant who is the object of his own concupiscence. Only the hero can distinguish the gem-like Monimia from the worthless maid, whose increasingly scandalous career, ending in prostitution on the streets of London, attracts the 'common conversation' deflected from Orlando's hidden treasure.

In these novels, then, surveillance is involved in sexual politics of a kind familiar from the gothic novels of the period: the heroines are threatened by villainous older men whose behaviour is associated with the profligacy of the feudal and anti-modern, and whose looks are predatory and licentious; whereas the desires of the enlightened heroes are marked by respectful self-restraint, and their surveillance is distanced and protective. In Smith's major novels after 1793 – and I have in mind *The Banished Man* (1794), *Marchmont* (1796), and *The Young Philosopher* (1798) – the role of surveillance is more complex, bound up with corruption in government and its means of social regulation, and yet directly associated with the difficulties of the novelist's private life. I don't want here to offer an extensive biographical narrative: Smith's life story has been ably documented by Florence Hilbish and Lorraine Fletcher.[16] I want rather to draw out some of the points which I think are helpful to an understanding of the treatment of spies and informers in the novels. For one of the striking features of Smith's work is the way that the intermeshing of national political issues with private life, which is of course the stock in trade of so many of the novels of the 1790s, is in her case also involved in her representation of herself as a writer who needs to appeal to mainstream opinion.

Smith is explicit about her need to write for money, and to conform to the requirements of booksellers who, she suggests, regard even liberal whiggish sentiments as incompatible with commercial success. She repeatedly reminds her readers that she writes under the booksellers' surveillance, that her novels are subject to censorship by the demands of the marketplace. On the one hand, Smith's politics do clearly change in the course of the decade. Like other liberal whigs, Smith's enthusiasm for the possibilities of revolutionary change in France shifts towards an emphasis on the need for political, legal and social reform in Britain in order for the country to live up to its own professed ideals and self-image. Her novels of the later 1790s turn from the national events she had addressed in *Desmond*, *The Old Manor House* and *The Banished Man*, towards the exploration of the way private life is disfigured by forms of surveillance and persecution that mark the pervasive influence of public corruption. On the other hand, Smith's personal experiences and private circumstances clearly inform this shift. As the first reviewers and readers of her novels noted, with varying degrees of sympathy or hostility, Smith never seemed to feel it necessary to exclude her own experiences, the calamities and injustices of her private life, from her novels. The forms of oppression with which her novels are, with increasing insistence, concerned, are linked directly and sometimes explicitly with her struggles to secure for her children the inheritance perplexed by the complications of her father-in-law's will. Lawyers and officers of the law, attorneys and their clerks, figure repeatedly in her fiction as the evil agents of persecution and oppression in situations that parallel her own. And she rarely misses an occasion to remind her readers of her dire financial position. In William Cowper's frequently cited description of her (borrowed of course from Webster), she wrote like a galley slave chained to her oar – though he also emphasized that she wrote with remarkable speed and correctness. Mary Hays, in her life of Smith, suggests the pride she took in the recognition that 'Her industry alone enabled her ... to support her family', and remarks that 'while she saw [her children] healthy and happy, her application to her desk was a matter of delight rather than of complaint'. But Hays acknowledges that as a result of the way Smith had to work 'her health began to suffer considerably.'[17]

What Smith emphasizes, however, in her fictional portraits of authors writing for money, are the constraints of conforming to the demands of publishers and readers. The publication of *Desmond* (1792) endangered what security or success she had achieved as a bankable author. Elizabeth Montagu, for example, wrote of it that: 'I am sorry to hear Mrs Charlotte Smiths [*sic*] Novel is so wildly Democratical. I have not read it, but find it offends all sober people. I am more mortified at this, as it affects her character than if it related merely to her Genius.'[18] Smith's character as a woman of acute sensibility, which was so important to the success of her poetry in particular – to the business of selling her sorrows which Jacqueline Labbe has discussed[19] – is damaged by the revolutionary enthusiasm and sexual politics of the novel. Cowper protested that he could see nothing in her politics with which he could disagree, and described the novel as a fine defence of the British constitution. Smith herself, in her Preface to *The Banished Man*, argued that though when she wrote *Desmond* she had been 'in an error' in her support for the revolution, she still believed that 'no native of England could help *then* rejoicing at the probability there was that the French nation would obtain, with very little bloodshed, that degree of freedom which we have been taught to value so highly'.[20] Like Cowper, perhaps, she implies that the politics of the novel proceed naturally and inevitably from the love of freedom as the birthright of the English nation. In a note she protests that her 'former work' has celebrated 'the constitution of England', which has 'proved itself to be the most calculated for general happiness' (*BM*, 1, pp. 94n, pp. 93–4).

In *The Banished Man*, however, the woman who heroically supports her family by her writing receives a letter from her bookseller or printer in which he tells her that he has changed the title of an ode to Liberty included in her novel because he has 'promis'd the trade that there shall be no liberty at all in the present work, without which asshurance they would not have delt for the same' (*BM* 2, p. 231).[21] The hero of Smith's novel *Marchmont* (1796), unjustly imprisoned for debt, contemplates earning some money by writing. He considers, however, 'that the principal dealers in literary traffic would hesitate at purchasing the work of a prisoner who was likely ... to vent in his writing some part of the discontent that imprisonment is very apt to engender'. Booksellers will be alarmed by any expression of discontent, he explains, because 'The passage from discontent to murmurs against ... oppression ... is very short; and murmurs may savour of seditious notions, and seditious notions might carry a man nobody knew whither.' He concludes by asking, 'What rich and substantial vender [*sic*] would hazard anything like this in these times?'[22] Marchmont's comments clearly signal the permeability of the distinction between private life and its discontents, and the discourses of public politics, which is apparent to the wary gaze of booksellers, alarmed that murmurs of personal unhappiness may easily be mistaken for, or indeed can quickly become, sedition. These incidents suggest that writers in positions like Smith's own, who are by necessity sensitive to their commercial position, are continually aware of the cautious surveillance of booksellers and printers alert to any possibility of political controversy in their work; and indeed that awareness marks the caution with which, in both of these incidents, she skirts around the question of whether murmurs of discontent or mentions of liberty in her writing are in fact politically charged, or whether the trade merely imagines that they are. Smith manages to distance her writing from possible involvement in political debate, and at the same time reinforces that possibility, by acknowledging commercial censorship.

It is important to the success of Smith's writing that she parade her personal sufferings in the public eye, for it is her character as much as her genius that is the key to its marketability; but the aspects of her situation that she chooses to advertise – her sufferings at the hands of those she identifies as 'the *weazles*, *wolves*, and *vultures*' of the law, and her need to comply with the requirements of commercial publishing – pull her fiction in two different directions. On one hand her writing claims transparently to reveal her character, to express her personal sufferings. She writes that: 'If a Writer can best describe who has suffered, I believe that all the evils arising from oppression, from fraud and chicane, I am above almost any person qualified to delineate', grounding her authority in her experience.[23] Her writing is sincere, personal, revelatory to a fault. On the other, her acknowledged submission to the commercial necessity for political caution characterizes her writing as indirect, even secretive. The transition between revealing personal misery, expressing the desire for political reform, and hinting, perhaps inadvertently, at 'seditious notions' that 'might carry a man nobody knew whither', characterizes her writing as analogous to Desmond's act of surveillance: ingenuous but indirect, candid yet covert. The intermeshing of Smith's personal situation and her political views, in the context of the culture of surveillance pervading the later 1790s, I want to suggest, resulted in the formation of a kind of English novel which, while it owed much to the picaresque, nation-building fictions of Fielding and Smollett, also looks forward to the genesis of the national tale, questioning the dominance and unity of Englishness not from its colonial or postcolonial margins but from within.

Katie Trumpener has pointed out the importance of *The Old Manor House* and *Desmond*, as well as of Radcliffe's *The Castles of Athlin and Dunbayne* (1789), to the formation of the 'central plot device' of the national tale, which she identifies as 'the spatialization of political choices, as a journey of discovery and homecoming through the British peripheries'; and she links Radcliffe's novel and *Desmond* directly to Sydney Owenson's *The Wild Irish Girl* (1806), which establishes what she describes as the 'basic plot: the contrast, attraction, and union of disparate cultural worlds'.[24] That link, I think, is significantly strengthened by the plot structures of Smith's later novels, *The Banished Man, Marchmont* and *The Young Philosopher*. In Owenson's *The Wild Irish Girl*, the English hero, Mortimer, begins on the most intense phase of his process of cultural and romantic education in Ireland when he attempts to watch the Princess Glorvina, the 'allegorical embodiment' of Ireland,[25] through a window of her father's crumbling castle. He falls, concussing himself, and he writes to his English correspondent that when he comes to he finds himself in the castle, 'But whether a prisoner of war, or taken up on suspicion of espionage, or to be offered as an appeasing sacrifice to the *manes* of the old Prince of Inismore, you must for a while suspend your patience to learn.'[26] Mortimer is received as a guest rather than as a prisoner of war, but whether he is a spy or a sacrificial atonement for the crimes of the English in Ireland is less clear. He presents himself as an itinerant landscape artist, and, as Claire Connolly observes, he takes advantage of this pose to sketch Glorvina without her knowing, and then 'delights in having captured both the spirit of the princess and that of her nation on canvas': in the same action he spies on Glorvina and on the cultural landscape of which she 'forms part'.

The hero is also of course absorbed in and seduced by the ancestral customs of the culture he observes, caught up in 'the difficulties and possibilities of colonial dialogue'.[27] His acts of looking undermine his position of national and gendered superiority, and blur his perception of the differences between English and Irish culture, while Glorvina seems to embody with increasing explicitness an idea of Irishness that is represented as both distinctively national and universal. So, for example, the hero writes that her proficiency as a linguist is a 'striking talent', an exceptional example of an 'aptitude' that is, he believes, 'peculiar to her country'; but he also stresses that he is not 'disgusted with her brogue' because 'her English, grammatically correct, and elegantly pure, is spoken with an accent that could never denote her country.' This is part of the process which, Connolly argues, 'displaces England from its position at the centre of the text': unlike the English, whose social fragmentation and provincialism is indicated by 'the barbarous and unintelligible dialect peculiar to each shire', all but the 'lower orders of society' in Ireland speak a 'purer and more grammatical English' than is heard 'in any part of England whatever'.[28] England is displaced, and Ireland appropriates its culturally superior characteristics. The hero, acting in his role as spy, continues to document Irishness with ethnographic precision, but he is fascinated by what he observes, and appropriated as an appeasing sacrifice to what Connolly identifies as a Grattanite vision of Irish national unity.[29] His dual characterization as spy and 'appeasing sacrifice' is central to the form of the national tale inaugurated by Owenson.

Smith's later novels, *Marchmont, The Young Philosopher* and *The Banished Man*, are all structured around surveillance reports, and suspicions of espionage, and the coercive influence of ancestral customs and prejudices. They can be read as inverted national tales which mark the fragmentation of

English culture under the pressure of an oppressive modernity. In *The Banished Man*, reactions to the presence of French emigrants in England, who are repeatedly suspected as spies, expose the mixture of fear and complacency that is the basis of national prejudice.To use Connolly's terms, the novel displaces the central position of England by contrasting English parochialism and xenophobia with the more extensive international sympathies of the principal characters, both liberal and conservative, who travel across national boundaries, between castles and country houses that spatialize 'political choices', and finally reject national differences in a series of marriages across national divisions. In both this novel and *Marchmont*, Smith's characters argue that the oppression suffered under the British constitution in its present abused and corrupted form is worse than that inflicted on France. In *The Banished Man*, the woman whose ordeals closely resemble Smith's own asserts that her experience of legal oppression has been comparable to that of those oppressed by 'the most odious ... characters in France', and 'may well cure me of national prejudice' (*BM* 3, p. 192). In *Marchmont*, the hero claims that though Robespierre or Danton 'had by a strange chance the power of doing more extensive mischief', they were 'less systematical scoundrels', less 'stained with crimes', than the agents of the law who persecute him (*M* 4, p. 411). He believes that his experiences in England and abroad have erased in him any 'disposition to indulge that national arrogance, and national prejudice, with which Englishmen in the middling or lower ranks of life are from their infancy impressed' (*M* 4, p. 101), and asserts that his encounters with 'the money-getting and money-saving part of the British nation' have led him to question 'if any country has less to boast of as to their genuine liberality and enlargement of mind than England' (*M* 4, pp. 70–1). Marchmont's alienated, cosmopolitan vision of England is, not surprisingly, mistaken for that of a spy (*M* 4, pp. 113–4). But the novel more authoritatively identifies 'the whole tribe of spies and sheriff's officers', seen 'creeping about, and asking this man, and asking t'other man' (*M* 2 pp. 80,73), as disruptive and oppressive agents, and condemns the lawyer who instructs them in language reminiscent of Vicesimus Knox's discussion. Knox argued that the '*whole* [legal] *profession*, with few exceptions' have become the tools of ministerial 'dirty work', and that they 'contribute to diffuse the spirit of despotism *more than any other* PROFESSION'.[30]

The narrative of *Marchmont* takes place within a landscape insistently characterized as the topographical representation of English national history, in which the hero is plotted both as 'an exile from society', compelled, he explains, 'either to live as a wretched vagabond, or submit to see my whole life wasted within the walls of a prison' (*M* 2, p. 125), and as a sacrifice to his ancestors – imprisoned for his father's debts, impoverished but sheltered by the ruins of his family house and his ancestors' Jacobite past, which the locals identify with the present Jacobin threat (*M* 2, pp. 73–4). Exiled from the present, his alienated and critical survey of England and France is counterpoised by the representation of the agents of the law as spies and informers, tools of the 'spirit of despotism' who attempt to enmesh him in their own corrupt conspiracy. The hero's sisters, and the heroine of the novel, are represented as oppressed by a feminine form of despotic surveillance. The sisters open a shop in Margate, as a result of what the heroine sees as 'that desire of independence, however humble, in which true and laudable pride really consists' (*M* 3, p. 157). The sister explains her belief that 'we shall be happier if we have something to employ us', than in 'just creeping through a vegetative sort of life in a cheap country town' (*M* 3, p. 159). But they are driven to abandon their aspirations to active independence by the intrusive gazes of curious society women, who reduce their virtuous industry to gossip-worthy spectacle. The possibilities of reading Smith's novels as early versions of an inverted English national tale, which makes surveillance of English society central to its plot, but displaces and decentralizes the politics and morals of that society, are apparent in both *Marchmont* and *The Banished Man*, but are most persuasive in *The Young Philosopher*, Smith's last major novel.

All of Smith's later novels engage their protagonists in travels within and beyond England, but in *The Young Philosopher*, their travels are exceptional in their extent, and in the detail with which they are narrated. The central characters spend time in England, Ireland, Scotland, Wales and America, and the heroine, Medora, travels the length of England following her abduction. Medora, the 'fair American' (*YP*, p. 78), was born in Lausanne, before her parents' move to America; her father is a Highland laird, and her mother, Mrs Glenmorris, whose tale makes up a significant proportion of the novel, was born in Florence. Mrs Glenmorris's father is a Dutch merchant, and though he appears to be Dutch only by virtue of his trade, the Dutch provinces are mentioned as 'his own country' (*YP*, p. 83). Only George Delmont, the young philosopher of the title, might be seen as the pattern for a sentimental ideal of Englishness: he cultivates and lives on his own small hereditary estate in the South Downs in virtuous retirement from the world, like Cincinnatus, as his brother sneeringly remarks (*YP*, p. 261); and an 'assemblage of almost every plant indigenous to England' is afforded by the 'great variety of ground' which makes up the farm (*YP*, p. 173).

Like the heroes of Smith's earlier novels, Delmont is praised as a 'citizen of the world ... divested not only of local prejudice, but ... of all prejudices' (*YP*, p. 169); and though he maintains his 'local attachment' to his estate (*YP*, p. 353), the ideal of English national character that his residence there represents is shown to be so beleaguered, by the end of the novel, that he is happy to move at least temporarily to America. Much of the novel is structured around explicit and implicit contrasts between notions of British oppression and American liberty, the progressive modernity of America, and, in Britain, a corrupting, oppressive modernity grafted onto the archaic barbarisms of the gothic past. Medora tells Delmont that, in contrast to America, in England there is always 'something which embitters our delight – Politics, and lawsuits, and old ladies finding out that we are people of bad character, and gossips repeating the malignant nonsense of other gossips' (*YP*, p. 154). The novel offers a historical genealogy as well as a spatialization of those evils through the parallel narratives of Mrs Glenmorris and Medora. Both heroines become enmeshed in elaborate conspiracies woven by malevolent older women: Mrs Glenmorris is persecuted first by her mother, who ruthlessly attempts to revive for her family the status enjoyed by her supposed Plantagenet ancestors – 'some of the most hateful characters in history' in the eyes of Mrs Glenmorris (*YP*, p. 93). Their castle, which, as Lorraine Fletcher has pointed out, is unmistakeably analogous to the British constitution, is rendered habitable by the enervating 'inventions of modern luxury', which obliterate 'all ideas of antiquity' as venerable (*YP*, p. 92), but leave its inhabitants prey to ridiculous superstitions and dangerous prejudices.

The unfortunate heroine is also persecuted by her husband's great aunt, who, Smith writes, 'was fortunate not to have lived a century and a half earlier, for she would undoubtedly have been in danger of being tormented, or killed as a female warlock' (*YP*, p. 111). Glenmorris himself is a highland laird whose education in England has taught him to reject 'feudal pride' but allowed him to retain the romantic idealism associated with Gaelic marginal identity (*YP*, p. 84). For his clan he is the benevolent focus of affective feudal loyalty, and under his stewardship they live in a state of impoverished but noble primitivism, inhabiting huts which are compared to wigwams (*YP*, p. 124). The great aunt, in contrast, is characterized by barbarous and oppressive primitivism, ignorant of 'modern improvement' (*YP*, p. 109). Nastily unclean and antisentimental, as a catholic and jacobite Scottish woman, she is shown to be governed by prejudice, family pride and 'the strange and wild dreams of local superstition' (*YP*, p. 109). When her son returns from fighting with the British army against the American rebels, he torments Mrs Glenmorris by detailing the means 'so disgraceful to humanity' by which 'the natives' of north America torture their prisoners, who may include Glenmorris, and as a result both the son and the great aunt are coloured with the barbarity attributed to the native Americans (*YP*, p. 115). The novel links highlanders and native Americans in a dialectic of purely virtuous or bestially impoverished barbarism familiar from the writings of theorists of the Scottish enlightenment, but implies that where the progressive improvements of European Americans have enabled them to disown the characteristics of native Americans, understood to be stuck in the eternal present of savagery, in Britain modern political despotism reinvigorates and perpetuates the oppressive barbarities of the gothic past.

The elderly women who engage in Gothic conspiracy against Mrs Glenmorris eventually succeed in securing her imprisonment in a madhouse, in an episode Smith compared with the confinement of the heroine of Wollstonecraft's *The Wrongs of Women* (published in the same year). Mrs Glenmorris only begins to recover from her derangement when her keepers 'insensibly relaxed in that vigilance which … so distressed her. Her guard at first trusted her to walk within her sight at some distance; then satisfied herself with looking after her now and then, and at length suffered her to walk or sit whole hours alone' (*YP*, p. 269). Mrs Glenmorris is oppressed and finally driven mad by the conspiracy of surveillance orchestrated by old women; she is the embodiment of an enlightened modernity for which America is the natural home, but is sacrificed to a distorted modern fantasy of the British ancestral past.

The narrative of Medora's persecution is more interesting because, though it is, as Nicola Watson points out the 'mirror-image of her mother's' it is, in some aspects at least, less 'intensely overdetermined'.[31] She is persecuted by the malicious gossip of a network of old women, who, Smith explains, hold

accommodating maxims of policy…so convenient, that they are adapted as well to the enlarged views of the statesman, who deluges half the world in blood, and sweeps millions from its bosom (for what he pleases to term the general good, or the balance of power) as to the minor projectors in private life, whose limited operations only allow them to contrive, how to render a few couple of simpletons miserable. (*YP*, pp. 190–1)

In Watson's words, Medora is subjected to 'a simulacrum of conservative plotting', orchestrated by a woman 'that lives at folks houses as half spy over the servants, half friend to the master – a tale-bearer, a gossip' (*YP*, p. 37). But the tale of Medora, unlike that of her mother, is a third- rather than first-person narrative, frequently mediated by the reports of a variety of onlookers and observers who display Smith's talent for suggesting the dialects and speech patterns of different social ranks and regions; and by no means all of these accounts are misleading or unsympathetic.

The hero, Medora's lover, like the protagonists of Smith's earlier novels, is disaffected, alienated from English society to a degree that leads others to accuse him of French views and principles, but he is rarely afforded opportunities for surveying his country, having retreated to his estate in order to avoid contact with it. When he tries to search for Medora in London, he is at a loss because he has never 'cultivated any acquaintance' (*YP*, p. 231), any friendships or alliances which might identify him with any group or class. He is almost as isolated and helpless as Mrs Glenmorris, who wanders the streets, 'her derangement of mind … becoming more and more visible', and exposing her to 'the rude gaze of the multitude' (*YP*, pp. 217–18). His brother tells him that his support for the 'Rights of men' has erased his class: there is, he says, 'nothing of nobility about thee but … blood, not even thy ideas – No haberdasher of small wares has more plebian notions!' (*YP*, p. 200). He is dependent on the reports precisely of shopkeepers and servants (who emerge as figures of some moral authority). A whole range of more or less important characters offer competing reports of aspects of society, or of Medora, its victim. What emerges from this is a sense of a society that is disunified, fragmented by differences of class, region and politics, by the absence of the virtues of openness and equality Glenmorris celebrates in America – a modern kind of public life in which Delmont, for all his republican virtues, is at a loss. When he does catch up with Medora, more as a result of luck than judgement, he spies her in the arms of another man, and goes through agonies of recrimination and self-reproach before he becomes aware that the man is her father – a comic mishap that emphasizes his naïvety, his inability to function in a world of contingency, of partial perceptions and rumours. But at the end of the novel, it is not so much the political virtues of America that attract the principle characters, but the possibility emigration offers them of turning away from society to enjoy 'uninterrupted domestic felicity' (*YP*, p. 352).

Medora, like her mother, is persecuted by spies and surveillance, but her safety, and the continuity of her character as the innocent representative of whiggish and American ideals of liberty, is also dependent on the reports and observations of socially marginalized onlookers – women, domestic servants, waggoners and innkeepers. Their reports, and sometimes their assistance, in contesting the plots and conspiracies of the network of old women, enable her to escape relatively unscathed from her abductor, despite the ineffectuality of the hero's efforts to help her. His disenchanted perceptions of social corruption merely serve to confirm his social isolation. Her salvation, like that of Anne Eliot in *Persuasion*, is dependent on gossip and on more or less covert surveillance, on behaviour that implies the confidence of intimate exchange, or the authority of privileged but not necessarily licensed perception, rather than anything more socially cohesive, any notion of the authority of candour, or of what had seemed the principal public virtues.

In conclusion I want to return briefly to *The Banished Man*, and the character of the hero's mother, which reads like a satire on the figure of the good housewife best described by Hannah More in her *Strictures* of 1799. Smith writes that Lady Ellesmere was 'indifferent... to what passed at a distance', but 'in the scene immediately near her she took the liveliest interest' (*BM* 2, p. 111). Ellesmere is disgusted by 'her attachment to insignificant things and insignificant people', her interest in local gossip, which is compared to the situation of 'prisoners long accustomed to darkness', who learn to 'distinguish objects around them' without light, 'and feel an interest in the habits of the animals or reptiles that inhabit their dungeon'. She weeps when Ellesmere leaves for France, but he comments that 'She has not a mind capable of figuring what she never saw'; if she did 'the most terrific drawings would soon be erased by the home scenes around her; and she would think more of what had happened at the next market town. Such is the effect of living always in a narrow circle, without any change of ideas'(*BM* 2, pp. 134, 132–3; 3.46–7) She epitomizes, then, that notion of femininity as characterized by a myopic focal range and a capacity to sympathize only with suffering that can be seen and felt, rather than merely imagined. She is curious about her neighbours, and subjects them to intense and detailed scrutiny, but her situation has made her incapable of surveying the world beyond.

Eleanor Ty suggests, in *Unsex'd Revolutionaries*, that, in comparison with Wollstonecraft, Smith is inconsistent in her 'critique of patriarchy ... because mothers are often shown to be just as guilty of tyranny and abuses as fathers are';[32] and it's certainly the case that in novel after novel Smith represents older women as malevolent or at least foolish. But the portraits of these women clearly need to be understood in the context of the political complexities of the novels in which they appear. In *The Banished Man*, Smith is at pains to make it clear that France has betrayed the ideals she had celebrated in *Desmond*, and the explicitness of her disillusionment with the revolution enables her to represent its original ideals as the basis for criticism of the conservative bigotry of English society, and of the oppressive form of government that nurtures it. The representation of older women in Smith's novels interweaves gendered and national politics, whether those women are engaged in struggles against forms of adversity that resemble Smith's own, or whether, like Lady Ellesmere, they are simply indifferent to what happens beyond 'the next market town', and condemned to narrow views by the limitations of their experience (*BM* 2, p. 133). Older women in Smith's fiction, like middle-class women in Wollstonecraft's second *Vindication*, are the focus for antifeminine strictures because this is the gendered currency of opposition to a politics that, in Knox's words, destroys 'all the sweet equality of social intercourse', and replaces it with a mischievous 'activity in trifles'.[33]

Perhaps the character of Lady Ellesmere alludes to *Caleb Williams*, which Smith mentions in her prefatory letter. When Caleb is imprisoned, of course, he reflects on the resources of his own mind in order to produce an individuating narrative of his personal history as well as a more expansive, universal survey, and concludes that in this way 'I eluded the squalid solitude of my dungeon, and wandered in idea through all the varieties of human society'.[34] In contrast to Caleb's enlightened capacity to enjoy the expansive interior landscape afforded by education, the occluded and benighted views of Ellesmere's mother suggest the behaviour Knox argued was imposed on those disempowered by despotic government. The account of her alludes most directly to Cowper's lines on the prisoner in the Bastille, who flies 'for refuge from distracting thought / To such amusements as ingenious woe / Contrives', and is obliged

> To turn purveyor to an overgorg'd
> And bloated spider, till the pamper'd pest
> Is made familiar, watches his approach,
> Comes at his call and serves him for a friend.[35]

Lady Ellesmere's situation resembles that of the prisoner perhaps because her husband and son are among the 'friends of arbitrary power' whom Knox condemned; she is a sacrifice to the *manes* of conservatism, deprived of any opportunity to survey the world beyond the next market town. Cowper comments that the prisoner's plight would drive him to 'beg for exile, or the pangs of death',[36] and the narrator of Smith's *Letters of a Solitary Wanderer* (1799, 1802) has indeed chosen exile from the outset.

In Smith's later novels, spies and suspicions of spies, and the reports of covert or unlicensed observers, become less directly political. In *The Banished Man* Frenchmen are taken for spies, and subjected to surveillance. In *Marchmont*, the hero's disinterested or disillusioned survey seems to conservative judges to be that of a spy because he exposes the divisiveness of their means of social control; of their use of the legal agents whom the narrative condemns as the spies of a despotic regime. In *The Young Philosopher*, older women, aided by corrupt lawyers and despotic laws, engage in conspiratorial espionage, and are, I have suggested, represented as the antipathetic victims and tools of a degree of political corruption that poisons the 'sweet equality' and openness of private life. They are signs of the spirit of despotism which Smith, like Knox, understood as a political evil, but which she also tied unambiguously to the travails of her personal history. But the novels also, and with increasing sureness, suggest that surveillance and covert observations have become the principle means of piecing together some form of social knowledge; that the disinterested, cosmopolitan survey of the liberal observer has been displaced into the competing and contradictory reports of interested gossips and disaffected onlookers. The spy, prisoner, exile, servant, or indeed the myopic woman becomes the unreliable retailer of partial information. The steady gaze no longer marks comprehensive understanding and social cohesion, but a continuous surveillance that records and instigates the psychopathology of paranoia. Smith writes a kind of inverted national tale in which the central position of a cohesive notion of Englishness is displaced, not by the cultures of its marginalized neighbours, colonies or excolonies, but by the atomized units of inward-looking domestic intimacy or individual isolation, of people bastilled by the social regulations of 'arbitrary power'. As a result, these are tales that give a heightened importance to the stranger's brief report, the exchanged glance, the covert and stolen look, as a means of constructing narratives of social difference.

## Notes

1  John Barrell, 'Visualising the Division of Labour: William Pyne's *Microcosm*', in his *The Birth of Pandora and the Division of Knowledge* (London: Macmillan, 1992), pp. 118, 116.

2  John Barrell, *Imagining the King's Death: Figurative Treason, Fantasies of Regicide, 1793–1796* (Oxford: Oxford University Press, 2000), pp. 51, 81.

3   John Barrell, 'Coffee-House Politicians', in *Journal of British Studies*, vol 43, no. 2 (April 2004), pp. 206–232.

4   Vicesimus Knox, *The Spirit of Despotism* (Morris-Town: Jacob Mann, 1799), section 24, p. 180; s. 1, pp. 11, 6; s. 13, p. 98; s. 35, p. 268; s. 14, pp. 108, 110.

5   'Mucius', 'To the editor of the Morning Chronicle', letter 1, 1 Feb. 1793, in William Godwin, *Uncollected Writings (1785–1822): Articles in Periodicals and Six Pamphlets*, intro., Jack W. Marken and Burton R. Pollin (Gainesville, FL: Scholars' facsimiles and reprints, 1968), pp. 111, 113.

6   See, for example, Gregory Dart's illuminating reading of the politics of *Caleb Williams* in his *Rousseau, Robespierre and English Romanticism* (Cambridge: Cambridge University Press, 1999), ch. 4.

7   Jane Austen, *Northanger Abbey, Lady Susan, The Watsons, and Sanditon*, ed., John Davie (Oxford: Oxford University Press, 1971, 1985), p. 159.

8   Albert Goodwin, *The Friends of Liberty: the English Democratic Movement in the Age of the French Revolution* (Cambridge, MA: Harvard University Press, 1979), p. 249.

9   On Erskine, see Lorraine Fletcher, *Charlotte Smith: A Critical Biography* (London: Palgrave Macmillan, 1998), pp. 237–8. On Wordsworth, see Nicholas Roe, *Wordsworth and Coleridge: The radical years* (Oxford: Clarendon Press, 1988), pp. 42–3.

10  T.J. Clark, *Farewell to an Idea: Episodes from a history of modernism* (New Haven, CT: Yale University Press, 1999), p. 8.

11  Charlotte Smith, *Desmond*, eds Antje Blank and Janet Todd (London: Pickering & Chatto, 1997), p. 230; further refs (*D*) in text to this edition.

12  Nicola Watson, *Revolution and the Form of the British Novel, 1790–1825: Intercepted Letters, Interrupted Seductions* (Oxford: Clarendon Press, 1994), p. 36, see p. 37.

13  The politics of *Desmond* have been the occasion for critical debate for some years. See for example, Diana Bowstead, 'Charlotte Smith's *Desmond*: The Epistolary Novel as Ideological Argument', in Mary Anne Schofield and Cecilia Macheski, eds, *Fetter'd or Free: British Women Novelists, 1670–1815* (Athens, OH: Ohio University Press, 1986), pp. 237–63; Chris Jones, *Radical Sensibility: Literature and Ideas in the 1790s* (London: Routledge, 1993); Alison Conway, 'Nationalism, Revolution, and the Female Body: Charlotte Smith's *Desmond*', *Women's Studies* (1995), 24, pp. 395–409; Eleanor Wikborg, 'Political Discourse versus Sentimental Romance: Ideology and Genre in Charlotte Smith's *Desmond* (1792)', *English Studies* (1997), 6, pp. 522–31.

14  Vivien Jones, ' "The Coquetry of Nature": Politics and the Picturesque in Women's Fiction', in *The Politics of the Picturesque: Literature, landscape and aesthetics since 1770*, eds Stephen Copley and Peter Garside (Cambridge: Cambridge University Press, 1994), pp. 132, 133.

15  Charlotte Smith, *The Old Manor House*, ed., Anne Henry Ehrenpreis, intro., Judith Phillips Stanton (Oxford: Oxford University Press, 1989), pp. 92–3; further refs in text to this edition.

16  See Fletcher, *Smith* (1998), and Florence M. Hilbish, *Charlotte Smith, Poet and Novelist (1749–1806)* (Philadelphia, PA: Pennsylvania University Press, 1941).

17  [Mary Hays], 'Mrs. Charlotte Smith', in *Public Characters of 1800–1801* (London: R. Phillips, 1807), pp. 62–3.

18  Elizabeth Montagu to Elizabeth Carter, MO 3702, [Sandleford], 22 July [1792], in Leonore Helen Ewert, 'Elizabeth Montagu to Elizabeth Carter: Literary Gossip and Critical Opinions from the Pen of the Queen of the Blues' (unpublished PhD dissertation, Claremont Graduate School and University Centre, 1968), p. 196.

19  See Jacqueline M. Labbe, 'Selling One's Sorrows: Charlotte Smith, Mary Robinson, and the Marketing of Poetry', *Wordsworth Circle*, 1994. See also Sarah Zimmerman, 'Charlotte Smith's Letters and the Practice of Self-Representation', *Princeton University Library Chronicle* (1991), 53(1), pp. 50–77.

20  Charlotte Smith, *The Banished Man. A Novel* 4 vols, (London: T. Cadell, 1794), Vol 2 'Avis au Lecteur', p. 10; further refs (*BM*) in text to this edition.

21  The letter is also a satire on the illiteracy of booksellers.

22  Charlotte Smith, *Marchmont: A Novel* 4 vols, (London: Sampson Low, 1796), Vol 4, p. 330. All further refs (*M*) in text to this edition.

23  Charlotte Smith, *The Young Philosopher*, ed., Elizabeth Kraft (Lexington: University Press of Kentucky, 1999), Preface, p. 5. All further refs (*YP*) in text to this edition.

24  Katie Trumpener, *Bardic Nationalism: The Romantic Novel and the British Empire* (Princeton, NJ: Princeton University Press, 1997), pp. 138, 141.

25  *Ibid.*, p. 141.

26  Sydney Owenson, Lady Morgan, *The Wild Irish Girl: A National Tale*, ed., with intro., Claire Connolly and Stephen Copley; foreword, Kevin Whelan (London: Pickering & Chatto, 2000), p. 43.

27  Claire Connolly, 'Introduction: The Politics of Love in the Wild Irish Girl', in Owenson, introduction, pp. xxxvi–vii, xlviii.

28  Owenson, p. 127; Connolly, Intro., p. 1.

29  See p. 185n, where Owenson notes La Tocnaye's observation, in his *Promenade d'un Français dans l'Irlande*, that parts of Ireland are 'less known than islands in the Pacific Ocean'. See Connolly, Intro., pp. liii–lv.

30  Knox, *Despotism* section 24, p. 180; s. 1, pp. 11, 6; s. 13, p. 98; s. 35, p. 268; s. 14, pp. 108, 110.

31  Watson argues that both narratives are 'intensely overdetermined', central to 'a novel which betrays the hopelessly beleaguered state of sentimental discourse at the end of the decade by systematically subjecting it to a simulacrum of conservative plotting'. I admire Watson's brief exposition of the novel, but I want to look in more detail at her account of it as a question of 'whether first-person narrative ... will come to carry enough authority to discredit the web of second- and third-hand gossip'. See Watson, *Form*, pp. 58–9.

32  Eleanor Ty, *Unsex'd Revolutionaries: Five Women Novelists of the 1790s* (Toronto: University of Toronto Press, 1993), p. 153.

33  For a fuller discussion of these issues see my *Small Change: Women, Learning, Patriotism, 1750–1810* (Chicago, IL: Chicago University Press, 2000), esp. Pt 4.

34  William Godwin, *Things As They Are: or The Adventures of Caleb Williams*, ed. and intro., Maurice Hundle (Harmondsworth: Penguin, 1988), p. 193. See 'Avis au Lecteur', *BM* 2, pp. vii and n.

35  William Cowper, *The Task*, Bk 5, 'The Winter Morning Walk', 11, pp. 415–17, 421–4, in William Cowper, *The Task and Selected Other Poems*, ed., James Sambrook (London: Longman, 1994).

36  *The Task*, Bk 5, 1, p. 434.

# 9
# Wordsworth and Empire – Just Joking
*David Simpson*

The dynamics of Empire and their presence in Romantic writing have been lately much inspected, and most people probably think they know what Wordsworth thought about them. He did not, one might say, think much about them at all, lining up with a number of other major writers who seem to have said very little on the difficult topics of slavery, imperialism, commerce and conquest. To be sure there is the vigorous critique of militarist empire-building in the 'Salisbury Plain' poem, along with the more or less sympathetic 1802 sonnets on Toussaint and on the 'female Passenger' exiled from France because of her race; but then there are those purple passages in *The Excursion* which might well continue to make us wince even if we convince ourselves that they are dramatic and not doctrinal, the property of the poem's speakers and not (or not simply) of its author. We may wince because it is after all the 'poet', and not one of the more obviously distanced characters, who launches into an encomium on the state and church of England – 'Hail to the State of England!' (BK. 6, 1.6)[1] – in a moment of hyperbole that elides the controversial unions of 1707 and 1800 with Scotland and Ireland, and quite forgets the earlier one with Wales. We are sensitive to these matters now. It is hard to make the case that this voice is not Wordsworth's own – for the poet says hardly anything in this poem, at least not enough to deserve the attribution of a dramatic personality clearly or interestingly distinct from that of the author.

At the same time, the poet's mild hope that the Church of England will continue to export 'sweet civility' to distant 'rustic wilds' (p. 187) looks rather modest next to the Wanderer's apparently compulsive predisposition towards the 'brighter scene' (9: 256; p. 294) and the good side of any and every situation (notoriously, the death of Margaret in Book 1). The Wanderer *is* a fully developed dramatic personality, and he is the one who waxes lyrical on the saving potential of a national education scheme and the subsequent export of an educated surplus population – the swarms from Britain's beehives – to the far-flung corners of the earth. The last book of *The Excursion*, furthermore, is a subtly disturbing narrative. The Wanderer's upbeat prospectus is followed by a quieter mood, a walk along the lakeshore, and a companion's doubts about whether an adequately elevated standard of national virtue could ever be obtained. The coming of evening brings a certain composure embodied in the picnic, the sunset, and the vision of the white ram. While there is no loud or explicit challenge to the Pastor's faith in the 'marvellous advance/Of good from evil' (9: 722–23, p. 310), there are darker intimations that qualify any easy conclusions. The evening star fails to appear (a withholding of something, we know not what), and the group disperses into its separate spheres. There is a cluster of images and cross-references to other Wordsworthian scenes that unsettles, quite distinctly although without melodrama, any simple ideological closure. The 'imperial front' of the 'snow-white ram' is reflected in the lake by which he stands, but the real and reflected images are eerily independent:

> Each had his glowing mountains, each his sky,
> And each seemed centre of his own fair world:
> Antipodes unconscious of each other.
>
> (9: 447–9, p. 300)

There is much to say about this figure; but for now, just remember 'antipodes'. The little group puts in to shore and builds a 'gipsy-fire' (9: 527, p. 303) that stimulates a sense of social solidarity between the adults and between the different generations – an idyllic trope to which Wordsworth refers elsewhere but which he also critically destroys in one of his most famous accusatory poems ('Gipsies'). Wordsworth was not sure about how to value the gipsy life. And, sure enough, this moment of improbable communal solidarity gives way to an orgy of plant-collecting:

> Rapaciously we gathered flowery spoils
> From land and water; lilies of each hue –
> Golden and white, that float upon the waves,
> And court the wind; and leaves of that shy plant,
> (Her flowers were shed) the lily of the vale,
> That loves the ground, and from the sun withholds
> Her pensive beauty; from the breeze her sweets.
>
> (9: 537–44, p. 304)

Pensive and shy no longer, but now exposed to the ravages of a gang of enthusiasts who seem to know no modesty; and does the parenthetical half line – 'Her flowers were shed' – serve to authorize the destruction of the plant, or does it suggest that the harvesters would have had those too had they still been blooming? Remember the 'flowery spoils'.

The Solitary makes a melancholic comment on the dying fire, emblem of mortal joys, but the repose of the others is maintained as they get back into the boat, cruise along the shore and 'into thickets peep/Where couch the spotted deer' (9: 562–3, p. 305). These acts of ravaging plants (recall the scene of 'Nutting') and peeping into private places put an odd spin on the moralizing of the local landscape as 'seemingly preserved/From all intrusion of the restless world/By rocks impassable and mountains huge' (9: 577–9, p. 305). For we have just seen two acts of obvious intrusion, one quite destructive and the other imagistically prurient although not inevitably criminal: Wordsworth does not usually make peeping a negative thing – plants do it – but one might nonetheless recall the physician-philosopher of 'A Poet's Epitaph' who is scolded for being 'one that would peep and botanize/Upon his mother's grave'.[2]

So we have here a group of intelligent and articulate lovers of rural life, 'seemingly' secure in a space protected from the 'restless world', who themselves act as agents of disturbance and molestation within the local economy of that very same space. Those who most value it, it seems, are those most prone to disrupt it. This set of concerns appears in various forms elsewhere in Wordsworth's poetry. I want to pick on one instance only. I asked you to remember the mention of antipodes and the incident of the 'flowery spoils'. These appear also in the fourth of the 'Poems on the Naming of Places', which will be the main topic of this essay. The poem recounts the story of a ramble along the 'eastern shore' of Grasmere lake on a 'calm September morning, ere the mist/Had altogether yielded to the sun' (*LB*, p. 248, 11. 3, 7–8). The mist is, predictably, the medium of optical illusion and misunderstanding, and assists the ramblers in deceiving themselves about the identity of the fisherman they encounter, who turns out not to be the idle able-bodied peasant of their moralizings but a wasted and worn old man too frail to work in the fields. Shallow and hasty moral judgment gives way to self-reproach, and in homage to this moment they give the place a 'memorial name', the name 'POINT RASH-JUDGMENT' (*LB*, p. 250).

There is a lot to say about this poem. I have written about it before as a symptom of Wordsworthian self-accusation and reflexivity, and the inevitably residual hubris thereof, and since then both Alan Bewell and Michael Wiley, at least, have broadened our sphere of reference by showing, respectively, the importance to Wordsworth of the anthropological encounter with the 'primitive other', and the situation of this Wordsworthian moment in the field of global exploration and empire.[3] The poem chronicles an incursion into what John Barrell has called 'the dark side of the landscape', the imprecisely figured territory to which the rural labourer is consigned as background or property of the major protagonists and possessors (actual or imaginary) of the land.[4] The shedding of light upon the dark side is itself startling enough; yet more so is its revelation of the moral failures of the poet figure and his rambler friends. But the poem is not just the record of a domestic encounter, an account of mistaking an ailing old man for a healthy young one, with all the small but serious dramas of class prejudice that devolve from this error. It is also another poetic investigation of the pursuit of 'flowery spoils' and a poem about the antipodes.

How is Grasmere lake to be read as the antipodes? Wordsworth tells us that the invention of 'POINT RASH-JUDGMENT' as the 'memorial name' for this act of moral aggression is one 'uncouth indeed/As e'er by Mariner was giv'n to Bay/Or Foreland on a new-discovered coast' (*LB*, p. 250). To invoke the naming of places along a 'new-discovered coast' in 1800 was to make an as good as explicit reference to Cook's three voyages in the South Pacific between 1768 and 1779–80. Accounts of the voyages were best-sellers among the affluent reading public – Hawkesworth's three-volume (1773) narrative earned him £6,000 as his copyright fee, the largest such payment for any book in the eighteenth century[5] – and much of Cook's time and imagination, at least as reported, was given over to bestowing names on the places he mapped and observed. The names are uncouth indeed, and while I have not found a Point Rash-Judgment, Wordsworth's name would fit right in with the names Cook and his crew did come up with. The inhospitable tip of South America gave him *Port Famine*; *Cape Tribulation* was so named 'because here begun all our troubles'; *Thirsty Sound* became so 'by reason we could find no fresh water'; and two 'small low Islands' became '*Hope Islands* because we were always in hopes of being able to reach these Islands'.[6] Thus, too, countless other sites: *Cape Turnagain* 'because here we returnd' and *Cape Kidnappers* where one of the ship's boys was almost captured by the natives (*Journals*, p. 77); *Cape Desolation* and *Cape Disappointment; Cape Flattery* and *Cape Foulweather*; and *Cape Circumcision*, which may or may not have been the extreme tip of the southern continent. To be sure there are the memorials to monarchs, mariners and suitable politicians and patrons, but many of Cook's names (like those recorded by Lewis and Clark on their trip through the American West 30 years later) devolve from entirely contingent and even personal circumstances, things that happened to him and his crew, and affected his feelings in a certain way. He would even change his mind. What began as the rather formal *Endeavour Bay*, named after the ship, became '*Poverty Bay* because it afforded us no one thing that we wanted' (*Journals*, p. 73).

One must find in this onomastic orgy a gross insensitivity to the names already given by others, most particularly native others, to these same spots. Cook's mission of 'map and move on' was seldom compatible with complex ethnolinguistic investigations of native naming habits, even had he any inclination to pursue them, which he seems not to have had, though he reproduces Polynesian names freely enough. One might also find here the nomination habits of an apostle of imperialism. Paul Carter however, thinks otherwise, and sees Cook's naming practices as very much at odds with the language of empire. He sees their improvizational and idiosyncratic features as preserving 'the difference between the order of nature and the order of culture' by not 'diminishing the otherness they make so readily accessible'.

They embody 'the figure of irony, a mode of description that passionately distances the observer from what he sees' because of the 'very violence of their metaphorical displacements'.[7] Carter is looking to Cook as the progenitor of 'Australia's spatial history', an 'open-ended, imaginative' genre that is not invested in founding colonies but in a series of mobile encounters with the landscape. So he perhaps overdoes the contrast between this and the static 'imperial gaze' attributed to Cook's shipmate Sir Joseph Banks (p. 33). After all, the evidence does not allow for simple distinctions between the one and the other, either in their effects or in their intentions. (Joseph Conrad also looked for a heroic moment of pure exploration as the precursor to profit and persecution.) The figure of irony appears again in Wordsworth's poem, whereby the protagonists are reported as if they half-recognize the pomposity of their self-rebuke ('uncouth indeed'), which thus cannot fully erase or compensate for the original misconception they are seeking to make up for. What is Wordsworth's citation of Cook and his kind telling us about the moral dynamics of going for a walk and passing opinions about those one sees along the way?

A number of things, some of which I hope to illuminate here. He is telling us first that one does not need to go to the ends of the earth in order to make certain things clear to oneself. The anthropological other begins at home, indeed right outside one's own front door. Wordsworth's poems are redolent with the aura of strangeness discovered in the most apparently familiar places, places one knows and regularly inhabits. Indeed, the familiar is already strange. It is so because of the cast of aroused imagination that any active mind will and must impose on what it finds to hand – a gibbet, a pile of clothes, a discharged soldier, a pile of stones. The same is then never quite the same, even when it is the foundation of a habit. But it is strange, too, because the local is always permeated by the figures of those who have themselves been the servants or followers of empire and foreign wars, figures who have been abroad and come home, mostly to find that either the place they left is not the same (as in 'The Brothers') or that they themselves have changed, or perhaps both at once. The old man fishing by the side of Grasmere lake is of course just that, an old man fishing. But his imaged association with the exotic inhabitants of distant lands – an association triggered by the way in which the ramblers do not know or recognize what they are seeing – is powerful for at least two reasons: because all perception is fallible and because the local landscape is now haunted by those who *have* come back from worlds elsewhere and been changed by them. You never know who you may be about to meet or where they have been.[8]

So it seems appropriate that the poem carefully presents the figure of the fisherman as optically challenging. There is a 'thin veil of glittering haze' that makes the man look 'tall and upright', which is perhaps what leads the walkers to assume that he is hale and hearty (*LB*, p. 249). As they approach, they find that his apparent stature is the result of emaciation, his figure almost that of a famine victim:

> We saw a Man worn down
> By sickness, gaunt and lean, with sunken cheeks
> And wasted limbs, his legs so long and lean
> That for my single self I look'd at them,
> Forgetful of the body they sustain'd.
>
> (*LB*, p. 249)

The mistake, then, is an understandable one. The rambling party has just registered the noise of the harvest, the 'busy mirth' of rustic labour, so that when they see the figure in the mist they have an associational pattern already in place – they assume that the man must have skipped work to go fishing. Even on a close-up viewing, the speaker of the poem has a hard time assembling body parts into a full human figure – he is fixated on the legs, to the point of forgetting the body they hold up. The man will not quite settle into recognition or familiarity – he remains a spectre, a shifting image. Consciously or otherwise – and I think that we should never under-estimate the artfulness of this most plainly speaking poet – this local 'mariner' reminds us of the lively debate about the limits of physical human nature that went along with the exploration of faraway places. Bernard Smith observes that 'there had accumulated by 1768 a formidable body of evidence that the natives of Patagonia were giants'.[9] Of course, one might say, as long as no one had set eyes on them. But in fact the belief was based not on hearsay but on actual sightings. Commodore Byron in 1764 described meeting a huge Patagonian chief and his report sponsored some imaginative illustration. Even when Banks set out deliberately to refute these ideas by taking actual measurements of the Fuegians, others like Hawkesworth himself felt justi-fied in concluding that there was so much evidence already in place that the existence of the Patagonian giants was quite plausible, and their existence continued to be credited even after Banks and Cook had published their findings.

Speculations about the physical size and health of geographically remote human beings were not of course driven simply by the desire for a statistical record. They were from the first implicated in arguments about the pros and cons of modern commercial societies in comparison with so-called primitive cultures, and were thus central to that important but now largely redistributed genre recognized in the eighteenth century by the name of *political economy*. According to those who took against modernity and upheld the Spartan ideal, physical strength and moral virtue could only flourish in precommercial societies committed to subsistence economies: physical, psychological and moral decay was the inevitable result of divided labour, luxury and depend-ence. (Hence the polemical power for some critics of the few hundred ragged Highlanders who made it down to Derby in 1745.) On the other side there were those who viewed complex commercial networks as civilizing forces, setting up relations between those who might otherwise remain strangers and thus contributing to the dissemination of cosmopolitan sympathy and mutual tolerance.[10] Wordsworth had his say on these topics, though his complex critique of modernity is not an issue in this poem. What is presented here is more basic – a scene in which the mere identification of the other, primitive or not, is both epistemologically confusing – what do we see when we see someone or something? – and ethically fraught – what does it mean to make judgments based on partial sightings informed by strong predispositions? In other words there is nothing here upon which a rational political economic preference or a scientific anthropology could be based, nothing stable enough to count as admissible evidence.

And nothing, by extension, that would allow Wordsworth to carry out the instructions given to James Cook at the start of his third voyage: to map, observe, collect and record as accurately and as often as possible, whether places, persons, plants, soils or animals.[11] This rage for order has been appropriately historicized as the guiding spirit of 'the Enlightenment', about which Wordsworth also had his say, mostly negatively. Cook's sailing companion on the first voyage, now almost as famous as Cook himself, was Joseph Banks, whose efforts increased the number of the world's identified plant species by around 25 per cent, and who then set himself up at Kew Gardens to receive the specimens of some 126 (identified) collectors who ranged over the entire globe excepting Antarctica.[12] This brings us back to the 'flowery spoils' motif in the last book of *The Excursion*, and to the botanical drama of the 'Point Rash-Judgment' poem, which can be seen to invoke a miniature Wordsworthian Botany Bay right on the poet's doorstep.

There is a good deal of botanizing in the poem. The ramblers take pleasure in watching dandelion seeds and thistle's beard skim across the surface of the water (*LB*, p. 248), and tremble on the edge of that riot of spoilation we have seen toward the end of *The Excursion*:

> – And often, trifling with a privilege
> Alike indulg'd to all, we paus'd, one now
> And now the other, to point out, perchance
> To pluck, some flower or water-weed, too fair
> Either to be divided from the place
> On which it grew, or to be left alone
> To its own beauty.
>
> (11.28–34, *LB*, p. 248)

The image of invasion is distinctly muted, there is no rapaciousness, no frenzy of collecting. But the assertion of equality and class neutrality (a 'privilege/Alike indulg'd to all') is ominous in the light of what is to come (and why should what is truly common remain a *privilege*), and the division of the mind is worth pondering: too fair to be picked but too fair to be left alone. What does one do? What should one do? To leave the flowers in place and to commit them to the mind's eye and the imaginative memory would fulfil the terms of the most famous of all Wordsworthian tropes – remember the daffodils consigned to the mind's eye. But here the flowers are picked. Banksian collectors had to pick flowers in order to do their jobs, at the service of the great task of classification. Wordsworth and his friends are not servants at the shrine of science, but rather gentlefolk at leisure: 'we/ Play'd with our time' in a 'vacant mood', the speaker tells us (*LB*, p. 248). James Jenkinson, one of Linnaeus's English translators, regarded botany as a perfect leisure activity for the affluent classes: 'If considered as an amusement, it seems extremely well-calculated to employ the vacant hours of the *country Gentleman*, being the most innocent, as well as the most salutary, that can excite the attention of the *human mind*.'[13] But Wordsworth's country gentlefolk are not quite innocent, their idleness and leisure are uncomfortable preconditions for the (erroneous) moral judgment they dispose on the fisherman. While it is the figure of the other that is deemed irresponsible for shirking the labours of the harvest, they are themselves already complicit in the society of those who subsist upon the labours of others, and Wordsworth purposively and carefully writes it this way, just as he does in 'Resolution and Independence' – another poem in which an old man takes on spectral form – and in the first book of *The Prelude*.

One salient significance of this critical self-dramatization is that it undercuts what was perhaps the basic conviction of the civic humanist tradition: that objective attitudes to the world can only be managed by those who operate from a position of effective disinterest, those who are sufficiently affluent and above mere need that they do not look to their environment to provide them with any of life's necessities, and who are unaffected by the distortions of perspective that come from occupying a specialized occupational slot in a highly divided labour system. The record of Wordsworth's complex ambivalence about his own place in the world in relation to these terms is to be found all over at least the early poetry, and this is no place to rehearse it.[14] Suffice it to say that in this poem the pose of gentlemanly disinterest is productive not of a more accurate observation of the world – the Royal Society assumption, if you will – but of a spectacular degree of *in*accuracy. Freedom from vested interest and from the deformations brought about by specialized work does not produce objectivity and a sure ability to subsume the particular instance within the general idea (one of the cornerstones of Lockean epistemology). Here it is leisure that allows the mind to be flooded with casual and unconscious associations, prejudices and projections of the sort that are always waiting in the wings but are seemingly more powerful when they are not brought to consciousness by some strenuous act of self-interrogation. Wordsworth suggests that it is not so easy to rid oneself of interestedness.

The fact that his ramblers have a good deal of it suggests either that the model does not work for those that it should work for (the leisured class whose image the strollers perform) or that should such a class exist somewhere then they do not belong to it. We may go on to surmise that no one could so belong, given a world in which rapid redistributions and realignments were occurring then as they have occurred since: that is the nature of democracy and capitalism. And that is what signals the demise of the Enlightenment fantasy of a place to stand from which pure observation can be imagined to take place. Neither picking the plants nor leaving them in place makes much difference: no science can be carried out by those who cannot trust themselves to 'see'. The environmental implications are left open and undeveloped, but it is hard to refrain from pointing out that no plant can continue to be 'too fair' once it has been picked.

In the lines following the ones we have just been discussing, there is more botanizing, along with a good bit of poeticizing. The poem continues thus:

> Many such there are,
> Fair ferns and flowers, and chiefly that tall plant
> So stately, of the Queen Osmunda nam'd,
> Plant lovelier in its own retir'd abode
> On Grasmere's beach, than Naiad by the side
> Of Grecian brook, or Lady of the Mere
> Sole-sitting by the shores of old Romance.
>
> (11.34–40, *LB*, p. 248)

How much did Wordsworth know about this tall and stately plant, classified by Linnaeus as *osmunda regalis*? Did he know, for instance, or did Linnaeus know, that there seems to have been no such person as Queen Osmunda? The common cognates king fern, royal fern, and Osmund the waterman, all incorporate male names; the *Dictionary of National Biography* gives three Osmunds, one Saxon king, one saint, and one bishop, but no entries under Osmunda. Nor have I found a record of a Swedish queen so named. Coleridge gives the form *osmund royal*, in a passage copied by Sara Hutchinson from William Withering's *Arrangement of British Plants*.[15]

Oddly enough, *osmunda regalis* belongs to a class Linnaeus called *cryptogamia*, those whose seeds remain hidden so that the plants are hard to sex. Linnaeus made a great matter of accurately sexing his plants, and upbraided others for their failures in this exact respect: 'The most eminent teachers of the science, attempting to discriminate the sexes, very often called the female plant the male; which affords the most decisive proof of their ignorance that could possibly have been given'. But Linnaeus himself made similar mistakes with the plants in *cryptogamia*, taking the male flowers for female.[16] There is a simple explanation for the attribution of Wordsworth's narrator. Erasmus Darwin renders the plant female:

The fair OSMUNDA seeks the silent dell,
The ivy canopy, and dripping cell;
There hid in shades *clandestine* rites approves,
Till the green progeny betrays her loves.[17]

*Osmunda*, says Darwin, is one of those plants whose sexual activities cannot be observed until the fruits appear. In other words, they withhold information of the sort that the zealous classifier most needs in order to tabulate his researches. I cannot prove that Wordsworth knew this, though I think we should not underestimate him. Further, the preface to the third edition of Withering's *Arrangement* promised 'new arrangements' of the *cryptogamia* 'in hopes of facilitating their investigation'.[18] And there is a teasing gathering of motifs around the sex of the plants. Alan Bewell among others has shown us that the matter was politicized and radically gendered in the 1790s – Darwin's botanical epic was taken to encode a critique of the social order and to extend an unseemly sex education to otherwise polite women readers.[19] Banks's behaviour on Cook's first voyage had also produced a conflation of scientific with sexual adventurism, both because of the general reputation of the Pacific Islands for easy sex, and because of Banks's own reported conduct with Queen Purea of Tahiti.[20] Botanizing after Banks, and again after Darwin, was a slightly scandalous occupation, notwithstanding its associations with gentlemanly leisure. There seems to be little of that in Wordsworth's poem. But it does pick out one of the very order of plants whose sexual functions seem to have stumped Linnaeus himself even as he was classifying it. Who invents *Queen* Osmunda? Wordsworth or his dramatic persona? It is hard to know, or to know how to tell. But if there is a coherent narrative of misbehavior and misidentification here, as I and others have said, then the fabulous etymology as a scholarly joke would be perfectly at home, especially given the hyperbole of the classical and Arthurian comparisons that follow it.

Perhaps, to the acquisitive botanizing imagination, all plants are figuratively feminized, passive before the acts of ravishment we have seen in the piling up of 'flowery spoils' in the last book of *The Excursion*, and which we know most famously from 'Nutting'. The philosopher of 'A Poet's Epitaph', he who would 'peep and botanize/Upon his mother's grave', is also a 'fingering slave', one who pries into private places uninvited (*LB*, p. 236). It is for the most part a male imagination that murders to dissect. But in this poem both sexes are implicated: the female companion – Dorothy of course – shares the 'same admonishment' (*LB*, p. 250) as the others. Gender may not be the primary issue here, but it is an issue. So is class. The leisure class mistakes the working class, and it is the leisure class that is supposed to uphold and carry out the work of global exploration and discovery – the very class that is theorized as educated and disinterested enough to get it right. Wordsworth makes this point not by accusing others, the 'uncouth' mariners, but himself and his own circle. It is a joke, this casting himself as an intrepid explorer of foreign places, but a serious one. We might have some sympathy and admiration for James Cook and his shipmates, piloting their converted Whitby colliers thousands of miles across uncharted oceans with a very unsure sense of where they were going – for, notwithstanding Cook's remarkable talents as a navigator, the specification of longitude was still at the experimental stage: Cook's second voyage (1772–75) carried with it prototypes of the complex maritime clocks that would be required for solving the longitude problem that had bedeviled all previous voyages.[21] Wordsworth, already identifying himself as the poet of local habitation and local knowledge, stumbles into errors a few hundred yards from his own front door. Nor does he attempt the comfort of ascribing a local name to the fern, in the spirit of the Heideggerian rootedness that James McCusick has found in Coleridge's writings as a conscious alternative to the dry Latinisms of Linnaeus.[22]

The joke is on the speaker and his friends, and it is a relatively forgiving one. After all, a lesson is learned and no damage is done except to the self-confidence of the exploring class, which is as it should be. The poem does, however, ask to be considered as among those (quite rare) commentaries Wordsworth offers on the matters of empire and global exploration. The standard accounts turn to the London sections of *The Prelude* and to the previously mentioned passages in *The Excursion* by way of filling out this topic. Alison Hickey's 1996 essay presciently observes that 'Wordsworth negotiates the hermeneutical relation between colonizer and colonized not on distant shores, but closer to home: in London, in familiar rural spots, in the territory of the mind', although she goes further than I would go in seeing *The Prelude*'s mention of 'Negro ladies in white muslin gowns' as 'an overdetermined image of the threatening immediacy of the body of the other'.[23] Saree Makdisi also finds a Wordsworth threatened by London as standing for 'the unrepresentable vastness of the world-system that has produced these objects and people'.[24] Hickey further reads the image of the white ram in the last book of *The Excursion*, by way of a Virgilian allusion, as a 'compelling miniature of Albion's noble race' reproducing itself elsewhere, albeit one that is 'precariously secured upon the threat of subversion'.[25] If there is such a trope at work, it is I think already subverted by what follows in the poem, which I have already discussed; and it is much more strongly qualified if my reading of the 'Point Rash-Judgment' poem is a credible one. Leaving London does not guarantee one's protective isolation; at best it allows the time and space needed to process the implications of one's misunderstandings. It is the possibility that the fisherman in the mist could be all sorts of persons, including the discharged veteran of foreign wars that Wordsworth's poems encounter elsewhere, that renders imperialism a local, domestic issue requiring moral vigilance even in the most apparently sequestered places. That he is a local man reinforces a connection between agricultural and military labour that renders all encounters unpredictable and potentially implicated in global politics. Reading the old man as a comic incarnation of the Patagonian giant, and Grasmere's local topography as a hyperbolic *terra incognita*, brings together the close at hand and the far flung, the local and the global, as subject not only to the same observational distortions but to a similarly exigent moral obligation. Botanical curiosity and incipient or actual spoilation add a further dimension to the situation, suggesting that taxonomical incompetence or ambiguity and not scientific truth might be the result of gathering specimens in north-west England as well as in Botany Bay. The self-accusation of Wordsworth's speaker works to disarm readerly outrage by seeming to do justice upon himself, while laughing very softly at the self-importance of doing just that. Had that lesson been heeded, the history of British India and of other British interventions might have been very different. Wordsworth has been packaged by a heritage industry that seeks to shore up a fortified local environment as *the* critically precious and protected place; his reputation has also endured the animadversions of politically attuned critics who have presented him as a defender of reactionary ideals. His own poetic understanding of his home in the world was a more complex and demanding one – at least, that is what I have tried to argue here.

## Notes

1 *The Complete Poetical Works of William Wordsworth*, eds E. de Selincourt and Helen Darbishire, 5 vols (Oxford: Clarendon Press, 1940–49), vol 5, p. 186. All further references to *the Excursion* in text are to CW, vol 5.

2 *'Lyrical Ballads' and Other Poems, 1797–1800*, eds James Butler and Karen Green (Ithaca and London: Cornell University Press, 1992), p. 236. [Henceforth *LB* in text.]

3 David Simpson, *Irony and Authority in Romantic Poetry* (London: Macmillan, 1979), pp. 72–6; Alan Bewell, *Wordsworth and the Enlightenment: Nature, Man and Society in the Experimental Poetry* (New Haven and London: Yale University Press, 1989), pp. 71–105; Michael Wiley, *Romantic Geography: Wordsworth and Anglo-European Spaces* (London: Macmillan, 1998), pp. 79–126.

4 John Barrell, *The Dark Side of the Landscape: The Rural Poor in English Painting, 1730–1840* (Cambridge: Cambridge University Press, 1980).

5 Greg Dening, *Mr. Bligh's Bad Language: Passion, Power and Theatre on the Bounty* (Cambridge: Cambridge University Press, 1992), p. 262.

6 *The Journals of Captain Cook*, ed. Philip Edwards (London: Penguin, 1999), pp. 32, 138, 135, 141. [Henceforth *Journals* in text.] The importance of Cook's narratives is the topic of Bernard Smith's *Imagining the Pacific: In the Wake of the Cook Voyages* (New Haven and London: Yale University Press, 1992). Smith suggests their influence upon 'The Ancient Mariner'.

7 Paul Carter, *The Road to Botany Bay: An Explanation of Landscape and History* (New York: Knopf, 1988), p. 31.

8 John Barrell's *The Infection of Thomas De Quincey: A Psychopathology of Imperialism* (New Haven and London: Yale University Press, 1991) is a powerful demonstration of the fact that one does not have to leave the country in order to absorb and reproduce the commonplaces of an imperialist culture.

9   Bernard Smith, *European Vision and the South Pacific, 1768–1850: A Study in the History of Art and Ideas* (London: Oxford University Press, 1969), p. 20.

10  The importance of this debate to the theory of fine art is the subject of John Barrell's *The Political Theory of Painting From Reynolds to Hazlitt: 'The Body of the Public'* (New Haven and London: Yale University Press, 1986).

11  Smith, *European Visions*, p. 14.

12  David Mackay, 'Agents of Empire: The Banksian Collectors and Evaluation of New Lands', in David Philip Miller and Peter Hanns Reill, eds, *Visions of Empire: Voyages, Botany, and Representations of Nature* (Cambridge: Cambridge University Press, 1996), pp. 38–57. See pp. 39, 43.

13  James Jenkinson, *A Generic and Specific Description of British Plants, Translated from the Genera et Species Plantarum of the Celebrated Linnaeus* (Kendal: T. Caslon, etc., 1775), p. ix.

14  This is the major topic of my *Wordsworth's Historical Imagination: The Poetry of Displacement* (New York and London: Methuen, 1987).

15  *The Notebooks of Samuel Taylor Coleridge, Volume One, 1794–1804*, ed. Kathleen Coburn (Princeton, NJ: Princeton University Press, 1957), N 863. Wordsworth owned the third edition (1796) of Withering's book, and in August 1801 he ordered two botanical microscopes advertized in the endpages. For information on the Wordsworth household's botanizing habits I am most grateful to Robert and Pamela Woof, Ann Lambert and Molly Lefebure.

16  *A Dissertation on the Sexes of Plants*. Translated from the Latin of Linnaeus by James Edward Smith (London: George Nicol, 1786), pp. 660. I am grateful to Marijane Osborne for help with the detective work on *osmunda regalis*.

17  Erasmus Darwin, *The Botanic Garden, Part II. Containing the Loves of the Plants, a Poem* (Lichfield: J. Jackson, 1789). Facsimile edn. Oxford and New York: Woodstock Books, 1991, p. 11.

18  William Withering, *An Arrangement of British Plants, According to the Latest Improvements of the Linnaean System, with an Easy Introduction to the Study of Botany*, 6th edn, 4 vols (London, 1818). The preface to the third edition is reprinted here (I: xvi).

19  Alan Bewell, ' "Jacobin Plants": Botany as Social Theory in the 1790s', *The Wordsworth Circle*, 20 (1989), pp. 132–9. The 1790s saw a huge increase in the number of publications on botanical subjects: see John Gascoigne, *Joseph Banks and the English Enlightenment: Useful Knowledge and Polite Culture* (Cambridge: Cambridge University Press, 1994), p. 109. Gascoigne also describes the competition between rival classification systems (pp. 98–107): not everyone subscribed to the Linnaean taxonomy. See also Judith Pascoe, 'Female Botanists and the Poetry of Charlotte Smith', in Carol Shiner Wilson and Joel Haefner, eds, *Re-Visioning Romanticism: British Women Writers, 1776–1837* (Philadelphia, PA: University of Pennsylvania Press, 1994), pp. 193–209. Nicola Trott, in 'Wordsworth's Loves of the Plants', in Nicola Trott and Seamus Perry, eds, *1800: The New Lyrical Ballads* (Houndmills: Palgrave Macmillan, 2001), pp. 141–68, thinks that 'Queen Osmunda' is an invented figure and suggests a purposively muted address on Wordsworth's part to the very visible debate about sex and botany. (p. 162).

20  Dening, *Mr. Bligh's Bad Language*, pp. 264–66.

21  See Dava Sobel and William J.H. Andrewes, *The Illustrated Longitude* (New York: Walker & Co., 1998), pp. 165–77.

22  James McCusick, 'Coleridge and the Economy of Nature', *Studies in Romanticism*, 35 (1996), pp. 375–92.

23  Alison Hickey, 'Dark Characters, Native Grounds: Wordsworth's Imagination of Imperialism', in Alan Richardson and Sonia Hofkosh, eds, *Romanticism, Race, and Imperial Culture, 1780–1834* (Bloomington and Indianapolis: Indiana University Press, 1986), pp. 284, 290.
24  Saree Makdisi, *Romantic Imperialism: Universal Empire and the Culture of Modernity* (Cambridge: Cambridge University Press, 1998), p. 32.
25  Hickey, 'Dark Characters', pp. 297, 300.

# 10
## Burns, Wordsworth and the Politics of Vernacular Poetry
*Nigel Leask**

In his poem 'At the Grave of Burns', written during his Scottish tour of 1803, Wordsworth made no secret of his indebtedness to Robert Burns, 'whose light I hailed when first it shone,/And showed my youth/How verse may build a princely throne/On humble truth'[1]. Paying homage by adopting Burns' trademark 'Standard Habbie' stanza[2], Wordsworth evoked the Lakeland peaks of Criffel and Skiddaw visible from both Grasmere and Burns' Dumfriesshire farm at Ellisland, musing that; 'Neighbours we were, and loving friends/We might have been'.[3] Despite this homage to Burns, Wordsworth believed, on the basis of his reading of James Currie's 'Life' prefixed to his 1800 edition of Burns' poems, that the poet had died an indigent alcoholic at Dumfries seven years before in 1796.[4] This explains Dorothy Wordsworth's comment, in her *Recollections of the 1803 Tour*, 'there is no thought surviving in connexion with Burns' daily life that is not heart-depressing'. Reports of the poverty of Burns' widow Jean and his surviving sons 'filled us with melancholy concern, which had a kind of connexion with ourselves', she added.[5] Dorothy registers familial anxiety concerning Burns' role as poetic *alter ego* for her brother Wordsworth, despite the fact that of the two poets' 'neighbourliness', and their possible friendship, thwarted by Burns' untimely death.

Since Russel Noyes's 1944 article 'Wordsworth and Burns', there have been suprisingly few attempts to bring into focus a commonly-observed sense of Burns' major influence on Wordsworth.[6] Notwithstanding all Wordsworth's talk of neighbourliness, a critical border-line has divided the two poets ever since the controversy following Burns' early death in 1796, often issuing in partisan defence of one against the other. This may be in part because the partisan line usually maps onto the political border between Scotland and England, privileging Burns as Scotland's 'national bard' against the English

---

* My thanks to Hamish Mathison and David Simpson for their comments on this essay.

or 'British' Wordsworth. But the line also follows the class and political divide, separating Burns the authentic 'plebeian' poet, whose politics became more rather than less radical in the years before his untimely death, and Wordsworth the middle-class radical, champion of the 'real language of men' during his revolutionary youth, before assuming the nefarious roles of 'lost leader' and Tory backwoodsman. Although Burns now scores massive points as the poetic spokesman for a small nation and a persecuted democratic movement, outside Scotland his poetry remains unjustifiably neglected in University literature departments, ostensibly because of the language difficulties facing non-Scots readers. Wordsworth, by contrast, is widely acknowledged as the major poet of British Romanticism; it's ironic that one of the few underdeveloped areas of Wordsworth studies is Wordsworth's Burns.

In this essay I'll sketch a different context for comparing the two poets by examining their respective ideas about vernacular poetry in relation to questions of social class, region and nation. In particular I'll examine two important mediations of Burns' poetry in the 1790s which, I argue, directly or indirectly influenced Wordsworth's reading of Burns, the first that of the Catholic philologist Alexander Geddes, the second the poet's posthumous editor James Currie. Both Burns and Wordsworth are renowned as poets of the vernacular in conscious rebellion against literary tradition – Burns's 'spark o' Nature's fire',[7] Wordsworth's professed bid to imitate 'the language of low and rustic life'. Olivia Smith has explored the political agenda behind Wordsworth's *Preface* in relation to its privileging of a plebeian rustic language against the neo-classical diction of the polite canon.[8] When set against Wordsworth's generalized concept of the vernacular, however, Burns's poetic language needs definition in regional, national *and* class terms. Carol MacGuirk describes it as a mixture of 'Ayrshire dialect, archaic Middle Scots, words derived from other Scottish dialects, sentimental idioms, and "high" English rhetoric'.[9] Burns drew extensively on the resources of both Scots and English literary tradition: but the diction of many of his best poems is also permeated with the vernacular speech of his own social class and region.[10] In order to understand the politics of Burns' language in the decades of the 1780s and 1790s, it is necessary to consider it in the context both of Enlightenment debates about language, and the eighteenth-century Scottish revival of vernacular poetry.

## Burns and Scottish vernacular poetry

The Scottish vernacular revival associated with the eighteenth-century poets Allan Ramsay, Robert Fergusson and Burns ran against the grain of the Scottish Enlightenment's obsession with defining a non-regional standard English. John Barrell, in his essay 'The Language Properly So Called' (the title is a quotation from Aberdeen rhetorician George Campbell), discusses the appeal by conservative writers like (the Scottish) Campbell, (English) Dr Johnson, and (Irish) Thomas Sheridan to the authority of common linguistic usage, where the word 'common' was understood to override local or occupational peculiarities, including what Sheridan termed 'the invidious distinction' of regional dialect.[11] 'Campbell estimated that only one in a hundred could speak the "reputable", "national", and "current" language', but, comments Barrell, 'his estimate is certainly a generous one.'[12] Janet Sorenson develops Barrell's point in *The Grammar of Empire*, arguing that the standard English 'above grossness and below refinement' promoted by the Scottish professors, and institutionalized in Dr Johnson's *Dictionary* (1755), was in this sense 'nobody's language'.[13]

Not only did the philosophers of Edinburgh, Glasgow and Aberdeen achieve distinction as writers of English prose (just as Scots-born James Thomson has achieved fame as a writer of English poetry), but David Hume, James Beattie and Sir John Sinclair all compiled lists of 'Scotticisms', or undesirably provincial idioms, to assist their fellow-countrymen in their linguistic 'improvement'. Scots 'scientific whigs' were proactively engaged as 'North Britons' in a modernizing Unionist project, instrumental in consolidating the Georgian state in the aftermath of the 1745 Jacobite rebellion. In this respect it is significant that when the Scottish Enlightenment did fly the flag of cultural nationalism, it was in the shape of James Macpherson's *Fingal* and *Temora*: 'ancient' Celtic epics soaked in nostalgia for a lost culture of 'sentimental savages', but 'translated' from Gaelic into standard, albeit primitivized English prose poetry.

All this raises the question as to exactly *why* Edinburgh literati like Professor Hugh Blair (former champion of *Ossian*) or Henry MacKenzie should in 1786 have welcomed Robert Burns with open arms as the author of a volume entitled *Poems, Chiefly in the Scottish Dialect*. That they did should surprise us, as well as the fact (Robert Crawford's point) that when Professors of Belles Lettres like Hugh Blair or William Greenfield suggested improvements to Burns' poetry, they left the Scots language of the poems intact, seeking rather the removal of 'oaths, indecencies, or 'quite inadmissible' references to the Scriptures'.[14] Evidently vernacular poetry was acceptable within polite Scottish culture, despite the strictures of the standardizers. Paradoxes abound in eighteenth-century Scottish attitudes to language, and we shouldn't forget that the vernacular poets Ramsay, Fergusson and Burns all published a considerable corpus of English verse which was influenced by Augustan and neo-Augustan models, some of it of high quality. F.W. Freeman has pointed out that 'anglicizers' like Adam Smith also patronized William Hamilton of Bangour, author of the vernacular ballad 'Braes of Yarrow', notwithstanding Smith's attack on Allan Ramsay and the ballad tradition on the grounds that 'it is the duty of a poet to write like a gentleman'.[15] James Beattie ('a veritable Jekyl and Hyde on questions of Scots language') composed a dedicatory epistle in Scots to Alexander Ross's *Helenore*; Lord Hailes edited *Ancient Scottish Poems* (1770), and William and Alexander Tytler patronized Burns.[16] All these men (with the exception of Oxford-educated Smith) still spoke broad Scots in private as well as 'polished' Anglo-Scots in public, at the same time as they sought to purge their written English prose of vulgar 'Scotticisms'.

Vernacular Scots poetry written in the 'informal' 'Standard Habbie' or 'Christis Kirk' stanza,[17] in common with Scots folk song and ballads, was of course quite distinct from the 'aureate' tradition of Scottish late-medieval and renaissance court poetry terminated by the departure of James VI and the Scottish Court to London in 1603. Matthew McDiarmid claims that the Scots revival originated in the late seventeenth century as 'a literary joke, an entertainment of the same order as macaronic or Hudibrastic verse',[18] privileging satire, informal Horatian epistle and, above all, pastoral. McDiarmid rightly emphasizes the links between Ramsay's Scots pastoral *The Gentle Shepherd* (1725) and the early eighteenth-century English debate about pastoral 'realism' conducted by Pope, Philips, Tickell and Gay. Both *The Gentle Shepherd* and the Scottish songs collected in Ramsay's *Tea-Table Miscellany* (1724–27) defended their vernacular idiom in Theocritan terms as pure 'Doric', compared to courtly English 'Attic' diction.[19] Ramsay and Fergusson appropriated the terms of the English pastoral debate as a vehicle for a new 'British canon' which promoted Scotland's prestige in post-Union Britain, at the same time often employing it as a tool to criticize the cultural 'standardization' of the Hanoverian regime (both poets had Jacobite sympathies).[20] Seeking to reconstruct the broken identity of Scottish poetry under the banner of pastoral 'realism', they created a synthetic language which undoubtedly showed a greater debt to the eighteenth-century spoken vernacular than to the 'aureate' diction of the Scots court.

Deprived of court patronage, the very 'headlessness' of eighteenth-century Scots poetry had the unintended effect of clearing a space for vernacular verse by 'vulgar' poets, like Robert Burns and his fellow Ayrshire 'bardies' John Lapraik, Davie Sillar and John Rankine. It's instructive to compare the fluid vernacular ease of their verse epistles (largely modelled on those of Ramsay and Hamilton of Gibertfield) with the linguistic stress evident in the writings of English plebeian poets from Stephen Duck to John Clare, as the latter struggled to accommodate vernacular English with the proprieties of Augustan poetic form and diction. Barrell cites Clare's frustrated response to his publisher when the latter sought to make his dialect conform with standard English; 'grammar in learning is like tyranny in government – confound the bitch I'll never be her slave'.[21] Provided he adhered to the convention (established earlier in the century by Allan Ramsay) limiting vernacular writing to 'lowly' pastoral genres like eclogue, elegy, epistle and song, Robert Burns enjoyed an advantage denied to the English Clare, and (in a somewhat different sense) Wordsworth.

Both in the Preface and poems of the 1786 Kilmarnock volume Burns declared his strong affiliation to the Scottish pastoral tradition of Ramsay and Fergusson. In his 'Epistle to J. Lapraik, An Old Scots Bard' he artfully turned his back on the polite pastoral of Theocritus and Virgil, wishing only 'for a spunk o' ALLAN'S [i.e. Ramsay's] glee,/Or FERGUSON'S, the bauld an' slee,/Or [in compliment to his correspondent] bright LAPRAIK'S, my friend to be,/If I can hit it!' (*BPS* [*Burns: Poems and Songs*], p. 68).[22] Yet despite the Preface's claim that he was 'unacquainted with the necessary requisites for commencing Poet by rule',[23] Burns showed great skill in extending the parameters of Scottish pastoral, exploiting the linguistic range it offered him, but developing its 'manners painting strains' in the direction of political and theological critique. The same is true of his literary self-image: as a relatively well-educated tenant farmer, Burns ranked above cottars and farm-labourers (including ploughmen) in the social hierarchy of rural Scotland. Although he never attended university (like Fergusson), his social origin was equal to that of Prof. James Beattie, and superior to Allan Ramsay, or his Edinburgh patron Dr Blacklock (the son of a bricklayer). Yet Burns carefully cultivated the role of the 'Heaven taught ploughman' promoted by Henry Mackenzie in *The Lounger* No. 97, a fact noted rather sardonically by his contemporary Robert Anderson.[24] Unlike many contemporary pastoral poets, of course, Burns really had worked at the plough on his father's failing farms, and his harsh experience of rural poverty is recorded in 'The Twa Dogs' and elsewhere. Burns contemplates the appalling prospect of destitution in 'Epistle to Davie, a Brother Poet' and in the 'Epistle to William Simson', he curses the 'whunstane hearts' of the 'Enbrugh Gentry' who had allowed Robert Fergusson to starve in a madhouse (BPS pp. 50, 73). Although proud of his command of literary English, elsewhere Burns effectively blamed the polite obsession with 'fine writing' (his wonderfully back-handed description of Prof. Hugh Blair's profession)[25] for betraying the poetry of the Scots tongue.

If the literary conventions of eighteenth-century Scottish pastoral represented one important factor determining vernacular Burns's acceptability in polite Edinburgh, another was the antiquarian interest in medieval language and literature so current in late eighteenth-century Scottish intellectual debate. Both tended to endorse a poetics of nostalgia. If standard English was a modernizing discourse, then polite Scottish antiquarianism, with its strong Whiggish and patriot leanings, offered a critical vocabulary for legitimizing the work of modern vernacular poets. In a variation of the temporalizing discourse employed by eighteenth-century exotic travel writing and anthropologists,[26] antiquarians validated the living speech of 'the vulgar' as a surviving form of 'Old Scots'. This often depended upon 'filtering out' the modernity of contemporary speech: in his introduction to *Antient Scotish Poems*, for example, the antiquarian John Pinkerton warned contemporary Scots poets not to confuse 'cant phrases' with 'old speech'; by all means 'use the words of the vulgar; but use ancient and grave idioms and manners. Remember this vulgar speech was once the speech of heroes'.[27] For Pinkerton, both Ramsay and Fergusson, inadequately learned in Scottish court poetry, failed the test, and doubtless he would have disapproved of Burns as well. Robert Heron, on the other hand, attributed the popularity of Burns' Kilmarnock volume to the particular quality of its 'phraseology'; 'at once, antique, familiar, and now rarely written...hence fitted for all the dignified and picturesque uses of poetry, without being disagreeably obscure'.[28]

On the one hand, antiquarianism supported the cause of the anglicizers by representing Scots as a language in the process of being 'improved' out of existence. This is evident in James Boswell's plan to compile a Scots dictionary, in the fear that 'the Scottish language is being lost every day, and in a short time will become quite unintelligible'.[29] On the other hand, it could support a more radical position which regarded modern Scots as a pure and uncorrupted dialect of English. This was a linguistic version of the political 'Norman Yoke' argument which championed ancient Anglo-Saxon liberty against modern political corruption; vernacular revivalism was construed as a patriotic 'cause of the people'. In Scotland this argument was often identified with cultural nationalism, albeit one usually content to assert a strong role for Scotland within the British Union, rather than advocating political separatism. Its most famous statement is the polemical claim which Smollett puts into the mouth of Lismahago in *Humphry Clinker* (1771); 'the English language was spoken with greater propriety at Edinburgh than in London... what we generally call the Scottish dialect was, in fact, true, genuine old English'.[30] This wasn't merely one of Lismahago's paradoxes. A decade later the same 'vernacularist' argument was being supported by the Whiggish Society of Antiquaries of Scotland, 'a Temple of Caledonian Virtue', founded in 1780 by David Erskine, Earl of Buchan (one of Burns most ardent and irritating aristocratic patrons).[31] In his study *A Language Suppressed*, Charles Jones draws attention to the writings of late eighteenth-century linguists Sylvester Douglas, John Callander, James Adams and Alexander Geddes (interestingly, the latter two both Roman Catholic priests) who advocated a 'Scottish Standard' against the anglicizers.[32] As we will see below, Geddes energetically pursued a radical form of 'Lismahago's' argument in the Society of Antiquaries' journal, by championing the Scottish poetry of Robert Burns.

Despite the fact that Mackenzie praised Burn's *The Vision* as 'almost English' in its 'high tone of feeling' and 'power and energy of expression',[33] the poem does in fact reveal some of the tensions underlying his attempt to accommodate pastoral and antiquarian discourses, as well as Burns' sense of their potential for a more radical critique. The poem's title echoes Allan Ramsay's *The Vision*, allegedly an early sixteenth-century translation of an earlier Latin poem, in which a warrior spirit rallies Scottish feeling against John Baliol's capitulation to the English Plantagenet invaders. Like Macpherson's *Ossian*, Ramsay's poem was an antiquarian forgery, a fact which serves to ironize *The Vision*'s own participation in the discourse of what Katie Trumpener has denominated 'Bardic Nationalism'.[34] Burns' first 'Duan' (canto) opens in Scots, brilliantly evoking the diurnal realities of agricultural labour which dishearten the rustic poet:

> The Thresher's weary *flingin-tree*,
> The lee-lang day had tir'd me;
> And when the Day had clos'd his e'e
> > Far I' the West,
> Ben 'I the *Spence*, right pensivelie,
> > I gaed to rest.
>
> There, lanely, by the ingle cheek,
> I sat and ey'd the spewing reek,
> That fill'd, wi' hoast-provoking smeek,
> > The auld, clay biggin;
> An' heard the restless rattons squeak
> > About the riggin.

(11.7–18)

On the point of giving up the unprofitable business of poetry ('stringing blethers up in rhyme,/For fools to sing') (1.23–4), the labour-exhausted poet is interrupted by a vision of the glamorous female Coila (named after Burns' native Kyle) 'the SCOTTISH MUSE', whose shapely leg nearly distracts his attention from her mantle, upon which is depicted a map of the topography of Ayrshire and its local worthies.[35] This regional hall of fame, considerably elaborated in the poem's second, Edinburgh edition, moves from the mythological Pictish King Cole and the Scots patriot William Wallace (Burns' nod to the antiquarians), through agricultural improvers Sir Thomas Miller and Col. William Fullerton, to intellectual luminaries Matthew and Dugald Stewart, former and present Professors of Moral Philosophy at Edinburgh University. In the main section of the poem devoted to the vision and Coila's speech, Burns drops the Scots language of the poem's opening, but the Standard Habbie stanza keep the reader in touch with the vernacular tradition

In the second 'Duan', Coila the rustic muse describes her lowly place in Scotia's hierarchy of the muses, or 'light aerial band' (Burns alludes to the sylphs in Pope's *Rape of the Lock*). Her loftier sisters watch over Scotland's civic elite; 'Some rouse the *Patriot* up to bare/Corruption's heart;/Some teach the *Bard*, a darling care,/The tuneful Art' (153–6). Her task, however, as a lowly-ranking member of the aerial band, is to inspire 'the rustic Bard, the lab'ring Hind,/The Artisan' (11.177–8). She has chosen Robert Burns to put her native Ayrshire on the poetic map of Scotland in pastoral verse; 'I taught thy manners-painting strains/The *loves*, the *ways* of simple swains' (11.241–2). Particularly when read in relation to the anti-pastoral strain of the poem's opening stanzas, this is (according to Liam McIlvanney) 'a manifesto for the kind of poet Burns knows his genteel public would wish him to be', rather than the kind of poetry which he might have preferred to write.[36] As such it conforms to the 'humble' pastoral limitations imposed upon Scots vernacular poetry by the Edinburgh professors of rhetoric. Coila continues to admonish the poet:

> Thou canst not learn, nor I can show,
> To paint with *Thomson*'s landscape glow;
> Or wake the bosom-melting throe
>    With *Shenstone*'s art;
> Or pour, with *Gray*, the moving flow
>    Warm on the heart.
>
> Yet all beneath th'unrivall'd Rose,
> The lowly Daisy sweetly blows;
> Tho' large the forest's Monarch throws
>    His army shade,
> Yet green the juicy Hawthorn grows
>    Adown the glade.
>
> (11.247–58)

Notwithstanding Burns' poor showing compared with Thomson, Shenstone and Gray, *The Vision* concludes with Coila crowning her rustic poet with a rustling green holly crown. Her exhortation that he should 'preserve the dignity of Man', 'And trust, the UNIVERSAL PLAN/Will all protect' (1.135; 137) elevates his calling to a sublime level beyond the traditional limits of pastoral. On the one hand, then, *The Vision*'s celebration of Scottish civic revival and agrarian patriotism appeals to gentlemanly antiquarians and patriots eager to affirm Scottish cultural nationalism, and Coila firmly states the pastoral conventions within which her chosen poet must work.

Nevertheless, like the 'juicy Hawthorn', Burns' plebeian radicalism stirs in the undergrowth. Coila the pastoral muse is evoked in earthier language in the 'Second Epistle to J. Lapraik', where she is described as 'The tapetless, ramfeezl'd hizzie,/She's saft at best an' something lazy' (BPS p. 69, 11.13–14), who implores the poet to take a break from rhyming to give her a rest. Reprimanding her, he insists 'I'll write, an' that a hearty blaud [screed],/this vera night;/So dinna ye affront your trade,/But rhyme it right' (BPS p. 70, 11.21–4). As McIlvanney notes, here the Muse is commanded *by* the poet rather than commanding him, her agency now that of incessant female artisanal labour, like the plebeian spinner with her 'rock and wee pickle tow' (distaff and reel) hard-pressed to spin rhymes.[37] Burns' own subordination in the cultural hierarchy is thus displaced via a metaphor based on the exploitation of female labour. Andrew Noble aptly contrast the 'Second Epistle to Lapraik' with the politeness and social deference of *The Vision*, 'a cry of defiant, satirical rage against the old land-owning class and the newly emerging bourgeoisie', the 'paughty feudal Thane' and the 'purse-proud' city-gent.[38]

I want to conclude this section by turning to a contemporary interpretation of *The Vision* which pushed pastoral deference and polite antiquarianism towards a more radical conclusion. Alexander Geddes's article 'Three Scottish Poems with a previous Dissertation on the Scoto-Saxon Dialect' was published in the first volume of the *Transactions of the Society of Antiquaries of Scotland* in 1792. The erudite, eccentric Geddes was a Catholic priest from Banffshire who fell out with the Catholic hierarchy over his controversial new translation of the Bible, which, it has been argued, was a major influence on Blake's 'Lambeth Prophecies'.[39] He was also a self-professed 'true Whig' who became a member of Joseph Johnson's radical London circle in the revolutionary 1790s.[40] Geddes's 'fragment theory' of the Bible (which Jerome McGann reads as a critique of Eichhorn's 'documentary' approach to the Biblical text), derived much of its force from the Scottish vernacular revival and the work of Aberdeen scholars like Thomas Blackwell, reading the Hebrew texts as orally transmitted 'in simple narrative or rustic songs' before being committed to writing.[41]

Geddes' dissertation rehearsed many of the familiar arguments of the vernacular revival, insisting that the 'Scoto-Saxon' language was originally identical to Anglo-Saxon. In a strong version of the 'Norman Yoke' argument, Geddes described William the Conqueror's struggle 'to abolish the language of his English subjects ... [but] the Saxon ... which has always been the language of freemen, tenaciously kept its ground, and in the end triumphed over its imperious rival'.[42] Geographically remote from the centre of power, Scotland remained relatively immune to the linguistic corruption introduced by the Norman invasion, so that at the Union of the Crowns Scots was 'equal in every respect, in some respects superior, to English'.[43] Geddes's 'Saxonist' polemic is a Caledonian version of John Horne Tooke's case in *Winged Words; or the Diversions of Purley* (1786–1805), a work of radical linguistic theory establishing Anglo-Saxon as the proper foundations for the English language, corrupted by Norman-French and abstract metaphysics.[44] For Geddes, an infusion of Scoto-Saxon, and a revival of Scottish poetry, might help to purify modern English (and, by implication, the venal British constitution) from its 'Norman' corruption, just as his use of the Samaritan Pentateuch as a base text for his Bible translation would purge theological corruptions added to the Vulgate by subservient priests and scribes.

Geddes insisted that Scoto-Saxon was superior to modern English in richness, energy and harmony. Challenging Swift's argument in his *Proposal for Correcting, Improving, and Ascertaining the English Tongue*, he argued that its profusion of monosyllables, 'rough, rigid, and inflexible as our oaks, are capable of supporting any burden'. Geddes regretted that Scots poetry, neglected by the learned since the Union of the Crowns, was 'a small grove to an immense forest', a metaphor clearly derived from lines 255–8 of Burns'

*A Vision*.[45] He also took the opportunity of promoting his reformed system of Scottish orthography, demonstrated in his appended translations of 'The First Eklog of Virgil' and 'First Idillion of Theokritus', and recommended that the Society of Antiquaries commission a 'Scoto-Saxon lexicon' to be gathered from all the regions of Scotland, to serve as the basis for a standardized Scots national language.[46]

The most significant part of Geddes article for my present purposes, however, is his long poetic 'Epistle to the President, Vice-President, and Members of the Scottish Society of Antiquaries, on being chosen as a corresponding Member'. The Epistle is written in Scots, although (fortunately) not using the reformed orthography. Despite his concern to praise his aristocratic Whig patrons (particularly the Earl of Buchan, eulogized for his 'love o' freedom ... far fre venal courts retir't'[47]), Geddes attributes the survival of the Scots language (personified as a noble but outcast woman) to the customary probity of the vulgar:

> For tho' tis true, that Mither-tongue
> Has had the melancholy fate,
> To be neglekit by the great,
> She still has fun an open door
> Amang the uncurruptit poor,
> Wha be na weent to treat wi' scorn
> A gentle woman bred and born;
> Bot bid her, thoch in tatters drest,
> A hearty welcome to their best[48]

The gendered personification of 'Mither-tongue' (and note that even radical Geddes holds to the antiquarian-nationalist discourse of the aristocratic origins of Scots) is sustained in his comparison of the Scots language to a 'blate an' bashfu' maid' who 'conceals her blushes wi' her plaid', compared with English, represented as a brazen hussy. The latter's language (with a debt to Defoe) is 'like her true-born Englishman/A vile promiscuous mungrel seed/Of Danish, Dutch, and Norman breed'.[49] Geddes goes on to point an accusing finger at the enlightened guardians of Scottish culture, demanding, in a bravura passage, whether the writings of Adam Smith, William Robertson, James Beattie or Thomas Reid would have lost anything by being written in Scots, rather than in 'mimic sud'ren dialect'.[50]

At this point, 'Coila's glory, self-taught BURNS' is hauled before the reader to vindicate literary Scots as safeguarded by the 'uncorrumptit poor'; 'Hale be thine heart, – thou wale o' swains,/That grace the Caledonian plain'.[51] In 1787 the Earl of Buchan had written patronisingly to Burns, admiring his 'little doric pieces ... in our provincial dialect', but urged the poet to 'keep your eye on Parnassus and drink deep of the fountains of Helicon, but beware of the Joys [*sic*] that is dedicated to the Jolly God of wine'.[52] In contrast, Geddes cautions Burns of the dangers of 'indolence an' pride/Nor cast thine aiten reed aside:/Bot trim, an' blaw it mair an' mair;/An court the Muses late and air:/... So sal thy name be handit down/With uther poets o' renoun;/An BURNS in gowden cyphers shine/Wi' INGLIS, LINDSAY, BALLANDYNE,/GILBRAITH, MONTGOM'RY: an far/Before the laif, ornate DUNBAR'.[53]

Geddes here appropriates Burns in a patriotic bid to elevate the humble tradition of eighteenth-century vernacular poetry (in contrast to Pinkerton, he'd already lavished praise on Ramsay and Fergusson) to a level with the courtly aureate tradition. He hopes that Burns' 'rare example' will serve to inspire 'our rising youths with rival fire': 'Then may some future DOUGLAS sing/A Christian, not a pagan king:/Scots hirds [shepherds] may Mantuan hirds defy,/And FERGUS with AENEAS vy!' A footnote explains that this refers to his hopes for a vernacular epic on King Fergus II, legendary founder of the Scottish royal line. The language of this great epic will be gleaned (like Geddes' Scoto-Saxon lexicon) from all the regions of Scotland 'purif[ied] as much as possible from vulgarism, and reduc[ed] ... to one uniform system of orthography and grammatical analogy'.[54] Its easy to see this sort of aspiration for Burns as being false to the poet's true character, but it does reflect the most cherished hopes of antiquarian revivalists, endowing Scots vernacular with the dignity of a national literary idiom as part of a political project to reform what they viewed as corrupt standard English. Although I've found no evidence that Wordsworth had any direct knowledge of Geddes' defence of 'Scoto-Saxon', in the next section I turn to his admiring (but ultimately ambivalent) relationship with the strain of vernacular nationalism which he championed.

## Wordsworth, Burns and Scottish vernacular

Although Burns's 1786 *Poems, Chiefly in the Scottish Dialect* was printed at John Wilson's provincial press at Kilmarnock, Burns added a glossary of Scots words (extended in the second, Edinburgh edition) which suggest that his ambitions for the volume extended beyond the south-west of Scotland and the Scottish metropolis to England. The fact that southern poet William Cowper made heavy weather of Burns' diction[55] has often been taken as evidence that he was unintelligible to English readers. This is explicitly denied by Burns' posthumous editor James Currie, a Liverpool physician of Scottish background, in a letter to the poet's friend John Syme of 16 September 1796; 'It would amaze you to witness the enthusiasm felt about Burns among many English people here. They understand him easily in all the English counties from Lancashire north; and he everywhere takes that strong hold on the heart which is the criterion of original genius.'[56] Wordsworth, who even in old age spoke with a distinct Lakeland accent, was one of those who had no difficulty with Burns, because 'familiarity with the dialect of the border counties of Cumberland and Westmoreland made it easy for me not only to understand but to feel [Burns' poems]'.[57] A letter from his sister Dorothy reveals that he had read the *Poems* by December 1787, whilst still a schoolboy at Hawkeshead Grammar School;[58] he later described how Burns 'powerfully counteracted the mischievous tendencies of [Erasmus] Darwin's dazzling manner, the extravagancies of the earlier drama of Schiller, and that of other German writers upon my taste and natural tendencies'.[59] Wordsworth frequently commended Burns as a painter of pastoral 'manners', defending him against the anti-pastoralism of Dr Johnson and other eighteenth-century critics of the genre.[60] He particularly admired Burns' idealized portrait of the domestic affections of the rural working class in his pastoral poem 'The Cotter's Saturday Night', to which I return in the conclusion.

Nevertheless, one striking difference from Burns lies in Wordsworth's avoidance of regional dialect in his own poetry. Obviously as an Englishman Wordsworth wouldn't have wanted to imitate Scots vernacular, but (in emulation of the Scottish vernacular poets) he might have sought to adapt the dialect of Lakeland rustics with which he was familiar, if he was serious about imitating the 'real language of men in a state of vivid sensation'. A precedent did exist in the work of Rev. Josiah Relph of Sebergham, whose poems in the Cumberland dialect were published in 1747, and again in a new edition, with woodcuts by Thomas Bewick, in 1798, although I've found no evidence that that Wordsworth read either. (The reprint was probably inspired by the success of Burns' vernacular poems.) Here's a stanza from Relph's pastoral 'St Agnes' Fast: or the Amorous Maiden' describing the maiden's superstitious bid to foresee the identity of her future husband:

> I laisted last aw Hallow-Even lang
> For growen nuts the busses neak'd amang;
> Wi' twea at last I met: to aither nut
> I gave a neame, and beith I'th' ingle put;
> Right bonnily he burnt nor flinch'd a-bit.
> An ah this cruel Roger comes not yet.[61]

Like Wordsworth, Relph was middle-class and university educated, combining an interest in local antiquities with his vocation as village schoolmaster and clergyman at Sebergham. In addition to pastorals, poems on local superstitions and songs, his volume included a translation of several of Horace's *Odes* into Cumberland dialect. Further investigation reveals that despite his Cumbrian roots, Relph's intellectual affiliation was with the Scottish literary scene. Educated at Glasgow University, the 1747 *Poems* were published in Glasgow, although the second edition came out at Carlisle. The editor of the 1798 volume commended Relph's Cumberland pastorals for their employment of 'the rich, strong, Doric dialect of this county...of all dialects, the most proper for pastoral', but then gave the game away by proposing that 'with a little more of sentiment in them, and perhaps tenderness, they would very nearly come up to that inimitably beautiful pastoral, *The Gentle Shepherd* of Allan Ramsay'.[62]

Wordsworth's university education was in Cambridge rather than Glasgow, so his own sense of identity as a Lakeland poet lacked the Scottish affiliation of his regional predecessor. In the preface to his 1800 edition of Burns (read by Wordsworth later in the same year), James Currie quoted the Scottish antiquary Ramsay of Ochtertyre on the advantage enjoyed by Scottish over English vernacular poems and songs; 'Songs in the dialect of Cumberland or Lancashire, could never be popular, because these dialects have never been spoken by persons of fashion. But till the middle of the present century, every Scotsman, from the peer to the peasant, spoke a truly Doric language'.[63] The Glasgow affiliation of Relph's Cumberland pastorals supports my contention that the Scottish vernacular influence on Wordsworth (largely mediated by Burns) offered a strong ideological counterweight to the literary hegemony of London, assisting him to formulate the poetic theory of the 1800 *Preface*. As Leith Davis argues, in the best extant study of the relationship of the two poets, 'Scotland and Burns symbolize a difference within Britain, which Wordsworth both acknowledges and attempts to deny by incorporating it into a universal scheme'.[64]

Wordsworth has really nothing to say about regional dialect in either the 1798 'Advertisement' or the 1800 'Preface' to *Lyrical Ballads*. In the latter, he even took pains to insist, for the benefit of his polite readers, that his imitation of the 'real language of men' here is 'purified...from what appear to be its real defects, from all lasting and rational causes of disgust'.[65] Moreover, apart from odd words usually derived from Cumberland dialect (*pike, sugh, intake, gill, clipping* and *tarn*), scattered through the poems, Wordsworth makes little use of vernacular diction in his poetry, and he generally avoids attempting (like Clare, Tennyson, Hardy or D. H. Lawrence) to represent spoken dialect in his dramatic poems. The only instance of a non-standard English poem in *Lyrical Ballads* is Coleridge's antiquarian 'Rime of the Ancyent Marinere', its orthography modernized in the 1800 edition, where it was relegated to placement near the end of the volume.

David Simpson, one of the few critics to comment on this issue, plausibly explains this in terms of Wordsworth's belief that 'dialect is itself an indicator of social difference, and would not thus have much assisted a poet who was consciously seeking to encourage his readers to meditate upon the essential similarities between man and man'.[66] Simpson argues that Wordsworth's commitment to a 'basic 'national' English' should be seen as part of a programme for reforming the language of poetry along broadly 'republican' lines.[67] Whilst this is undoubtedly true of the Priestley/Paine/Cobbett axis of radical language theory, the examples of Burns and Geddes shows that 'republican' language didn't always insist on erasing its vernacular roots in this way. It was, of course, easier for Scots, Irish and Welsh, than regional English writers, to proclaim their alternative 'imagined communities' in vernacular poetry which promoted patriot ideologies of 'bardic nationalism'.

Although it has generally been read as an attack on the democratic politics behind Wordsworth's bid to imitate 'the language of the vulgar', Francis Jeffrey's celebrated 1802 *Edinburgh Review* article on the Lake Poets reveals his distaste at the spectacle of an English poet 'imitating' Scottish vernacular poetry (or, more simply, Burns) as part of a campaign to reform English poetic diction. Wordsworth's compositions, he wrote, are 'like that of a person who is attempting to speak in an obsolete or provincial dialect' but who 'betrays himself by expressions of occasional purity and elegance'.[68] In a later, 1809 review of Cromek's *Reliques of Burns*, Jeffrey sought to drive a wedge between Burns' vernacular and Wordsworth's 'real language of men' by reiterating Ramsay of Ochtertyre's point:

> we beg leave... to observe, that [Burns'] Scotch is not to be considered as a provincial dialect, the vehicle only of rustic vulgarity and rude local humour. It is the language of a whole country, – long an independent kingdom, and still separate in laws, character and manners...Scotch is, in reality, a highly poetical language...it is an ignorant, as well as a illiberal prejudice, which would seek to confound it with the barbarous dialects of Yorkshire or Devon.[69]

Although Jeffrey has already had a notorious stab at Burns' radical politics, in the final paragraph of his review he sets up a comparison between the 'authentic rustics of Burns', 'Cottar's Saturday Night', and Wordsworth's 'fantastical personages of hysterical schoolmasters and sententious leech-gatherers'.[70] Whilst Jeffrey's critical views embodied many of the Unionist principles of the Edinburgh Anglicizers, he was willing to pardon Burns' radicalism in the interests of promoting Scottish cultural nationalism within the Union, and Wordsworth seemed to offer himself as a sacrificial victim in that cause. Seen through the partisan lenses of the *Edinburgh Review*, Burns was the national poet, Wordsworth the provincial.

We know that Wordsworth was justifiably infuriated by Jeffrey's review, and (as Leith Davis has pointed out) his subsequent hatred of Scottish *literati* like Jeffrey and Currie further complicated his relationship with Burns.[71] Wordsworth's 1816 *Letter to a Friend of Burns*, for example, used Burns as a stalking horse for a savage retaliatory attack on Jeffrey which compared him with Robespierre and Bonaparte: Wordsworth's sense of 'neighbourliness' with Burns was reinforced in terms of the empathy he felt for another poet unjustly used by the Edinburgh critics. But, as Hazlitt noted, '[Wordsworth] is...anxious to get [Burns]out of the unhallowed clutches of the Edinburgh

Reviewers...only to bring him before a graver and higher tribunal, which is his own'.[72]

In a sense, though, Jeffrey did indicate a real problem in Wordsworth's poetic theory and practice. In defining a positive alternative to the neo-Augustan 'poetic diction' which he believed to have vitiated English poetry, Wordsworth needed to devise an alternative language for poetry which was (impossibly) based on a rustic lower-class vernacular that was not a regional dialect. In one respect, then, Burns' vernacular pastoral (which, as we have seen, Wordsworth valued so highly) presented itself as a powerful model, although Wordsworth's own cultural location excluded him from identification with Burns' Scottish tradition, leaving the English poet open to charges of provincialism. The problem of Wordsworthian vernacular was succinctly underlined by Coleridge in the *Biographia Literaria* when he wrote that 'a rustic's language, purified from all provincialism and grossness, and so far re-constructed as to be made consistent with the rules of grammar...will not differ from the language of any other man of common-sense...except as the notions the rustic has to convey are fewer and more indiscriminate.'[73] Coleridge, filtering the 'Preface' of its radicalism, established the conditions for the subsequent acceptance of Wordsworth's critique of poetic diction as a new standard English. If, in the end, Wordsworth's 'experiment' with poetic language was hugely successful, it was mainly because Coleridge's *Biographia* renamed the vernacularist 'real language of men' as a 'lingua communis'. Coleridge located Wordsworth within a conventional tradition of pastoral or meditative poetry, having dismantled the 'Preface's' Burnesian claim to imitate the language of 'low and rustic life', and the radical patriot politics which accompanied that claim.[74]

## Conclusion: the old leech-gatherer

In considering the influence of Burns on Wordsworth, scholars have tended to overlook the fact that Currie's 1800 edition (almost as much as Burns' 1787 volume itself) had a crucial impact on the genesis and arguments of the 1800 'Preface' to *Lyrical Ballads*, as well as several of the poems added to the second edition. Coleridge had met and admired Currie through their mutual friend William Roscoe during his visit to Liverpool in July 1800, en route to the Lake district, where, in September 1800, he began the discussions with Wordsworth which gave birth to the co-authored 'Preface' over the next couple of months. Wordsworth's Commonplace Book shows that by 29 September 1800 he had 'transcribed various fragments from Burns using the second volume of Currie's edition, so it is clear that he, too, had read the work by this time'.[75] These were also incidentally the crucial months when Wordsworth composed *Michael* (included in the 1800 volume), one' of 'a series of pastorals, the scene of which was laid amongst the mountains of Cumberland and Westmoreland',[76] in response to Burns' Ayrshire pastorals.

Space doesn't permit me any detailed analysis here of the influence of Currie's introductory 'Life of Burns' (which Coleridge praised as a 'masterly specimen of philosophical biography'),[77] or his 'Observations on the Character and Condition of the Scottish Peasantry', on Wordsworth and Coleridge's 1800 'Preface'. Suffice it to say that Currie's description of the domestic affections, national feeling and purity of expression amongst the Scottish peasantry (who 'possess a degree of intelligence not generally found among the same class of men in the other countries of Europe'[78]) strongly anticipates Wordsworth's idealized view of the language of 'low and rustic life'.[79]

Just as Currie analysed the social conditions for Burns' Scottish pastorals, so Wordsworth's 1801 *Letter to Charles Fox* sought to contextualize *Michael* and *The Brothers*, in relation to 'the domestic affections...amongst a class of men who are now almost confined to the North of England...small independent proprietors of land here called statesmen...Their little tract of land serves as a kind of permanent rallying point for their domestic feelings ... This class of men is rapidly disappearing.'[80] The character of the exemplary 'statesman' *Michael* in particular appears to absorb much of the Calvinist piety and 'republican' independence of Burns' old Cottar in his pastoral *The Cottar's Saturday Night*. But the tragic narrative of the fate of Michael's 'patrimonial fields', and the urban dissolution of his son Luke, draws rather on Currie's biography of the poet himself, especially his account of Burns' rapid decline as soon as he leaves his farm; 'in Dumfries, temptations to the *sin that so easily beset him*, continually presented themselves; and his irregularities grew by degrees into habits'.[81]

Despite his strong criticism of Currie and 'biographical criticism' in the 1816 *Letter to a Friend of Burns*, Wordsworth's comments on the poet are swayed by Currie's account of Burns' decline into vice and alcoholism. Prised free from the protective enclosure of Geddes' or Jeffrey's 'temple of Caledonian fame', Burns' personal flaws now seem to carry the burden of Wordsworth's own anxieties. Wordsworth elsewhere hinted that Burns' fate was prompted by an internal moral flaw summed up in Coila's seductive doctrine (expressed in lines 239–40 of *The Vision*) that 'the *light* that led astray/Was *light* from Heaven'; no doubt Wordsworth's memory of his 'illicit' affair with Annette Vallon and his own revolutionary sympathies played a part here.[82] But *The Vision* seems to have been a particularly troubling poem for Wordsworth for other reasons, perhaps in part because it located the poetry of 'low and rustic life' within the framework of a distinctly Scottish civic discourse. I want to close by suggesting that in his 1807 poem *Resolution and Independence* Wordsworth returned to the *The Vision* in meditating upon his relationship with the vernacular tradition, even if, in the end, his 'egotistical sublime' triumphed over the Burnesian drive for strong cultural location. It is after all Burns – as well as the teenage suicide Thomas Chatterton – who is evoked at the poet's moment of crisis, as he thinks 'Of him who walked in glory and in joy,/Following his plough, along the mountain-side:/

By our own spirits are we deified:/We Poets in our youth begin in gladness;/ But thereof come in the end despondency and madness'.[83]

Wordsworth maps the poem's narrative of resolution onto the architecture of Burns' *The Vision*. We might recall how Burns' poet comes into his cottage exhausted and depressed from a day's threshing, resolving to abandon poetry (already a rebuke to his Wordsworthian antitype who fears that he lives unproductively off the labour of others). Both Burns and Wordsworth, then, are crippled by an anxiety of vocation: as we've seen, Burns's is resolved by the apparition of Coila, the 'tight, outlandish Hizzie' who imparts the (seductive) doctrine of the 'light that leads astray', before crowning him with the holly wreath of rustic bardship. Wordsworth's vision of the old Leech-gatherer, an instance of the lowest form of economic survival possible in the rural economy, offers a very different, altogether less seductive, kind of 'resolution':

> His words came feebly, from a feeble chest,
> But each in solemn order followed each,
> With something of a lofty utterance drest –
> Choice word and measured phrase, above the reach
> Of ordinary men; a stately speech
> Such as grave Livers do in Scotland use,
> Religious men, who give to God and man their dues.
>
> (ll.92–8)

Wordsworth's poems are littered with stately-speaking Scottish characters, like the Pedlar in *The Excursion*; 'Among the hills of Athol he was born . . . on a small, hereditary farm'.[84] (In an earlier draft, the pedlar 'repeat[ed] the songs of Burns' as he strutted over the hills, 'his eyes/Flashing poetic fire'.[85]) But in reworking the resolution of Burns' *The Vision*, Wordsworth seems to have conjured up one figure from Burns' poetry to allay anxieties raised by another, for behind the Leech-gatherer's 'grave livers' stands the old Cottar reading 'the sacred page'; '*Or Job's* pathetic plaint, and wailing cry;/Or rapt *Isiah's* [sic] wild, seraphic fire;/Or other *Holy Seers* that tune the *sacred lyre*' (BPS p. 120, 11.124–6). Burns' seductive Coila is banished, replaced by an idealized, pious and patriarchal figure of rustic life whose stately diction is that of the Authorized Version rather than the Merry Muses of Caledonia. But what makes this passage such an appropriate conclusion to my essay is the fact that Wordsworth's final couplet is couched as a simile; '*such as* grave livers do in Scotland use'. The visionary Leech-gatherer doesn't actually speak 'the stately speech' of Scotland, but rather a nondescript language which resembles it, the regional affiliation of which cannot otherwise be named.

I've argued that Wordsworths 'real language of men' is dependent upon the cultural politics of Burns' Scottish vernacular just as it struggles to resist it. Not only does 'The Leech-gatherer's' resolution speak volumes about Burns' massive influence on Wordsworth as paramount poet of British romanticism, it also reminds us that the British literary canon emerged from a conflict of national as well as regional and class vernaculars, and that the complexity of these struggles isn't adequately encompassed by a model which proclaims the inexorable triumph of standard over vernacular English. The question is far from closed, but the complexity of the issues at stake should be easier for us to grasp within the devolving culture of the British *post-imperium*.

## Notes

1  *Wordsworth: The Poems*, 3 vols., ed. John O. Hayden (Harmondsworth: Penguin, 1977), I, 588, 11.33–6.
2  A six-line stanza with two rhymes; three iambic tetrameters rhyming aaa, followed by a dimeter, rhyming b, another tetrameter rhyming a, and a dimeter rhyming b. The stanza is named after Robert Sempill of Beltree's (?1600?–1660) mock elegy for Habbie Simson, Piper of Kilbarchan
3  *Ibid.*, 11.41–2.
4  Wordsworth later attacked Currie for publicly parading Burns' 'pernicious habits', but the poems about Burns written during and after the Scottish tour, particularly 'To the Sons of Burns' 11.39–42, effectively reiterate his moralistic criticism. See 'A Letter to a Friend of Burns' (1816) in *Wordsworth's Selected Prose*, ed. John Hayden (Harmonsworth: Penguin, 1988), p. 416 and 'To the Sons of Burns', *Poems*, I, 659.
5  *Recollections of a Tour Made in Scotland*, intro, notes and photographs by Carol Kyros Walker (New Haven and London: Yale University Press, 1997), pp. 43, 44.
6  'Wordsworth and Burns', *PMLA* lix (1944), pp. 813–32. Noyes claimed that his essay was the 'first full and accurate account of Wordsworth's literary debt to Burns' (p. 813). See also Mary Jacobus's excellent remarks in *Tradition and Experiment in Wordsworth's Lyrical Ballads, 1798* (Oxford: Clarendon Press, 1976), pp. 90–1, 202–5, 253–4, Andrew Noble, 'Wordsworth and Burns', in *Critical Essays on Robert Burns*, ed. Carol McGuirk (New York: G.K. Hall, 1998), pp. 49–62, and Leith Davis, *Acts of Union: Scotland and the Literary Negotiation of the British Nation, 1707–1830* (Stanford University Press, 1998), chap. 5.
7  'Epistle to J. Lapraik', l.73. All references are to *Burns: Poems and Songs*, ed. James Kinsley (Oxford: Oxford University Press, 1969), p. 67. [Henceforth *BPS* in text.]
8  *The Politics of Language, 1791–1819*, p. 224.
9  *Robert Burns and the Sentimental Era* (Athens, CA: University of Georgia Press, 1985), p. xxii.
10  See also Raymond Bentman 'Burns' Use of Scottish Diction', *From Sensibility to Romanticism*, ed. Frederick W. Hilles and Harold Bloom (Oxford: Oxford University Press, 1956), p. 239.
11  John Barrell, 'The Language Properly So-called: the Authority of Common Usage' in *English Literature in History, 1730–80; An Equal, Wide Survey* (London: Hutchinson, 1983), pp. 110–75; Thomas Sheridan, *Lectures on Elocution* (London, 1762), p. 31
12  Barrell, p. 133.
13  Sorenson, *The Grammar of Empire in 18th Century British Writing* (Cambridge: Cambridge University Press, 2000), p. 95. See also Barrell, *ibid.*, p. 34.

14  Robert Crawford, *Devolving English Literature*, 2nd edn (Edinburgh: Edinburgh University Press, 2000), p. 101

15  Quoted in *The Bee*, Wed. 11 May 1791, Appendix 1 of Adam Smith's *Lectures on Rhetoric and Belles Lettres*, ed. J.G. Bryce (Indianapolis: Liberty Fund, 1985), p. 230. Wordsworth singled out Smith's remark for attack in his 1802 'Letter to John Wilson', *Selected Prose*, p. 311.

16  F.W. Freeman, *Robert Fergusson and the Scots Humanist Compromise* (Edinburgh University Press, 1984), p. 6.

17  For 'Standard Habbie' see note 2; the 'Christis Kirk' stanza alludes to the late fifteenth-century *Christ's Kirk on the Green*, a poem in Middle Scots often attributed to King James V. See Douglas Dunn, " 'A Very Scottish Kind of Dash': Burns' Native Metric," in Robert Crawford, (ed.), *Robert Burns and Cultural Authority* (Edinburgh: Polygon, 1999), pp. 58–85.

18  In his excellent introduction to *The Poems of Robert Fergusson*, 2 vols (Edinburgh and London: W. Blackwood, 1954), I, p. 118.

19  *Ibid.*, pp. 151–60. See also John Barrell's *Dark Side of the Landscape: The rural Poor in English Painting 1730–1840* (Cambridge: Cambridge University Press, 1980), pp. 8–12.

20  See Steve Newman, 'The Scots Songs of Alan Ramsay: Lyrick Transformation, Popular Culture, and the Boundaries of the Scottish Enlightenment', *Modern Language Quarterly*, 63: 3 (Sept. 2002), pp. 277–314, 288, and Susan Manning's excellent 'Robert Fergusson and 18th Century Poetry', in *Heaven-Taught Fergusson': Robert Burns's Favourite Scottish Poet*, ed. Robert Crawford (Phantassie, E. Lothian: Tuckwell, 2003), pp. 87–112.

21  Barrell, *op cit.*, p. 112.

22  See also Burns's tribute to Allan Ramsay as father of Scottish pastoral in his 'Poem on Pastoral Poetry', 11.32–54 (*BPS*, pp. 155–6).

23  *The Canongate Burns*, ed. Andrew Noble and Patrick Scott Hogg (Edinburgh: Canongate Books, 2001), p. 3.

24  *The Lounger*, No. 97, Saturday, Dec. 9th, 1786, (London; 1794), III, p. 272. See Donald Low *Robert Burns: The Critical Heritage* (London and Boston: Routledge & Kegan Paul, 1974), pp. 8–9.

25  *Letters of Robert Burns*, ed. J. De Lancey Ferguson, 2nd edn. by G. Ross Roy, 2 vols (Oxford: Clarendon Press, 1985), I, p. 440.

26  See my *Curiosity and the Aesthetics of Travel Writing 1770–1840: From an Antique Land* (Oxford: Oxford University Press, 2002), pp. 43–53.

27  'An Essay on the Origins of Scotish [*sic*] Poetry' in *Antient Scotish Poems*, 2 vols (London, 1786), I, p. cxlii. See also Colin Kidd, 'Race, Theology, and Revival: Scots Philology and its Contexts in the Age of Pinkerton and Jamieson', *Scottish Studies Review*, 3, 2 (Autumn 2002), pp. 20–33.

28  *A Memoir of the Life of the late Robert Burns*, published as an appendix to Hans Hecht *Robert Burns: The Man and his Work* (1936) (reprint Ayr: Alloway Publishing Ltd, 1971), p. 266.

29  *Boswell in Holland, 1763–4*, ed. Frederick Pottle (London: Heinemann, 1952), p. 161.

30  *Humphry Clinker*, ed. Peter Miles (London: J.M. Dent, 1993), p. 203. Lismahago also criticized the economic effects of the Union, and supported Bute's ministry, both positions associated with Smollett himself.

31  For an authoritative account of the cultural politics of the Society of Antiquaries, and Buchan's role in particular, see Steven Shapin, 'Property, Patronage, and the

Politics of Science: The Founding of the Royal Society of Edinburgh', *British Journal for the History of Science*, vii (1974), pp. 1–41.

32  Charles Jones, *A Language Suppressed: The Pronunciation of the Scots Language in the 18th Century* (Edinburgh: John Donald, 1995), particularly pp. 13–21.

33  *The Lounger*, 97 (Saturday, 9 Dec 1786), p. 267.

34  *Bardic Nationalism: The Romantic Novel and the British Empire* (Princeton University Press, 1997).

35  Gerard Carruthers explores the influence of Thomson's *Seasons* on this passage. See 'James Thomson and 18th Century Scottish Literary Identity' in Richard Terry, ed., *James Thomson: Essays for the Tercentenary* (Liverpool University Press, 2000), pp. 165–90; 182–3.

36  Liam McIlvanney, *Burns the Radical: Poetry and Politics in Late 18th Century Scotland* (Phantassie, E. Lothian: Tuckwell Press Ltd, 2002), p. 72.

37  *Ibid.*, p. 74.

38  *Canongate Burns*, p. 141.

39  See John Mason Goode, *Memoirs of the Life and Writings of Rev. Alexander Geddes, LL.D.* (London, 1803); Charles Jones, *A Language Suppressed*, pp. 15–18; and Jerome McGann, 'The Idea of an Indeterminate Text: Blake's Bible of Hell and Dr Alexander Geddes', in *Social Values and Poetic Acts: The Historical Judgement of Literary Work* (Cambridge, MA: Harvard University Press, 1988), pp. 152–72.

40  In 'Alexander Geddes and the Burns' "Lost Poems" Controversy', *Studies in Scottish Literature* 31 (1999), 81–5, Gerard Carruthers identifies Geddes as the author of several political poems published in the *Morning Chronicle* in 1794 and 1795, attributed to Burns by Patrick Scott Hogg in his book *Burns' Lost Poems* (Clydeside Press, 1997). Partly on the strength of these poems, Carruthers claims Geddes as 'after Burns the second most significant Scottish poet of the 1790s' (p. 82).

41  McGann, p. 169.

42  'Three Scottish Poems, with a previous Dissertation on the Scoto-Saxon Dialect', *Arachaeologica Scotica, or Transactions of the Society of Antiquaries of Scotland*, Vol. 1 (Edinburgh 1792), pp. 402–68, p. 407.

43  *Ibid.*, p. 416.

44  For Tooke's influence on Wordsworth and Coleridge, see Olivia Smith, *Politics of Language*, ch. 6.

45  *Ibid.*, p. 420.

46  *Ibid.*, p. 439.

47  *Ibid.*, p. 455.

48  *Ibid.*, p. 444.

49  *Ibid.*, p. 447.

50  *Ibid.*, p. 449.

51  *Ibid.*, p. 453.

52  Ian McKintyre, *Dirt and Deity: A Life of Robert Burns* (London: HarperCollins, 1996) p. 126.

53  Geddes, p. 453.

54  *Ibid.*, p. 455.

55  See Low, *The Critical Heritage*, p. 91.

56  Quoted by Robert D. Thornton, in *James Currie 'The Entire Stranger' and Robert Burns*, (Edinburgh: Oliver & Boyd, 1963), p. 352.

57  Low, p. 162.

58  *Ibid.*, p. 92.

59  *Ibid.*, p. 163.

60   See particularly his 27 Feb. 1799 letter to Coleridge reprinted in Low, p. 131.
61   *A Miscellany of Poems, consisting of Original Poems, Translations, Pastorals in the Cumberland Dialect, Familiar Epistles, Fables, Songs, and Epigrams, with Preface and Glossary* (Glasgow: Robert Foulis, 1747), p. 95. The theme is common to both Burns' 'Halloween' and Keats' 'St Agnes Eve'.
62   *Poems, by the Rev. Josiah Relph of Sebergham, with the life of the autho*r (Carlisle, 1798), p. xix. See also E.R. Denwood and M. Denwood, eds, *Oor Mak O'Took: An Anthology of Lakeland Dialect Poems, 1747–1946* (Carlisle, 1946).
63   James Currie, *Complete Works of Robert Burns, with an Account of his Life, and a Criticism on his Writings, to which are added, some Observations on the Character and Condition of the Scottish Peasantry* (Aberdeen: George Clerk & Son, 1847), p. 108.
64   Leith Davis, *Acts of Unions*, p. 129.
65   Wordsworth and Coleridge, *Lyrical Ballads*, ed. R.L. Brett and A.R. Jones, 2nd edn (London: Routledge, (1991), p. 245.
66   *Wordsworth's Historical Imagination: The Poetry of Displacement* (New York and London: Methuen, 1987), p. 102.
67   *Ibid.*, p. 104. See also Barrell on the awkwardness of Priestley and other dissenting theorists on the question of dialect, *English Literature in History*, pp. 161–5.
68   *Edinburgh Reviews*, 1 (Oct. 1802), p. 68.
69   Low, *Critical Heritage*, p. 186.
70   *Ibid.*, p. 195.
71   *Acts of Union*, pp. 135–41.
72   Hazlitt, 'Burns, and the Old English Ballads', in *Lectures on the English Poets and Spirit of the Age* (London: Dent, 1920), p. 128.
73   *Biographia Literaria*, ed. Nigel Leask (London: Everyman, 1997), p. 209.
74   See my *Politics of Imagination in Coleridge's Critical Thought* (London: Macmillan, 1988), pp. 46–74.
75   Daniel Sanjev Roberts, 'Literature, Medical Science and Politics, 1795–1800: *Lyrical Ballads* and Currie's Works of Robert Burns', in Cedric Barfoot, ed., *A Natural Delineation of Human Passions': Lyrical Ballads 1798–1998* (Amsterdam: Rodopi Press, 2003), pp. 115–28, p. 120. Thanks to Daniel Roberts for sending me a copy of his essay, to which I owe my remarks on Currie's influence on the 1800 *Lyrical Ballads*.
76   Footnote to 'The Brothers', *Lyrical Ballads*, p. 135.
77   Low, p. 108.
78   Currie, p. x.
79   *Lyrical Ballads*, p. 245.
80   *Wordsworth, Selected Prose*, p. 164. Note that this explicitly *excludes* Currie's Scottish peasantry. In a longer version of this essay I compare forms of customary land tenure in Scotland and England underpinning Wordsworth's remark.
81   Currie, p. 80.
82   *Canongate Burns*, p. 69, The line is (mis)quoted in 11.41–2 of 'To the Sons of Burns', *Wordsworth: The Poems*, I, p. 659.
83   *Ibid.*, I, p. 553.
84   *Ibid.*, III, p. 43.
85   Stephen Parrish, *The Art of the Lyrical Ballads* (Cambridge, MA: Harvard University Press, 1973), p. 125.

# 11
# Organic Form and its Consequences

*Frances Ferguson*

In the spring 2001 issue of *Critical Inquiry*, Mary Poovey reopened the question of organic form and its functioning in literary criticism.[1] She began by quoting an account of the model system in biology, which the authors described as 'an object or process selected for intensive research as an exemplar of a widely observed feature of life (or disease)'. The authors she cited noted the importance of model organisms (such as mice) for laboratory research, insofar as laboratory research is interested in identifying typical problems and solutions, and they noted as well the self-reinforcing character of model systems. Even self-consciousness and criticism of such systems, they said, tended only to strengthen the hold of the model system on practice. After quoting them, Poovey went on to ask: 'Does contemporary literary criticism have a model system?'

Her answer, that it does, and her further specification, that the model is that of organic form, are, I think, entirely persuasive. In her account, the rise of discursive specialization in the nineteenth century involves not just the emergence of autonomous intellectual disciplines out of what she calls 'the relative lack of discursive specialization in eighteen-century British writing' (Poovey, 2001, p. 412); she also notes that such autonomy rests on a foundational borrowing. 'Like all organizational paradigms', Poovey writes, 'these tropes come from other systems of naming and ordering the world, where their figurative dimension is not necessarily prominent' (p. 410). Literature, she argues, may have adopted the particular trope of organic form in an act of misappropriation, but its presumption has not prevented it from functioning to set cultural and professional values. Illegitimate in itself, it has become an implement for social arbiters. Thus, Poovey observes that the notion has come to serve as a tool with which to separate some readers from others. The deployment of the notion of 'organic form' has, in particular, enabled a distinction between readers and *readers*, There are the lay readers who might read novels, poems and journalism alike for topicality or moralism or both, and, on the other hand, there are professional literary critics who read for form while shunning moralism.

Some might, with simple if shame-faced resignation, accept Poovey's account of the historical determinism that has led 'the trope of the organic whole and the genre of the romantic lyric' to enjoy what she calls 'a virtual monopoly in the literary criticism published by professionals in the U.S.' (p. 437). Or they might accept her diagnosis of what it means to be a practicing literary critic and wear it as a badge of honour, much like consumers actually ordering from catalogues that they have received unsolicited in the mail. Yet it is clear that Poovey is not simply holding up a mirror to literary critics so that they can reluctantly accept or enthusiastically admire their own reflections. She is also, as she says in her closing remarks, hoping 'both to discover the limitations of the disciplinary orthodoxies we have inherited and to devise new methodologies that put different metaphors to a different use' (p. 438).

Some readers might want to dismiss Poovey's diagnosis – and mine – as mistaken and to say that she and I are worrying about an illness from which we have long since recovered, that we are merely dwelling on a kind of intellectual flu from which we bounced back some time ago. After all, it has been some time since gender studies began criticizing the presuppositions of implicit biologisms that suggested the 'natural' superiority of certain forms of organization to others, and various historicisms (Marxist and New) have made it axiomatic that history is made rather than grown. Furthermore, the deconstructive attack on the notion might seem to have done a definitive job of dispatching it, because deconstruction targeted it on two fronts. If deconstruction first criticized organic form as an implicit effort to make cultural products look natural, hence unalterable by human efforts, it also had another weapon in its arsenal. For even if one were to reduce one's claims for organic form and concede that it was just a metaphor, deconstruction readily answered that even metaphors were constructions that mistakenly suggested that concepts could be given stability and that thus blocked the recognition of language's constant processes of distribution. And were these demurrals not enough, some readers might object that poetry – particularly lyric poetry – has not enjoyed centre-stage for some decades now and that prose – particularly the prose of the novel – has become the reigning model literary object. For all the apparent evidence of the decline of the idea of organic form, however, I think that Poovey is absolutely right to see that it continues to have a purchase on our understanding of literary objects and our organizations of that understanding.[2] Moreover, I think that she addresses her argument to the right target – the question of beliefs and how we get them, lose them, and find them intractable, or find them comparatively unaffected by argument.

In this essay I will not be able to rehearse the various points that Poovey makes in the course of her subtle and interesting discussion. For my purposes here and now, it is enough to stress her attention to the relationship between literary professionalization and religious belief. Explaining how a professionalizing biology in nineteenth-century England deployed techniques for observing organisms, she notes how the resultant account of evolution ran into headlong conflict with the creationist doctrine that organisms replicated themselves according to plans laid down for them during the six days of divine creation as described in the *Book of Genesis*. Professional science, she observes, developed a theory of organic change that contained the theory of evolution *in nuce*. In the process it advanced in such a way as to exact a price from religious belief. In saying this, Poovey recounts a history that is familiar to readers who have no more familiarity with Victorian literature than the poems of Tennyson's *In Memoriam*. Yet she also advances a more controversial claim – that literary criticism emulated the professionalism of the biological sciences and self-consciously tried to eliminate religious and moral concerns from its purview. Although literature had no 'facts' to observe and discover that would challenge religious orthodoxy, literary criticism increasingly took its own seriousness to rest on distinguishing itself from a moralism that could run while it read. Criticism thus banished St Paul and various divines to embrace a professionalized status for Ariel. Recounting Biblical stories might provide parables for moral guidance, and the literature of moral uplift might offer secularized versions of such writing. Literary criticism would, however, come to professionalize itself by staring in the face the requirement that an attention to form – specifically, organic form – would involve sloughing off reference to the particular problems that individuals might face in their lives.

Poovey finds evidence to support her view in much of the most influential criticism of the last century, and she could easily find more. By the time that W.K. Wimsatt wrote an essay called 'Organic Form: Some Questions about a Metaphor' (which was published in collections in 1972 and in 1973), he discussed the question of 'organic form' as one professional to others.[3] He was relying on the histories of others, he said, because he took 'history as an object...before us, almost palpably, upon the table', so that he could 'choose [his] own exhibits' (Wimsatt, 1973, p. 13). He then proceeded to make a series of theoretical claims. His first was that what was organic had to do with form rather than content – so that Wordsworth's writing might plausibly be seen as exemplifying organic form even though he did not use the term, while a 'Currier and Ives print of watermelon vines, trumpet flowers, and humming birds' might present 'organic forms' without our being disposed 'to argue that it thereby *has* high artistic form' (p. 19). His second claim, which he made by quoting G.N.G. Orsini, was that organic form could only be applied to 'the finished product', that it had no relevance to the psychological or compositional aspects of art that Coleridge had concerned himself with in his early deployment of organic form in an English context. As Wimsatt said, this view amounted to yet another rejection of what he said he had 'fallen into the habit of referring to as the "intentional" or the "genetic" fallacy' (p. 22). Finally, he endorsed a generous or loose interpretation of the analogy between poems and organisms. Claiming that Orsini was right to remark the moment in the *Critique of Judgment* in which Kant observes 'that a work of human art differs from a natural organism in that the latter is self-organizing, that it can repair itself when damaged, and that it reproduces itself' (p. 24), Wimsatt called attention to the limits of the analogy. Organic form as it is represented by 'neo-Kantian idealist voices' (p. 34) might describe the interanimation of literary works by their various parts but that was only true for 'perfect' literature. Wimsatt, however, breezily dismissed claims to perfection. With 'English poetry as we know it – [that of] Shakespeare, for instance, or Pope', however, he thought that the facts of uneven poetic execution required that a modern critic 'find the organic structure of the poem, perhaps paradoxically, a notably loose, stretchable, and adjustable kind of organic form' (p. 34).

Perhaps the most remarkable feature of Wimsatt's discussion is his high degree of ambivalence about the notion of organic form. As his wry charac-terization of perfection suggests, he treats perfection and organic form alike as ideas and ideals that must inevitably misrepresent what he takes to be the practice of poetry – poems as they are. Insofar as the notion of organic form is associated with what he calls 'the absolute idealist doctrines – no life in the part without the whole, no substitution of one part for another, and the like', he distances himself from it (p. 26). Yet he does defend the notion when he confines it to what he terms 'a very purified post-Kantian version of the aesthetic properties: the individuality and uniqueness of each aesthetic whole, the priority of the whole to the parts, the congruence and interdependence of parts with part and of parts with the whole, the unique-ness or irreplaceability of parts and their non-existence prior to the aesthetic whole or outside it' (*Ibid.*). Indeed, Wimsatt goes so far as to say that 'if we had never heard of organic form, we should today be under the necessity of inventing it' (pp. 26–7). His reasons for thinking about its necessity, however, are somewhat surprising. No 'literary critic is likely to rebel against the ideas he has associated with organic form', so long, that is, as a literary critic knows enough critical history 'to appreciate the embarrassments for criticism created by the more extreme versions of legislation according to the classical literary kinds, or of evaluation according to the classical ornamental rhetoric, or of explanation according to economic, sociological, or other historical categories, or according to any theological, anthropological, or psychological archetypes' (p. 26).

My point in quoting as much of Wimsatt's discussion as I have is to call attention to what may look like a startling omission of argument. For Wimsatt neither addressed the assumptions of the non-organic modes nor did he argue against them. Instead, he proceeded in a rigorously comparative mode. A God surveying the kind of creation that Wimsatt saw would not have seen that it was good, but would have seen that it was better than another alter-native. He would have seen that it was comparatively good. Indeed, this comparative procedure enabled Wimsatt to mount an energetic defense of a reading that Talbot Donaldson had advanced for a disputed passage in the *Wife of Bath*'s tale when he explained his editorial decisions. Even though the 'key word [happened] to occur in three [supposedly] "bad" manuscripts among the total of fifty-two', that key word [was] the reading 'that [made] good sense' – by way of making better sense than the alternative. Wimsatt's account of Donaldson's position, in other words, not only set itself in opposition to idealism. It could accept a modified idealism if one had arrived at a generally idealist position through techniques that classical utilitarianism had developed and honed. If, in 'The Intentional Fallacy', Wimsatt and Beardsley had argued that 'The proof of the poem, as of the pudding, is that it works',[4] that statement of the apparent primacy of the poem *in itself* rested on the kind of comparative analysis that someone like Bentham regularly produced when he opined, in a passage that Wimsatt had once cited, that poetry might be no better than pushpin, if one were considering simply the amount of pleasure that the two activities might generate.

And one consequence of the application of comparison was that one did not need to be able to say much about the nature of any of one's options; one needed merely to identify one available possibility as preferable to or inferior to some other. In that sense, the comparative method was committedly agnostic. It suspended claims about existence. Utilitarian comparativism set itself free from the requirement for justification and evidence of the plausibility of one's belief, as William James famously demonstrated in his essay 'The Will to Believe' when he claimed that religious belief might be, from a comparative, utilitarian perspective, more effective for an individual than non-belief. The distance of this position from any argument designed to prove the existence of God is substantial, because James simply does not concern himself with whether God does or does not exist. Moreover, he sidesteps all the emotional apparatus in which an individual might tax herself with deficient faith as if there were a standard of religious faith that persons might fall short of. The existence of God ceases to be a notion that is formulated as a proposition about existence, with arguments that affirm or deny.[5] Rather, we have that same gesture that Wimsatt used in explanation of his commitment to 'organic form' even as he was explicitly disagreeing with almost everything that might be seen as a plausible explanation of the content of the notion: Is religious belief preferable to the absence of belief? Is a commitment to organic form better than a commitment to classical literary kinds or classical ornamental rhetoric or explanation 'according to economic sociological, or other historical categories, or according to any theological, anthropological, or psychological archetypes'?

Indeed, at this point, we might observe that a tension has developed in Wimsatt's discussion between the notion of organic form as any kind of a model object and as a methodology. The emphasis on a model object involves a loose and practical Platonizing; it identifies entities that are said to have greater or lesser resemblance to other entities on the basis of shared properties. When objects become model objects, they can perform that function because they are being credited with having recognizably similar content to other (usually larger and more complex) objects. Indeed, this has been the understanding that even the strongest arguments against the notion of organic form have involved. Roland Barthes, Jacques Derrida and Paul De Man objected to the notion of organic form, in part because they took it to involve an illegitimate analogy between natural givenness and artificial production. Artifice was continually seen to try to borrow or prop itself on forms that, in being natural, had some claim to reality, to an actuality less open to suspicion than the world of artifice and society in which persons can misrepresent themselves and their views. Barthes, Derrida and De Man took people to whore after nature, or, perhaps better, to pimp for it, because people imagined that nature did not lie and thus might disclose its content with peculiar reliability.[6] Thus, Barthes, Derrida and DeMan treated the naturalization of culture as if it were the equivalent of counterfeited designer clothing. Naturalized culture, in their view, operated with a guilty consciousness of its own imitativeness, or should do. From their perspectives, it thus seemed that the project of criticism ought to be conceived as the project of coming to understand what sorts of claims about the properties of objects one was underwriting in pressing such analogies farther than they ought to go.

The post-structuralist critique – that various forms of artifice were continually trying to claim a content they didn't have by insisting on their 'naturalness' – was profoundly influential. Morever, if one looks at Wimsatt's essay 'The Structure of Romantic Nature Imagery', one can see that their suspicion of the use of nature had strong precedent. Wimsatt talked in that essay as if the sharp descriptions of eighteenth-century poetry had given way to the blurry descriptions in Romanticism, to descriptions of natural surfaces that became, improbably enough, the occasion for speaking of greater subjective depth.[7] There Wimsatt described poetic technique and form but ultimately left the impression that these were different ways of representing poetic content that were like focused and unfocused camera lenses. Yet, if one were trying to compile statements about the content of literature in general or poetry in particular from Wimsatt's essay on organic form, the task would be a very difficult one indeed. Wimsatt characterizes neither Shakespeare nor Pope. He never comes close to mentioning a standard for judging literature or criticism. Instead, he pursues his comparativism so relentlessly that the essay has an odd swagger to it, as if he were ultimately saying, 'I don't know what it is, but I know it's the best'.

The peculiar result is that Wimsatt defends values that seem to be unconnected to facts. And many critics have thus plausibly searched for the real commitments that underlay and motivated the value judgments that were so aggressively held. Yet Wimsatt's practice foregrounds problems that have been particularly live for both criticism and literature itself since the eighteenth century, in that it insistently divests itself of commitments that might be exposed. For the point of professionalization as he practices it is not to create a class of experts who can recognize and applaud organic form when they see it in poems or novels, but to deploy organic form – specifically by assembling a canon – so that they can make different poems and novels work not just by being what they are in themselves but by continually calling up what they are in comparison to some other poem, some other novel. Professional credentials in some fields – I think here of law, for example – involve the mastery of certain formulas, the professional jargon that treats a particular combination of words as if it were a key cut so that it would open a particular lock.[8] Yet it is a remarkable feature of New Critical practice that it developed and invoked so few terms of art and that its technical phrases – 'intentional fallacy', 'genetic fallacy', 'affective fallacy' – all described putatively bad ways of thinking about literature rather than good or bad features of literature itself. The sole professionalized and professionalizing contribution that New Criticism offered to literary criticism was the notion of a canon, a collection of texts that together constituted literature, with literature being conceived in essentially ahistorical terms.

The New Critical notion of the canon was the device that itself instantiated organic form and provided an account of how individual poems or novels might be put to work, might come to be especially meaningful on account of their intertextual relations to other texts. What now looks like Wimsatt's unguarded candour in speaking about 'imperfect' literature like Pope's or Shakespeare's was in effect already a way of identifying the 'work' that a poem or a pudding or anything else might do as an action that could only be perceived if one set it into a larger field in which constant comparisons would allow it to 'work' and 'act'. The canon enabled individual poems to look ambitious whether or not their authors had been ambitious for them, because it created a field of value that could work upon individual texts in much the way that a market economy works on individual goods and services. Professionalism and professionalization involved identifying and stabilizing that market.

The stakes of Wimsatt's critical gesture may become most readily apparent, however, if we consider two different artistic forms that enjoyed exponential growth in the eighteenth century – the novel (particularly in the narrow characterization that Ian Watt gave of it and that has in recent years been continually criticized for its narrowness) and the landscape garden.[9] Both of these represent a dramatic break with previous accounts of artistic imitation, for neither, however much they seem to commit themselves to reproduction of the actual world in drawing their materials from daily life and in using nature to imitate nature, worried about whether they could adequately imitate original objects of perception. As is famously the case, the eighteenth-century novel changed even its standard naming practices. Instead of using the kinds of names that would be recognizable in an iconographic tradition that included the lives of heroes and saints and all their associated paraphernalia, the novel used names drawn from the vernacular. And the landscape tradition moved in a similar direction. It divested itself of traditional iconography and began to announce its commitment to seeing that 'all nature was a garden'. If both of these artistic currents have been said to appeal to the lower classes or the advancing bourgeoisie who might not be expected to recognize the iconographical references of the learned, their appeal was perhaps even more direct. For their real accomplishment as arts was to 'discover' their subjects, to utter to them words that we would associate with Hollywood pick-up lines, 'You ought to be in pictures'. For the fictitious editors that Richardson and Rousseau employed were not, in the final analysis, fictions at all. The new role for novelists and landscape gardeners alike was that of editors, people who did not so much idealize actual domestic scenes and natural growth, but edit them. Indeed, they called attention to the way their editorial efforts attempted to create a hyper-actuality. The world of ordinary life and the world of ordinary landscape, however interesting and beautiful they might be, were *inadequate to themselves*. Even if they were as 'perfect' as the stanzas of Pope, the dramas of Shakespeare or the most beautiful natural sites, that achievement came to look imperfect in the hands of novelistic and garden editors, who saw that things could always be improved, or, oxymoronically, made more perfect.

Organic form, in other words, became more a method than a description of the true nature of objects, as both picturesque viewing and epistolary novels insisted upon working the margin in which one view would look comparable to and competitive with another view. As John Barrell observed in his *The Idea of Landscape and the Sense of Place 1730–1840: An Approach to the Poetry of John Clare*, the word 'landscape' is 'a painter's word' that marked the difference between the merely visible and the picturable.[10] John Dixon Hunt tells us that 'the term "picturesque" in English. . .was originally used to refer to material that was suitable for inclusion in a painting or, by extension, material in the actual world that could be conceived or viewed as if it were already part of a picture'.[11] And if picturesque travellers spent a good deal of time changing their 'station backward & forward, till [they] had obtained a good [foreground]', and agriculturalists and landscape gardeners went so far as to move earth and stream to improve a landscape, Barrell explains that their efforts weren't simply a foolish fashion. 'What did matter', he writes, 'was the ability to conceive a landscape as a pictorial composition, and that this was so is further suggested by the enthusiasm with which collectors tolerated the numerous bad imitations of Claude, bad copies, and even bad forgeries' (Barrell, 1972, pp. 5–6). The actual painting did not matter. What was uppermost was 'a style of conception but not a quality of realisation' (p. 6).[12]

I want to underscore the importance of Barrell's recognition that the eighteenth century was already developing its own version of what the twentieth century would call conceptual art, and I want as well to offer a brief addendum to indicate how I think his remarks should be understood. For it would be easy to understand the rise of 'a style of conception' to mean that the poetry (or the landscaping) doesn't matter. This characterization seems to me mistaken, because Barrell's account also points to an important feature of the editorializing of novels and landscapes that I earlier mentioned – that both novelistic and landscaping art in the eighteenth century create themselves as canons, miniature archives that continually compare one version and another to ask if this, now, isn't better. Gilpin, for instance, needs to produce an account of the less-good way of seeing a particular scene, not because he needs to demonstrate that he has laboured to produce it, but because he needs to establish a comparison. And this same process appears even more insistently in the novels of Richardson and Rousseau, which are themselves almost nothing but an archive containing the possibility of comparing what one said then with what one said later to see which seemed preferable. The epistolary novelist and the landscape artists, in other words, redefine the notion of a canon. No longer does it refer to a collection of sacred or approved texts that should be used as the basis for imitative action. Epistolary novelists and landscape artists replace that understanding with the notion of an archive in which the various exhibits are to be compared with one another and in which texts and gardens create their own internal historical trail. Moreover, that historical trail is not designed to provide support for a particular meaning in the way that a contract drawn up in the past might be understood to do. Instead of asking, in the manner of Christian fundamentalists, 'What would Jesus do?' or, in the manner of readers of a contract, 'What did they actually mean by using these words as the sign of agreement?', the epistolary novelist and the picturesque connoisseur continually present character and observers as their own editors, thinking always about 'what I should have said' and 'how it should have looked'.

In *The Idea of Landscape*, Barrell did not explicitly take up the question of organic form as a distinct aesthetic metaphor, but his concerns there are especially pertinent to my view of organic form, because he consistently broached the question of the impact of our taste in representations on our ways of acting in the world. Specifically, he traced the process through which the chief way of valuing a landscape came to lie in thinking about how to alter it, to see landscape gardening as what Capability Brown called 'place-making' and to see that fashion in taste replacing the older interest in paintings and drawings that were essentially portraits of distinguished houses. 'The paintings of Claude, Poussin, and their imitators', Barrell writes, 'did invite ... a specifically formal appreciation, and it was chiefly in response to the work of these men that the English connoisseur of the eighteenth century developed his characteristic way of looking at landscape... *A* landscape was fitted into *the* established set of landscape patterns, and so became part of the *universal* landscape, which included any tract of land the connoisseur chose to examine'(p. 7).

It is a key feature of Barrell's analysis that he was not tracking down specific paintings of Claude's that Gilpin, say, had seen or might have seen. Indeed, as I mentioned earlier, he was more interested in the cumulative effect of various instances of an aesthetic fashion, so that he could talk precisely about the way in which the fashionableness of what we see leads us to see it not just as natural but as *applicable*. Thus, he called attention to the fact that viewing many landscape paintings by Poussin, Rosa and Claude did not merely enable members of the sophisticated reading and viewing public to recognize various paintings as the work of those artists. Instead, such viewing led them to '[reconstruct] the landscape in the imagination', so that understanding the basic 'principles of composition' gave them skills that they did not exercise in producing exact descriptions of unique examples but instead deployed in a generalizing and universalizing way (pp. 7–8). Ultimately, participating in an aesthetic fashion did not involve merely metaphorical action, or mental labour. For, on Barrell's argument, aesthetic fashion itself helped to shape the very unmetaphorical activity of enclosing fields and distinguishing the various different portions of what had once looked like mere terrain. In the process, it created a great deal of work for surveyors, valuers, and the like. If aesthetic experience was not the cause of the agricultural revolution of the late eighteenth and early nineteenth centuries, it profoundly shaped the kinds of perceptions that would look beautiful and the kinds of effects that would look right on a field. Claude and his imitators led the way, Barrell suggests, for the photo-shoots to which we have become accustomed, in which Ralph Lauren or Calvin Klein design clothes of a certain sort and have them photographed in a landscape that is not a mere context for them but an active echo of their colours and principles of composition.

What Barrell described was an ideology that was all the more effective for not merely borrowing authority but arriving at its evaluations through a circuitous route, like the Protestantism that Weber identified in the spirit of capital. For if the patterns of evaluation that he discerned in the aesthetic perception of landscapes would never have been able to identify themselves exactly as utilitarian, Barrell demonstrated their very considerable if indirect effect in the promotion of the capacity to seeing what things 'actually' were and might be. Nothing in his account is more important, however, than his insistence upon action. As Barrell speaks of the extent to which observation is active in the experience of the picturesque, we can see the basis for two distinct practical phenomena. The first consequence of what Barrell described as a loose application of generalization constructed from memory was to create a world in which everyone saw herself as an artist. Jane Austen archly suggested as much in her description of Emma and Harriet's charades as evidence that we live in an 'age of literature', and Flaubert later organized

*Bouvard and Pecuchet* around the notion that people have become incapable of valuing any knowledge that they don't themselves try to put into practice. It is the world in which people imagine that altering a recipe is nobler than following it. The second consequence is the construction of an archive that enables comparison to take place easily. Barrell's emphasis fell on the sense that Gilpin and Gainsborough had developed a way of altering the land-scape that 'had become so habitual that it was no longer even noticed', but he also observed the fact that they were unembarrassed about recounting their efforts and describing them as effortful (p. 47). It became habitual to alter the landscape in certain ways, but the internal archive called upon connoisseurs to see the difference between untouched and touched, between touched and retouched. In the process, the archive gave scenes a life-story, so that natural scenes were not merely composed of organic nature but were also credited with ongoing life. If the assumption of picturesque observation was that it actualized natural scenes, the reason why its habits of observation so easily became imperceptible was that it was an example of a significantly more pervasive practice, the utilitarian assembly of an organized array whose elements would display themselves – whether simultaneously or by recourse to their own historical stages – so that it was possible to make com-parisons, to feel that one was choosing among alternatives.

It would be hard to overstate the importance of the development of utilitarian comparative choice, because it simplified choices and actions so effectively. No-one needed large-scale commitments or religious doctrines to explain their choices, because it was simply a matter of choosing between this and that, or this and those. In that sense, ideas – whether they applied to religious notions or individual self-reflection – removed themselves from discussion. Utilitarian techniques for setting up comparisons were uncon-cerned to establish accounts of the properties or essences of objects. Instead, they made organic form a *method* that could be applied with minimal attention to what objects or persons really were or meant.

And if utilitarianism promoted professionalization, in part by showing how to make the process of judging significantly easier, its force also mani-fested itself in a much less professional and professionalizable world – the world of plants. For the problem with the analogy between plants and poems does not lie in the fact that poems cannot repair themselves the way that plants and animals can (after all, Donaldson's editorial practice that Wimsatt cited in his essay on organic form suggested that poems do indeed provide the means for their own repair). Instead, the real difficulty appears in the unidirectional character of the way in which people talk about the organic metaphor, as if its only force derived from the attempt to describe products of human art as if they were products of nature.

The organic metaphor operated, I want to observe, not just as a projection of the attributes of organic objects in Goethe's botanical writings from the 1780s and 1790s. Goethe also introduced the organic method into his account of his research, so that he was able to develop an early version of a theory of evolution.[13] His botanical researches, he said, enabled him to see 'symptoms of a ceaselessly advancing organization, hurrying from life to life' (Goethe, 1989, p. 105). He identified organic bodies as those that 'have the characteristic of producing their like by themselves or from themselves' (p. 86), yet his main concern was with the *changes* (my emphasis) that organic bodies effect on themselves. His travels in Italy had made it possible for him to see that the same trees looked different in Germany and in Italy; and those differences seemed to him to constitute a good reason for thinking that plants were 'perfecting' themselves under the influence of their environments. If Hume had found the cornerstone of human behaviour to consist in our alertness to utility, Goethe looked at different botanical specimens and arrived at a similar conclusion for plants. Trees, he saw, might develop narrower leaves in drier climates, broader leaves in wetter ones. Goethe could thus imagine an *Urpflanz* and an *Urteil*, but those images of aboriginal plants and animals were constructs that served to dramatize how much plants and animals had changed under the pressure of their environments. Plants had repeatedly, he said, made choices.

It may sound like a mere play on words for me to describe Goethe as having invested plants with the power of choice. And the charge would certainly be well-placed if we were to understand the notion of choice in terms of the exercise of free will and genuinely autonomous judgment. Yet when Goethe complained that humans exaggerated the importance of their own place in the universe when they labelled certain plants 'weeds' (p. 82), he was pointing to the fact that weeds are plants that are extraordinarily abundant in certain environments because they have made what would appear to be very good choices. He was, in short, wondering why we have contempt for what we might plausibly see as conspicuous success at finding the materials of their own sustenance.

The claim that I am advancing here is that, even though Goethe used a language of self-perfection more than a language of 'success', he was able to develop a early version of evolutionary theory because he was applying to the plant world essentially utilitarian techniques for depicting choice. And if it might seem that he was anthropomorphizing plants in suggesting that they could make choices, he was also suggesting how plant-like and animal-like most people were in most of their choices. Goethe's account of the self-development of plants made it clear how far utilitarian techniques had simplified choice, enabling cats and dogs and trees to choose.

What I mean in saying this is that utilitarianism developed the notion of the importance of an environment in understanding what it was to make a choice. A plant, having no consciousness, could not assert its own interests, preferences and beliefs. A central position of classical utilitarianism – particularly as represented in Hume and Bentham – was that persons were frequently not asserting their own beliefs, their own perceptions of their self-interest, or constant preferences when they made choices. Rather, choices were made in a context or environment, and the environment narrowed the range of options available to anyone. Indeed, Bentham, in only one illustration of this insight, devised the first significant account of sentence-meaning in English, which was the first full-blown formulation of the notion that words draw their meaning from their use in sentences. In his view, no word has meaning outside the environment of a sentence. And although Wimsatt later described poetry as a verbal situation in which a complex of meaning is handled all at once, Bentham could easily have accepted that description as an accurate account of sentences, which make it easy for us to see what the verbs and nouns are within a sentence and not to worry that this word or that could be used as either. Choices, in the utilitarian account, scarcely needed to be conscious, because they were made almost effortlessly. Whether one was a plant, a lower animal or a human, one did not need to identify an absolute good; one could continually choose because these highly articulated contexts were continually delimiting one's choices, making choice look like a minimal gesture.

If Goethe made choosing so easy that even a plant could do it, he was participating in the same general perspective on choice that Bentham had perfected in his Panoptic classrooms. A philosophical commitment to individual autonomy in the form of a faculty of choice might recruit choice for morality, but Bentham rigorously simplified choice, and made individuality a product rather than a point of origin. For if Goethe had seen what he called 'ceaselessly advancing organization, hurrying from life to life', Bentham saw that locating choice within a social organization had the same effect on humans that it did on plants: choices became practical rather than moral, virtually automatic rather than expressive of free will or large-scale belief.[14]

In the Panopticon, Bentham assembled persons to create a machine for choosing. Bentham's Panoptic classroom was machine-like less because of its Gradgrind-like regularity than because of its so clearly making choices approximate inevitability. In its standard format of oral examination – examination in which every student's answer was announced before every other student as well as the teacher or monitor, the Panoptic classroom circulated one sustained activity – spelling or doing sums – through a series of persons. And this procedure made it possible for students not just to participate in the process of spelling or doing sums but to see the comparative value of their action. Students were not compared against perfection. They were compared against one another, so that educational facts were constantly being assigned a value. Susie was first in the class in math, Johnny was seventh in his class at doing sums. Every examination, multiplied through what Bentham projected as an infinite number of subjects, identified the value of each person's performance and described that value in terms of the least controversial or dubitable arrangement possible – the sequence of numbers as they are used to count. This is to say that evaluation, which had once and recurrently seemed to open an abyss of subjectivity in which individuals were the sole ascribers of value, was repeatedly presented as public and objective. Susie wasn't the only one who would recognize her position as first in math; everyone else in the class would recognize her as well.

Now Bentham described this process as one of according appropriate proportional shares of general regard to individuals. And there is no doubt that his Panoptic social structures were aimed at individuating their participants. Every time two or more individuals were indistinguishable, the examination had to be renewed. Ties were reached, only to be resolved. Yet the crucial point to be made is that Bentham was, by virtue of his process of assembling and analysing the activities of a set of persons, treating his social structures in much the same way that Goethe treated his trees. If the first impression was of the whole – be it tree or classroom – the closing of the set of persons as of the organism involved opening it to internal differentiation. Goethe would notice the difference among various kinds of internal tissues, Bentham would make the differences among individual performances perspicuous.

The analogy between a collection of different kinds of tissues in an organism and a collection of different persons in a classroom might seem to be merely that – an analogy. But it was highly consequential, because it did not simply gesture towards the notion of vitality that underwrote the recognition that organisms 'produce their like by themselves and from themselves' (Goethe, p. 86). Rather, both the botanical interest in organic form and the utilitarian interest in producing social structures that used a perception of the whole to make individual differences perceptible led to a new attention to action. Knowing trees or persons no longer revolved around identifying something or someone as yet another instance of the concept 'cornus' (dogwood) or 'homo sapiens'. Instead, knowing plants or persons involved seeing how the various elements of a plant or social group relied on one another and acted together. In botany, that meant thinking of the different kinds of tissue in the organism as dynamic, generating growth and change out of their interaction. In the social organization, it meant assembling a class of persons to be an audience noticing and capturing action for one another. Knowledge – such as spelling a word correctly, for instance – might be necessary, yet Panoptic examination treated knowledge as incidental, necessary but insufficient. For the Panoptic educational organism aimed to have no facts that weren't collapsed into values, that appropriated what an individual knew and also mined the unthought of the assembled group.

The distinctive contribution of the notion of organic form – in biology and in utilitarian social structures – was the identification of value as something beyond the reach of individual elements or persons. And it is this use of the notion that has become both generative and problematic for art, poetry and criticism. For if Bentham's development of utilitarian comparative techniques was designed to rescue the physical and perceptible world from the corrosions of religious belief, it has been hard for modern materialism to identify a place for thought, much less for critique. Indeed, Wimsatt (writing with Monroe Beardsley) adopts a position that is highly skeptical of all characterizations of literary meaning. Although Wimsatt says, in his essay on organic form, that explication is the 'practical point of criticism', he writes in 'The Intentional Fallacy' as if 'the very uncertainty of exegesis' means not just that the poet cannot plausibly be consulted about the poem's meaning, but that critics can only be consulted with caution. What Wimsatt calls 'the objective way in criticism' thus comes to rest not on meaning but being, a view that came to be captured in the assertion that 'a poem must not mean but be'. And a poem 'is', for Wimsatt in 'The Intentional Fallacy', on the basis of a critical judgment of its success: 'Judging a poem is like judging a pudding or a machine. One demands that it work.' Indeed, as Wimsatt and Beardsley went on, 'Poetry is a feat of style by which a complex of meaning is handled all at once', and, it 'succeeds because all or most of what is said or implied is relevant', so that the achievement of style is to make meaning feel simultaneous, rather than like a process of unfolding. Being overcomes meaning, but being is itself a product of a method that shifts attention from thinking to doing and that sees choices not as the result of our ideas and intentions but simply as the effect of perceptible differences in objects.[15]

I have been accumulating examples to suggest that the organic metaphor has been influential – indeed determinative – in literary criticism largely because it taps into a utilitarian tradition that is good at creating structures that notice the smallest gestures, treats them as actions, and makes the perception of the relative values of actions seem both inevitable and incidental. But, of course, poetry scarcely works by producing a consistent collective action – such as spelling or doing sums – that can be used to rank the relative performances of its elements. Characteristically, there is no one word that could be said to 'win' a poem (though Benjamin sometimes imagined that criticism might proceed along approximately those lines with novels). The perception of the interrelationship among the parts generally involves the sense that they are all, more or less, both indispensable and unrankable. (Pound must edit *The Waste-Land* until its parts can be seen in that way.) But that very tendency to treat poems – or novels or paintings – as if they were indissoluble and effectively atomic has created a pressure to produce the canon as we know it, a framework that enables us to say the individual works of art work. This framework has enabled us to perceive the activity of simple words or phrases, has given us not just intertextuality but also the sense of the 'liveness' of slight gestures. The production of a literary work has come to involve the reproduction of the literary canon, insofar as the existence of the canon has become an integral part of the very possibility of seeing that any literature works.

The ethical consequences of the organic metaphor, I want to observe in conclusion, are that it has enabled a conception of activity that doesn't make literature involve a retreat from the world. Instead, literature has come to participate in its own form of busy-ness. Ethics, in the utilitarian sense that someone like Foucault picks up on, is content to talk about action rather than moral judgments about the goodness and badness of actions. Yet if literary criticism has plausibly pursued moral neutrality in its adoption of utilitarian techniques, it has also opened an intensely evaluative moment for the critic – the moment of the judgment that an art object works. And that moment is all the more problematic not because it is subjective, but because it has no way of evaluating its evaluation. Criticism, in its New Critical utilitarian aspect and in the mode of critique, recapitulates the debate between Bentham and Kant that prompted Kant to argue that a sense of one's duty could not be derived from the perception of the good.

If utilitarianism sought to liberate both persons and artifacts from belief and to return them to the physical world, it effected a change in aesthetics that is more significant than the shift from emblem to expression that is usually characterized as the movement from a typological account to a personal and effusive mode. For Wimsatt's modern utilitarianism relies, if only implicitly, on the notion of a community of belief as much as a religion-based typology does. It simply removes statements of what the beliefs might be and what a poem might mean from the realm of the articulable. Utilitarianism as a methodology replaced beliefs with actions, and reasons to choose with evidence that one had chosen (or been chosen). It is thus, as they say, no accident that Robert Smithson repudiated what he (rightly) called the utilitarianism of 'the art history of the recent past', which assembles 'the remains of Europe' to give the recent past its appearance of activity.[16] If utilitarianism managed to eliminate theatrical questions about the extent to which people had the beliefs that they seemed to be acting on, it established a constant scene of activity in which things and persons alike could act in the theatre of comparison. No wonder, then, that the conceptual art of Smithson and others went out of doors. He was not seeking nature but an end to both belief and doctrine, on the one hand, and to action and busyness, on the other.

## Notes

1  Mary Poovey, 'The Model System of Contemporary Literary Criticism', *Critical Inquiry*, 27 (Spring 2001), pp. 408–38.

2  I am grateful to David Simpson for having asked that I address the question of the apparently obsolete nature of my topic. He is surely right to pose the skeptical question to the topic and to its 'liveness' for much recent criticism. Mary Poovey and I, in our different ways, aim to draw attention to the sense that its eclipse has (however wrongly) been more apparent than real. I see my essay as an effort to explore some of the thinking that made the notion of organic form a particularly

live topic for much of the second half of the twentieth century, and to explain
how that debate ought to inflect our search for other models.

3 W.K. Wimsatt, 'Organic Form: Some Questions about a Metaphor', in *Romanticism:
Vistas, Instances, Continuities,* ed. David Thorburn and Geoffrey Hartman (Ithaca,
NY: Cornell University Press, 1973), pp. 13–37.

4 In W.K. The Wimsatt, The Versal Icon: Studies in the Meaning of Poetry (Lexington,
KY: University of Kentucky Press, 1994), p. 4.

5 I cite James's essay because it is perhaps the best known of a series of considerations of the usefulness of religion. The first and most important of these is Jeremy
Bentham's *An Analysis of the Influence of Natural Religion on the Temporal Happiness
of Mankind,* which largely disappeared from view after Bentham published it
under the pseudonym Philip Beauchamp in 1822. It has recently been published
as *The Influence of Natural Religion on the Temporal Happiness of Mankind,* ed. Delos
McKown (Amherst, NY: Prometheus Books, 2003). See also John Stuart Mill's
'The Utility of Religion', in *Essays on Ethics, Religion and Society,* ed.
J.M. Robson, *Collected Works of John Stuart Mill,* X (Toronto: University of
Toronto Press, 1969), pp. 403–28.

6 Key texts are Roland Barthes, *Mythologies* (Paris: Editions du Seuil, 1957); Derrida,
*The Truth in Painting,* trans. Geoff Bennington and Ian McLeod (Chicago, IL:
University of Chicago Press, 1987); and Paul De Man, 'Form and Intent in the
American New Criticism', in *Blindness and Insight: Essays in the Rhetoric of Contempor-
ary Criticism* (New York: Oxford University Press, 1971), pp. 20–35.

7 W.K. Wimsatt, 'The Structure of Romantic Nature Imagery', in *English Romantic
Poets: Modern Essays in Criticism,* ed. M.H. Abrams (New York: Oxford University
Press, 1960), pp. 25–36.

8 The professions that Kant described as those of the higher faculties – law, medicine,
and theology – all correspond to this model insofar as they are all professions of
the book. See Immanuel Kant, *The Conflict of the Faculties,* trans. Mary Gregor
(Lincoln, NE: University of Nebraska Press,1979). See also the discussions of
Kant's *Conflict* in Bill Readings, *The University in Ruins* (Cambridge, MA: Harvard
University Press, 1996), esp. pp. 56–9; and Ian Hunter, *Rival Enlightenments: Civil
and Metaphysical Philosophy in Early Modern Germany* (Cambridge: Cambridge
University Press, 2001), pp. 375–6.

9 Ian Watt, *The Rise of the Novel* (Berkeley, CA: University of California Press, 1957).
The most sweeping challenge to Watt's narrowly characterized tradition of the
novel is Michael McKeon's *The Origins of the English Novel: 1660–1740* (Baltimore,
MD: Johns Hopkins University Press, 1987).

10 John Barrell, *The Idea of Landscape and the Sense of Place: 1730–1840: An Approach
to the Poetry of John Clare,* (Cambridge: Cambridge University Press, 1972) p. 1.
Barrell's opening pages develop this notion with great subtlety and exactitude.

11 John Dixon Hunt, ' "Ut Pictura Poesis": The Garden and the Picturesque
(1710–1750)', in *The History of Garden Design: The Western Tradition from the
Renaissance to the Present Day,* ed. Monique Mosser and Georges Teyssot (London:
Thames & Hudson, 2000), p. 231.

12 Barrell, *Idea of Landscape,* pp. 5–6. He quotes from a Gilpin fragment published in
C.P. Barbier, *William Gilpin* (Oxford, 1963), p. 177.

13 Johann Wolfgang von Goethe, *Goethe's Botanical Writings,* trans. Bertha Mueller
(Woodbridge, CT: Ox Bow Press, 1989).

14 My account here intersects with post-structuralist discussions of the non-human
and mechanical as models for human choice. See particularly Gilles Deleuze

and Felix Guattari, *Anti-Oedipus: Capitalism and Schizophrenia* (Minneapolis, MN: University of Minnesota Press, 1983).

15   W.K. Wimsatt and Monroe Beardsley, *The Verbal Icon,* pp. 4, 8,16.

16   Robert Smithson, *The Collected Writings*, ed. Jack Flam (Berkeley, CA: University of California Press, 1996), p. 42.

# Index

Note: page references in **bold** refer to illustrations.

Price, Uvedale   15, 17, 40–1, 53, 70
Purea, Queen   197
Pyne, William Henry   64, 67, 69

Radcliffe, Ann   177
Ramsay, Allan   203, 204, 205, 206, 207
Rankine, John   205
Ray, Martha   131–5, 137–41, 144, 145
religion
    Evangelical Christianity   86–7, 90–1
    French painting and   101–10
Relph, Josiah   213–14
Rendell, Jane   67
Repton, Humphry   15, 42
Restout, Jan   103, 105
    *The Supper at Emmaus*   103, **104**
Richards, I.A.   5
Richardson, Samuel   4, 139
Ross, Alexander   204
Rowlandson, Thomas   52, 75, 78
Ruskin, John, on Turner   13, 14, 28, 31

*salons*   97
Sandby, Paul   15
Sandby, Thomas   17
    *South Prospect of the Town of Nottingham*   17, **18**
Sandwich, Earl of   131–2, 133, 134
Scarlett, James   25
Scottish vernacular   203–19
Shanes, Eric   14, 31
Shee, Martin Archer   76
Shelley, Mary   3
Sheridan, Thomas   148–9, 204
    Kelly Riot and   150–2
    Sheridan's Case   148, 150, 152, 160–5
Shesgreen, Sean   74
Sillar, Davie   205
Simpson, David   214
Sinclair, John   204
Sloman, Susan   52, 53
Smiles, Sam   23
Smith, Adam   173, 204, 205
Smith, Bernard   193

Smith, Charlotte   8, 170–85
    *The Banished Man*   174, 175, 176, 178, 179, 180, 183–4, 185
    *Desmond*   173–4, 175, 176, 184
    *Letters of a Solitary Wanderer*   185
    *Marchmont*   174, 176, 178, 179–80, 185
    *The Old Manor House*   173–5
    *The Young Philosopher*   174, 178, 180–3, 185
Smith, Greg   71
Smith, J.T.   52
Smith, Olivia   203
Smithson, Robert   238
Smollet, Tobias   207
Soane, John   40
Society of Painters in Water Colours (SPWC)   64, 71, 76, 83
Solkin, David   10
Somerset, Isabella   53
Sorenson, Janet   204
spies   169–85
Sterne, Laurence   137
Stewart, Dugald   208
Stewart, Matthew   208
structuralism   228
surveillance   169–85
Swift, Jonathan   4, 5, 210

Taine, Hippolyte   152
taste   9–11
theatres   *see* actors and acting
Thicknesse, Phillip   52
Thompson, E.P.   2, 3
Thomson, James   204
Thoroton, Robert   17, 25
Throsby, J.   18, 21
Tickell, Thomas   63
Tooke, John Horne   210
Trumpener, Katie   177, 208
Turner, Joseph W.M.   7, 12–32, 53
    *Bacharach on the Rhine*   29, **30**
    *Birmingham*   16
    *Coventry*   23
    *The Fallacies of Hope*   21
    *Nottingham* (1795)   **13**, 16–21
    *Nottingham, Nottinghamshire* (1833)   **14**, 23–31, 32
    *Ploughing Up Turnips Near Slough*   12